Christ&
TheModernMind

Edited by Robert W. Smith

InterVarsity Press
Downers Grove, Illinois 60515

InterVarsity Press
is the book publishing
division of Inter-Varsity
Christian Fellowship.

ISBN 0-87784-863-7

Library of Congress
Catalog Card Number:
70-186349

Printed in the United
States of America

Contents

Preface

When an undergraduate enters a university, he meets many attractive ideas and options for life both inside and outside the classroom. Many newcomers to the campus are not able to sort out the good and the bad, the fact and the opinion. It all comes so fast—and so authoritatively—that they are tempted either to scrap earlier ideas and accept "Dr. Brown's" word or to retreat into a shell of insecurity, refusing to modify their earlier views.

This book attempts to provide some guidelines which will make a student's college experience more exciting, challenging, and rewarding. Not all that one finds in the Athens of learning will be false, nor is all that he retains from his prior Jerusalem true. But we hope to show that Jesus Christ relates to all life, including the university's curricula.

In times past, Christians, often with little effort and less incisiveness, have mouthed the well-known dictum that "the fear of the Lord is the beginning of knowledge" (Prov. 1:7), but they have found it more difficult to translate its meaning into the life of the undergraduate. They have understood, perhaps vaguely, that God in some way stood behind truth, life, and the world, but precisely how in relation to an academic discipline, many have found difficult to explain.

Because our present state of knowledge is incomplete, we cannot comprehend the unity of truth possible perhaps a century from now nor the unity that some scholars alleged in the Renaissance. We do know, however, that solid faith in God as he is revealed in Jesus Christ provides a perspective on one's education unattainable by human insight alone. Christianity and scholarship comprise two sides of the same coin of God's truth: A Christian commitment reminds the scholar that all truth ultimately comes from God, while scholarship cautions the believer not to descend to superstition and fanaticism. These commitments do not preclude, but rather supplement, each other.

This series of essays grows out of the conviction that Christ wants to be Lord of all life, including that of the undergraduate struggling with ideas in a classroom normally hostile to Christianity.

Recent studies, as well as classroom observation, show that students in the last third of the twentieth century are primarily concerned about their personal development, and not in the acquisition of knowledge. Many are bored with traditional instruction widely used for 2,000 years. The scholars and scientists writing for this work firmly believe that learning and personal development in the university can walk together unabashedly in the whole man, simply because, as the apostle Paul set forth clearly to the Colossians, Christ is the cohesive principle of the universe, and faith is the nexus in the union of God and his creatures.

Jewish rabbis long ago taught that ignorance and piety face opposite directions in life and pursue contrary goals, simply because the uninformed person cannot understand what God has done in countless ways and ages. Thus the fool argues for a non-theistic basis of knowledge primarily because he is unmoved to look deeply into learning and creation. We need today, in an age of anti-intellectualism, a Christian philosophy of education to help undergraduates to relate their faith to their academic interests. A commitment to God or to ultimate values will last only so long as God is seen to be related to one's intellectual life and to the needs of his contemporaries.

Leaders of the Reformation—Luther, Calvin, Knox, and Melanchthon—were themselves men of the mind as well as the heart. Modern Christians should be no less. Though we can never argue a man into the kingdom, it does not follow that we should abandon all arguments about the kingdom. Faith alone saves, but the faith that saves is not alone—as the apostle James so eloquently reminded us. Nor is faith enough for the growth of a student; that same faith must have an object and that object a content for study. God implants within each student the basic desire not only to know him in revelation but also in creation.

Does such a trust, once made, tie one to a past reference point in a world dynamic and constantly changing? Perhaps, but such a bond is necessary for a person to live life to the fullest. Even the most permissive radical student wants assurances that past relationships are not altogether ephemeral. Those who insist that in maturing they have graduated from the school of faith to the school of knowledge may need to remember that a timeless God presides over both. Authority and liberty, faith and scholarship, ultimately are solidly wedded. Perhaps the only true radical on today's campus is the Christian student who sees ultimate and effective change as possible only when man looks beyond himself to Another who alone understands all issues of life and motivations of man. Christ can suggest new and dynamic ways to apply ageless principles to contemporary issues.

No professor in the classroom, library, or laboratory can honestly claim an unbiased approach to his discipline, whether he teaches in the humanities, social sciences, or natural sciences. Each knots his thread before he sews the fabric of learning in his discipline. Moreover, if he could be neutral—and no scholar worth his credentials would ever so maintain—his no-stand would itself constitute a position.

Understandably, each author in the following studies looks at his discipline from the vantage point of a Christian scholar or scientist. Each holds in great respect the library, laboratory, and field trip which introduce men to new ideas and principles. But each, like Paul, would remind both his students and colleagues that constant searching without formulating at least tentative answers may carry the air of objectivity and scholarship, but in reality be little more than a respectable "cop-out" of the educational process.

From the outset we have felt it important to provide undergraduates with handles for better grasping college course work. We have deliberately avoided the area of pre-professional training and the more extensive and detailed treatment of minor issues in specific subjects. Rather, we are addressing the undergraduate liberal arts student who may not yet have chosen his major program of study, or if he has chosen it, may not know much about it. But we trust that his major advisor or graduate friend will not be misled by the contents.

As editor and authors, we do not expect every reader to read every chapter, at least at one sitting. But we see something here for virtually every liberal arts undergraduate, and perhaps something for his older counterpart in graduate or professional school.

Each of the essays has been read by at least three different sets of eyes: the author's, a first reader's, and the editor's. We are particularly indebted to the first readers whose helpful insights—sometimes strikingly so—improved the final products. Finally, deep appreciation extends to men and women of the staff of Inter-Varsity Christian Fellowship, particularly to the itinerant staff, for suggesting authors. To all of these our deepest thanks in aiding a series of studies whose purpose from the outset has been to show that Athens and Jerusalem, to use Tertullian's phrase, do indeed have much in common.

Robert W. Smith, Chairman
Department of Speech and Theatre
Alma College

I. The Humanities

Baird W. Whitlock

The Humanities

The humanities lie at the heart of Christian thought and expression. At one time during the development of our civilization that sentence could have been stated the other way around. Then, Christian thought and expression were the heart of the humanities. But, now, that is no longer so, nor has it been since at least the eighteenth century.

As we examine Christian perspectives in the humanities, therefore, we shall range far beyond the limits of what Christian churches normally consider their field of work. It has been said rightly that there is no such thing as the secular in the life of the Christian. And it can also be said that there is no non-humanistic Christianity. The Christian is automatically entangled in the problems of the humanities whether or not he knows it, and the thoughtful Christian, like any other student, cannot evade the problems and criticisms raised by the findings of humanistic study.

Obviously such broad generalizations require some limitation. For the purposes of this discussion, we shall include among the humanities the study of literature and language, oral and written; music and drama, written and performed; art, both as object and action; philosophy and religion. "Humanistic" will, in this context, refer to the study and expression of man in these fields; no one should misunderstand and substitute the nineteenth-century concept of humanism, which was a philosophical stance centering on man divorced from divinity or the supernatural.

what are the humanities?

The term "humanities" originally referred to the study of classical languages and literature. (In Europe that usage still predominates.) It implied both the discipline required to master the languages involved and the intellectual acumen to understand the ideas and concepts set forth in classical literature. In American education today, the term is used either to cover all or part of the subjects mentioned above or to designate the kind of study which attempts to bring together in some inter-related way the separate subject areas. Such interdisciplinary study is often concerned with a culture in its entirety, such as Periclean Athens or the Middle Ages or the Baroque.

In any attempt to see a total culture, the study of the various "humanities" is central, although it does not, of course, eliminate the activities of the sciences and the social sciences. If we attempt to find what Christian perspectives obtain for the modern student, we are necessarily faced with trying to see our culture as a whole; and, I would suggest, we should see the humanities as an important area of that culture.

Immediately we perceive the split, conscious or otherwise, fortunate or unfortunate, between the humanities as they form an actual part of the culture of our civilization (the books we read, the paintings we see, the music we listen to) and the humanities as they constitute a study of those artifacts and activities. The college student cannot avoid the problem, however, since today he competes on both sides of the bifurcation. He must grapple with the obvious difficulties or withdraw. He may dislike intensely the modern literature he must read, or he may be angered at the inability of older faculty to understand the lyrics of Bob Dylan, for example. He may see senselessness in much modern painting, or he may think an art teacher lingers in the nineteenth century for not appreciating a Jackson Pollack. He may hold that a teacher who talks earnestly about the God-is-dead movement is either a heretic or a nincompoop, or he may presume that anyone who teaches religion who does not keep up with current religious debates is not relevant to his needs.

philosophy and religion

The problems the modern student encounters are probably those faced by students of every age, but they seem particularly sharp today. They are the problems of identity, the meaning of life, relationship and alienation, relevance—in short, the issues of philosophy and religion in their deepest sense. The dichotomy between philosophy and religion is difficult and often meaningless. But that does not mean that study in the two areas coincide. The modes of inquiry, the methods of investigation, usually differ. In philosophy we toil to discover how we know, how we relate to other entities, the principle of reality, and the nature of being. In religion and theology we are concerned with the essence of revelation, the existence and nature of God and man's relationship with him. At one time philosophy served as the handmaiden of theology; now theology is considered a small segment of philosophy. The world is not noticeably better off for the change.

The ultimate questions of philosophy and religion are, of course, the same, and they remain the ultimate questions of each of us. Perhaps the most perceptive statement on education was made by Socrates: "The unexamined life is not worth living." One astonishing and discouraging quality of some students is their unwillingness to see the absolute necessity of putting their minds to work in their religious beliefs.

This is not to say that the academic discipline of philosophy necessarily aids Christian thought and behavior. Anyone aware of current trends in philosophy knows that, if anything, the opposite is more the case. But the questions it raises are basic to religious life and must and can be answered by the Christian if he lives rather than merely exists in the modern world.

We can probably safely declare that no significant Christian writer has been untouched by the major philosophic trends of his day. Paul was certainly well trained in Greek philosophy and literature and used Greek poets for his quotations. St. Augustine worked his way through Manicheism and came out the other side before his conversion, and that experience helped him in spreading his Christian beliefs. One could almost argue that his study of Plato and Cicero led him to Christianity. His study determined most of his ethical and theological positions, which, in turn, have had perhaps the greatest single influence on the history of Christian thought of any non-biblical writer. Similar instances could be cited of writers throughout the Middle Ages, the Renaissance and the Reformation. It remains true of theologians today as well as the major Christian apologists like C. S. Lewis.

The student, especially the Christian student, has a double intellectual obligation: He must seek to understand himself, his relationship to other men and the world, and his relationship with God in terms which bring satisfaction and comprehension to himself, and, moreover, he must come to understand the questions and problems of other men so that he can offer some solutions. Whether the others wish to accept these Christian solutions is up to them. Nonetheless, the Christian is obligated to others. In Donne's words, "No man is an island."

The Christian has the theological compulsion of communication. But he cannot communicate if he does not know the philosophic stance of the person with whom he wishes to communicate. This does not imply that one need agree with another's philosophic system in order to communicate with him; but he should know what the other person thinks in order to communicate meaningfully. If I am to talk with a Buddhist, I should know something about Buddhism, or I may find to my surprise that he simply gobbles up my Christianity into his Buddhism (and from his point of view he has every right to do so, albeit disconcerting to a Westerner). So, if I am talking with an existentialist I shall waste my time if I talk in terms of absolutes which he "absolutely" (or relatively) denies. I will need to get around to the absolute, but if I start there, I stop the conversation immediately.

Sometimes, as is often the case in logical positivism, one must realize that if he gives in to certain methodologies (for example, the uses of words in certain sharply-defined, limited ways), he will never be able to get back to a Christian position. One cannot use the categories of the logical positivist and come up with a Christian religious position, as C. S. Lewis discovered to his dismay when he tried it in one debate at Oxford.

Perhaps stressing the importance of philosophy for the Christian student is like flogging a dead horse because it would seem so obvious; but it remains true that for many students the study of philosophy is the most threatening element of a college career and avoided most assiduously. And even more avoided is the study of theology, both Christian and non-Christian. As the world diminishes in size, the teachings of other world religions become better known. Already in our country the teachings of Zen Buddhism have powerfully affected young people. All major world religions contain attractive elements (they would hardly have become such if they did not), and the Christian student must come to understand these rival religious positions if he is to remain an effective Christian among those holding these views. I am quite willing to prophesy that within twenty years Christianity will be a minority religion in the United States (in terms of committed Christians, it almost certainly is now). The Christian untrained in other religious systems and conclusions will have a small voice in reaching others.

literature and language

It is impossible to draw a clear line of demarcation between philosophy and literature. College departments may seek to set limits, but such boundaries ultimately prove unsuccessful. In the same way, it is impossible to dichotomize the study of literature and language because they are inseparable. Indeed, one of the recent major movements in literary study has been the understanding that the way language works may basically determine our comprehension of literary modes. This has always been true of older works and those in translation. In order to read Chaucer, one simply must know how Middle English works. Seventeenth-century critics thought Chaucer was an interesting but unpolished poet because they did not know how to pronounce the earlier language. The problem of translation continues, for language alters just as customs and cultures do. For example, an adherence to the King James translation of the Bible is a matter of literary taste and cultural conditioning. That is not to say that one may not think that the King James is a better translation than some other version, but that words change in meaning. All of us have come to know that words do not, in spite of the dictionary, carry specific, understandable meanings by themselves.

We know that words carry different interpretations within different contexts; words "mean" according to the verbal groupings in which they appear. One typical example from the King James translation is the word "prevent." Today this word generally means to stop or hinder someone or something. But even with us, it can carry a sympathetic meaning, as when we want to prevent a child from hurting himself or an unfriendly meaning, as when we want to prevent an enemy from hurting us. Most of us know that in sixteenth- and seventeenth-century usage, and hence in the King James translation, the word conveyed the basic meaning of its Latin source "prevenio," to arrive before. When God "prevents" in the Bible, he simply gets there first. We must find from the context the reason for that early arrival: Does it show his supremacy? Is he saving us from our own mistakes? Does he wish to cut off an unworthy act? Only the context will show us that.

Once we understand language and how it works—and also how it operates on us in subtle emotional ways—we stand better prepared to get to the meaning of literature in a deeper way. A great many different kinds of approaches to literature have gained currency in recent years. There is the application of psychological approaches to the understanding of characters and authors, or the use of sociological concepts in dealing with novels, etc.

But two of the most interesting literary approaches are those of the New Critics (no longer so new after over twenty years of argument) and those who emphasize the traditions of literary genres (certain literary forms which have developed their own definitions and restrictions). Both have real implications for the Christian student, not only as he handles any literary work, but also as he reads the Bible.

The New Criticism of literature emphasized the validity of the work of art in itself. It cleared away the mass of anecdotes about authors and unprovable statements concerning why the works were written, and claimed that the only knowledge one needed about a poem or story was contained in the poem or story itself. There were necessary limits to that claim, of course; for example, one had to know what the words meant. Indeed the whole movement went too far. As we have already noticed, language and literature take place in contexts, and any attempt to remove all contexts simply overdoes it. But the emphasis on appreciating literature for its own sake rather than for who wrote it and why it was an important influence, is one which, hopefully, will remain.

The genre approach differs considerably. It posits that an author carries some of the intended meaning in the very form he adopts for his writing. Sometimes the one certain clue that a poet wishes the reader to see his work as a love poem will be its sonnet form. A writer's use of irony and satire may often be made clear only when the reader recognizes the use of the wrong genre. Pope's *Rape of the Lock,* an epic poem about the cutting off of a lock of hair, is a case in point.

Understanding genre is indispensable in reading the Bible. There is, in storytelling, a very clear and concise genre that has developed in many different cultures; we call it a parable. A parable simulates another literary genre, an allegory, but it has a different purpose and a different goal. An allegory presents a story with a second meaning in a kind of one-to-one relationship. In *Pilgrim's Progress,* for example, whenever Christian undergoes some difficulty or danger in his trip, this carries with it a theological meaning or concept.

But a parable does not do this—or at least it is not designed to do it. A parable's story carries with it a *single* implied meaning. Whenever Christ explained his parables, he did exactly this; he showed the single meaning that the parable entailed. In other words, literary study can help clear up one very bad habit of preachers: emphasizing what was of little concern in the story. The parable of the prodigal son does *not* deal with the older brother, nor does the parable of the Good Samaritan concern the man who has fallen among thieves.

But students today have real problems in their study of modern literature as they do in the study and appreciation of all modern art forms. The writer, composer, or artist no longer considers it necessary to be clear or even to be comprehensible. In many cases he shifts the burden completely onto the viewer, listener, or reader. Moreover, in many cases the subject matter has shifted radically. There is decreasingly less art which allows the reader any sense of relaxation or escape. A student today usually finds it difficult to decide whether his parents are mature enough to read what he must read for class. The same is true of the appreciation of modern art and music.

some of the arts

At one time all major forms of art and music in the Western world were tied intimately to the church and to Christian experience. In our own age we have become so accustomed to the secularized community that we look back in disbelief to an age which found a major third in music so sensual and licentious that it was not allowed either in church music or in music that a polite society would listen to. The Renaissance supposedly changed all that, but it didn't. The overwhelming majority of works of art of the Renaissance, in music, painting, sculpture, and architecture, are religious in subject matter and intent. True, secular and pagan subjects returned, but then they had never completely left the arts or literature. The drinking songs and love ballads of the Middle Ages found their roots in Ovid and Virgil more than in Solomon's Song of Songs or Ecclesiastes. The carefully and lovingly carved nude figures in the cathedral miserichords or those of the tympani of the great church portals derived from feelings that Paul would never have admired in Christian clergyman or layman.

In the same way, the Ranaissance, although it reveled in human beauty and thought of all times and ages, sought to express man's relationship to God in standards of beauty never surpassed before or after. Modern art scholarship has returned the Renaissance to its proper place within the traditions of the Christian community of the Western world. It has also taught us a good deal about the nature of the creative act and the expression of the individual in his attempt to relate to his God.

One complaint leveled against the humanities in the past has been that within the academic community it has been concerned solely or largely with the past. The charge was, to a large extent, a valid one, but it is no longer. Courses in modern art, for example, are now as commonplace as courses in the Renaissance. Moreover, the application of artistic ideas and practices of the past are relevant to present circumstances and standards. The study of art, especially religious art, yields a major result for the Christian who is interested in the life of the church.

Only those periods which seem to lack genuine religious drive use art objects from other periods of time. A community vitalized by religion expresses that religion in the artistic media of its own time. When the construction of a cathedral spanned many hundreds of years (usually the case), each part of it was built in the style of the age in which it was constructed, not in the style of an earlier part of the church. So a great cathedral like Peterborough or Ely will usually contain elements of Romanesque, Gothic, Flamboyant, and possibly Renaissance, while interior paintings and decoration may indicate the style of Mannerism, Baroque, and Rococo. In the late eighteenth and nineteenth centuries, as the strength of the church in the community declined, church architecture more and more took on the characteristics of past ages, and so we find fake Gothic churches, fake colonial churches, fake Greek temple churches, and so on. The study of art shows that a vital church uses contemporary expression both in its architecture and in its decoration.

As in philosophy and religion, there is an increased emphasis on oriental and other non-Western art forms in contemporary art courses. This is paralleled by more attention to Indian music, both in music which we associate with the traditional concert hall and in popular rock and roll groups. The academic study of music lags behind many of the other humanities, since the music actually being written and listened to is usually not that being studied and heard in class. Music history courses consider themselves modern when they deal with Stravinsky and Schoenberg in their earlier phases, and most harmony courses go as far as traditional harmony in its altered forms, in other words, up to the late nineteenth century.

Moreover, the two major movements of modern music—serial music and aleatoric music—remain unknowns for most students. This does not argue that either the mathematic rigidities of serial music or the potentially chaotic chances of aleatoric music are the best thing that could happen to music. They may be the worst. But they are what is happening, and the academic world remains largely untouched by it all. We must not forget that the first full mass of the church came from folk music, and that church music has always gained new impetus from secular musical forms, slight as they might be. The varieties of musical experience open to the student today is breathtaking, however, and perhaps richer than in any previous period of history.

the other arts

I have so far concentrated on music, art history, and literature as finished products, but such an approach limits us both historically and in modern educational theory. With studio classes in art, performance groups in music, and theatrical groups and speech activities becoming increasingly important as academic areas, one should not speak as if the student were trapped in educational passivity. We have recently learned in academe what everyone has known since the beginning of time, that men communicate in different ways and that those various ways are all valid if they achieve their purpose. If I cannot correctly express a warning for someone to fall down before a hand grenade goes off, I can more wisely communicate by knocking him down than by working on my sentence construction. Indeed, if, as a social worker, I really want to help an underprivileged group, I had better *not* be too correct in my expression. "It is I" may be correct, but if I use it in the wrong context, I may alienate the very people I want to help. But more important, we have learned that nonverbal means of communication are often just as effective educational tools as verbal, and with that realization the creative arts have come into their own in the academic community.

When all is said and done, though, we remain basically a verbal and oral culture. The training in speech has, therefore, been an important element in college education, often becoming a joint requirement with writing in freshman programs. Part of its growth has stemmed from the increasing recognition that proper training in speech is not the old finishing-school emphasis on elocution, but a process of researching, evaluating, organizing, and presenting of materials in the most comprehensible and effective manner. As we spend most of our lives communicating orally, the importance of learning how to do so most effectively is obvious enough.

Effective speech calls all sorts of elements of personal expression into play. Like good writing, good speech uses general patterns to allow the individual to express himself best as an individual, not as a copy of someone else. This is the point at which good writing, imaginative writing, and good speech play together as valuable assets for the Christian student. Religion, any religion, is a personal experience. This does not argue that all is relative; rather, that each person experiences God as an individual. If he is to communicate his experience to anyone else—and this is really the only message that is meaningful in religion—he must be able to make himself understood and felt.

But writing and speaking are not the only ways. One fault of the Reformation was that it narrowed the number of ways that a person in a congregation could express himself in his public worship and testimony. He could now speak, sing (perhaps in the choir if he had a good enough voice), or, if he had the necessary training, play the piano or organ. Gone were the church orchestras except in the very rare community, gone the art objects that one could carve or paint (and even if it were a small carving a hundred and thirty feet up in the air in the vault of the cathedral, God could still see it).

All branches of the church are now coming back to something like the earlier position. The viols may not be back in large numbers, but the guitars are. Church halls and Sunday school rooms now carry a decor of paintings and other objects restoring to life the symbols on which the church has always fed spiritually.

Drama has become one of the most effective voices of the church, and there is no irony in this. Western drama began not in Greece—although there, too, it came out of religious worship —but in the service of the mass and grew within the confines of the church itself until it simply became too large and popular for the church to handle.

Television has been a valuable medium for the presentation of dramatic messages in a meaningful and direct way to the public. College religious groups have discovered that their witness can be made more effective by means of dramatic productions. Plays have always been able to bring home messages more powerfully than other means of communication, and they retain that power. The Theatre of the Absurd has done as much as any art form to confront today's students with the necessity of facing the ultimate problems of life's meanings.

At the same time such creativity and imagination carries an inherent danger because it can substitute the means for the end. The early church was right: Some combinations of chords have purely sensual pleasure about them (play a major third triad on the piano and then flat the third into a minor triad and feel the difference). That doesn't make them wrong, but it does perhaps lessen our attention to the religious message. Paintings of religious subjects may often be so aesthetically pleasing that we lose their subject meaning. Botticelli has painted an Annunciation with the Virgin Mary so beautiful that the subject is immaterial; I'm simply enchanted with the girl. (And there is a painting of Hagar in the Scottish National Gallery that will convince you that Abraham was wrong in choosing Sarah.) The medium can distort the message.

problems in the humanities

I wish to end with some thoughts on problems faced by the Christian student at this point in history, especially as he faces the study of the humanities. I have no easy answers, but I have some difficult questions. First, I think he must face one important fact: rejection. The Christian student today is in about the same position as the Roman pagan in the mid-fourth century. He is part of a culture which is changing around him. Instead of being part of a religious majority, he is part of a coming minority.

He may be in even a worse position. Twenty years ago the Christian student was under attack by his peers; today he is more often laughed at. Attack has always been easy to stand against; laughter is much harder. The Christian group which talks about the theological issues of the Virgin Birth is regarded in the same way Christians would regard a student group who met downtown each Tuesday night and discussed seriously the problem of whether Venus was born on a half shell rising from the Mediterranean Sea or whether she issued forth from the waters of Lake Tithonus. This does not in any way minimize the importance of discussing the Virgin Birth, but it does put it into a context of an academic world which couldn't care less.

Further, the Christian student has a twofold role that has never been easy; he must live in the world and be deeply committed to all those in that world (if he does not, he has broken Christ's commandment to love his fellow men), yet he is not to be *of* that world. He is not to be conformed, but transformed. He must communicate and understand, but he must be a new creature, not corrupted by the communications of others. He is a man, with all of man's weaknesses and faults, but he has been enjoined to be perfect, even as God is perfect. How is he to be in the world but not of it? Should he take the hippie way out and interpret "be ye separate" as an injunction to drop out? Obviously not. His role is much harder.

Most of the literature which he will read will have elements which his parents will label filth and pornography. Most of the philosophy which he will study will emphasize the relativity of all knowledge, experience, and existence, which his parents and minister will label sacrilege. Much of the music and art, even the drama and movies, if he goes to the best-done works, may be unintelligible to him, in many cases purposely so. These his elders will label garbage. In most of his art, music history, and literature courses, as well as many of his philosophy courses, he will find that he is being trained in the techniques of form rather than in the interpretation of meaning, which he, if he is still alive, will label dead.

Is the situation hopeless? The Christian answers, No, if he thinks about it very long. The ultimate meaninglessness of life is death, but to the Christian, death is anything but meaningless. There are perhaps some saving graces for the Christian student to remember, although they will not make his life any easier. In the first place, literature has changed little throughout history; the language may be a bit rawer than it was in the nineteenth century, but no worse than in Shakespeare, Chaucer, Aristophanes, and the Bible (where almost all of the current four letter words show up with amazing ease). Much of the biblical story is filled with incidents which, if recorded in the modern idiom, would shock almost any casual churchgoer. Why is homosexuality frightening on a stage, but permissible in the pulpit when read in the Bible? Biblical incest relationships are rather common fare.

Moreover, of philosophy, one can say that relativity in one form or another has always been a potent force from the very beginning of Greek philosophy. Moreover, our own relativity is derived from a scientific formula in which the concept of relativity works because there is an absolute on which it is based, namely the speed of light. Christianity has never absolutized personal experience but only the nature of God. Who would be so blind as to argue that God reveals himself in the same way in Genesis and the gospel of John? This in no way negates the absoluteness of God himself.

One must admit that the problem is harder in art, music, and drama. The artist often says he has broken completely from the past, that he is striving for something completely new. The student must listen to this claim even when he does not agree with it. For one thing, it will keep him alive to the possibility of new changes and forms within which to work. Paul exhorted the Christian not to be conformed to the world, but Christians seem to spend most of their time trying to adapt. Modern art is more biblical than that.

But where the Christian student must rebel is against the system that substitutes form for meaning, methodology for content. Christ argued that the Sabbath was made for man, not man for the Sabbath. Form is there for the communication of content, not the other way around. When this order is reversed, the humanities cease to be humanistic, and the student must reassert the basic principle.

Virginia Lowell Grabill

English Literature

A recent textbook depicts a father admonishing his off-to-college daughter to beware of her English teacher: "English teachers lead people astray." His comment reflects an attitude that poetry, fiction, and drama are at best pleasant leisure-fillers and at worst pretty lures of the devil. Such denigrations of "nonpractical" writing reveal an idea held often unconsciously by people reared on the Yankee virtues: that all that is not work—even money- or goods-producing work—is evil, that the chief end of man is duty and duty is work. Even with machines far stronger and more consistent than men, the need to be always physically "busy" is hard for the parent generation to escape. But students reared with a TV set in every room are less likely to think of leisure as, ipso facto, evil.

Among leisure activities, those concentrating on the aesthetic seem especially natural and appropriate for Christians or others interested in living fully if one observes the color of sky and grass, the balanced form of evergreens, the rhythm of planets and gazelles, the melody of meadowlark and waterfall. The urge in men to produce art may indeed echo whatever caused God—looking on a world "without form" and empty and dark—to create intricate forms, fill emptiness with beauty, and make darkness light. Thus for people who worship God as creator of sunsets, snowflakes, and baby smiles and, in a real sense, of the plans for a magnificent temple, of descriptions of the ineffable, of parables, and of poetry, the creation of the aesthetic should not be difficult to accept as worthy work or the appreciation of it as worthy pleasure.

More clearly than other arts, though, literature has—from classical times at least—claimed two purposes: to delight and also to teach by so wedding content and form as to arouse and satisfy sense, emotion, and mind. The Latin word for the creative writer, *vates,* means both "poet" and "prophet," and literary artists have felt that a prophetic responsibility as well as a delighting privilege came with the creative gift. Shelley called literature "the record of the best and happiest moments of the happiest and best minds"; Matthew Arnold, "the best that has been thought and said in the world," a "criticism of life" which can give man meaning and consolation. Tennyson saw it as the poet's duty to shoot lighted arrows of wisdom into a dark world. Coleridge understood imagination as the part of man closest to the divine. Thus literature—far from being simply a leisure-time filler—at its best helps men live meaningfully and richly. The quality of literature depends on the artist's ability to see men, the universe, and God as they really are and to communicate this vision whole.

Even in the most important of his own writing, the student struggles with matters of man and universe and God. Therefore, even though a student's contact with the English Department be limited to a course in expository writing, English is not commas and term papers but the cultivation of vivid sensation, logical thought, and honest evaluation—all matters essential to the Christian and other men who desire abundant life. Intelligent, thoughtful freshmen can produce essays not lacking in the characteristics of literature when they say important things clearly, honestly, logically, and attractively.

If, then, the English teacher does "lead people astray," as he no doubt does sometimes, one must agree that doing so is not inherent in his subject matter. Indeed, his subject matter requires him to deal not with a narrow specialty but with ideas and emotions vital to all men. Further, since man's relationship (if any) to God (if any) is certainly vital, the English teacher—unlike his counterpart of physics, economics, or education—cannot ignore religion, even if he does not believe in any particular one.

what does an english course demand?

If the literature or writing class is well taught, the student's role is not to give unsupported opinions. It is to learn and also to think—about his own identity and purpose, the presence of good and evil in the world, justice and forgiveness, freedom and responsibility and order, power and love, the beautiful and the ugly, democracy and aristocracy, the pragmatic and the idealistic, sexuality and spirituality, innocence and wisdom, intelligence and industry, ambition and humility, joy and suffering, conserving and discovering, purity and guilt, life after death, and so on.

For any student, this may be the first time of really confronting some of these subjects for himself, even though he may have more or less had opinions on them—opinions of his parents, his church, his peers, or opinions on principle opposed to one or more of these. One student may delight in the freedom to build a unique philosophy and style of life for himself, accepting and rejecting ideas and feelings as he wishes; another may feel utter fright at even reading, lest in the delight of the aesthetic and the thrill of dangerous ideas he lose what he believes.

The one who starts off joyfully needs to remember that pat answers will not be there for the taking because men have struggled in every age with these subjects. He will need to realize that an idea is not right or wrong simply because he has never heard of it before or because an intelligent, sensitive writer or teacher holds it. He must beware of accepting one thrillingly new idea after another without noticing how it fits with those he has already embraced. A student frightened lest he lose what he has needs to remember that his loyalty is to truth—not to what he now holds to be truth—and that he reads to experience truth, not to polish his old ideas for propagation.

In the experience of reading an essay carefully, empathizing with characters in a play or story, trying to wring every nuance of sensation and feeling and meaning from a poem, a student must involve himself; such involvement is not without discomfort and danger. He begins to realize that his experience of life is neither unique nor complete, that some of his previous ideas and feelings are untenable when he weighs them against others and that some are among the best men have found. If he would be a man, he must seek and, at least to some questions, find answers and commit himself; if he would be a Christian, he must accept God's grace; if he would be intellectually and spiritually mature, he must "try the spirits," examine the world, and in God's name "subdue" it.

what has christianity to do with english?

Since most of the literature read in college English courses was written during nominally Christian eras by people who presumed their readers were in some sense Christian, a student uneducated in the Bible will have some catching up to do if he is to understand allusions to Saul, David, Bathsheba, Jonathan, Job, Abraham, Isaac, the beloved disciple, etc., to such items as the walls of Jericho, the scapegoat, the sun's standing still, the coat of many colors, etc., and to terms like *prodigal, shibboleth, ichabod.* Further, he will be likely to miss the depth of important literary symbols made from Bible materials like the garden, the serpent, the Cross, and the Resurrection. The student without belief in Christianity may have to suspend his disbelief if he is to fully understand important work frankly based in personal faith in Christ and in belief in miracle, heaven and hell, the Incarnation, sin and grace, etc.: like Donne's "Batter My Heart," Herbert's "The Collar," Milton's *Paradise Lost* and *Paradise Regained,* Swift's "The Abolishing of Christianity," Hopkins' "Caged Skylark," Browning's "Saul," and Eliot's "Four Quartets," to mention only a few.

Whether a work is explicitly religious or not—and most literature is not unless one defines *religious* very broadly—a student must know or learn the major Christian doctrines if he is to interpret and evaluate the literature of the Western world properly. For example, Christianity teaches that man is both base and made in God's image—the latter at least suggesting potential for good actions; it further teaches that man cannot, despite this potential, pull himself to God-likeness by his own effort. It shows God as both immanent and transcendent and points out man's duty to love God and his neighbor. Various writers point up certain of these facets; Wordsworth sees God near; Pope sees him afar. Emerson sees man's goodness; Hardy and Dreiser see his inability to be good; Dickens, Shelley, Ibsen, and Goethe emphasize what man can do for his fellows. Not to see both sides of these subjects is to miss the truth—truth which Christianity clearly displays—as certain writers have been able to communicate, as Milton does in depicting that freedom is found only in slavery to God, as Dostoevsky does in showing the importance of the individual and of his spiritual death, as Tolstoy does in showing the importance of individuals and of God's great plan, as Hopkins does in finding God in both the magnificent and the slight, and as Swift does in showing what a man is without grace and what he is with grace.

Just as one student may have problems because he lacks biblical knowledge, so another may miss Christian insights in literature because he is busy making moral judgments on the author's life. The fact that Coleridge was addicted to drugs may make a student miss or reject the sin-and-salvation theme of "The Ancient Mariner" and thus be both a poorer critic and a less obedient Christian. The fact that Lord Byron's sex life could hardly be said to follow St. Paul's injunctions does not subtract from the beauty and power of his "The Destruction of Sennacherib." Truth is not confined to triumphant Christians; a sinner who writes well can provide both instruction and delight to the saint. Moreover, not all Christian writers are good writers any more than all Christian cooks are good cooks. A student who takes Christianity seriously must beware of insisting that a poem is good merely because he believes what it says, though poorly. Lines of rhymed or rhythmic cliches do not teach or delight, no matter what their subject.

Moreover, one should be careful lest he miss the delight and teaching of a work because it does not include the whole of Christian doctrine. Even sermons are not expected to do that! Furthermore, one should not expect that a writer who is truly Christian will always write on patently religious themes any more than he would expect a Christian cook to always be making bread and wine.

Students sometimes wonder why literature seems more often to show man's sinfulness than his goodness or God's grace. Perhaps this is so because literature reveals truth and more men are in sin than in grace ("few there be that find" life); perhaps writers know that even characters in grace are realistic and are more attractive to most people when they are sinning than when they are not.

is shakespeare christian?

To illustrate some of the foregoing thoughts about the importance of Christianity in the interpretation and evaluation of literature, let us look briefly at three of the most often studied works of the writer acknowledged for three and a half centuries to be the best: Shakespeare's *King Lear, Macbeth,* and *Othello,* each a painful vision of the human condition. A sensitive reader can hardly leave these powerful statements of what evil can do to a man without feeling the need for Christian grace. In each the content—that man is a sinner in need of grace—and the dramatic form combine to make a powerful intellectual and emotional experience of teaching and delighting.

In *King Lear,* Shakespeare creates a pagan, pre-Christian world in which the basic human elements struggle, the noble being repeatedly thwarted. After four acts of purgatorial suffering, Lear depicts himself thus:

> I am bound
> Upon a wheel of fire, that mine own tears
> Do scald like molten lead. (IV, 7)

Though the play is not overtly or explicitly Christian, it is a powerful communication of Christian teaching for it shows clearly and forcefully the world of man preyed upon by the animal within.

Macbeth is a sensitive, intelligent, imaginative person who knowingly puts himself outside of grace; the play then views his earthly damnation, a meaningless succession of unredeemed, godless minutes. Upon hearing of Lady Macbeth's suicide, he describes his own state:

> Tomorrow, and tomorrow, and tomorrow
> Creeps in this petty pace from day to day
> To the last syllable of recorded time;
> And all our yesterdays have lighted fools
> The way to dusty death. Out, out brief candle!
> Life's but a walking shadow, a poor player
> That struts and frets his hour upon the stage
> And then is heard no more. It is a tale
> Told by an idiot, full of sound and fury,
> Signifying nothing. (V, 5)

Surely this is the Christian view of the man who has turned from God and righteousness.

Almost like a morality play, *Othello* makes clear an important aspect of the Christian story: Man is weak and vacillating, beset by temptation on his pilgrimage through life. At the beginning of the play Othello is seen as a man of moral and spiritual strength in a cultivated Christian community. He marries Desdemona, the symbol of grace, in a love union of peace. Then Iago enters to destroy both the harmony and Othello himself by causing him to lose his faith in Desdemona. The temptation and its consequences make a clear and moving study of man's fall. The dramatic moment when Othello realizes his imminent damnation elicits profound pity from any reader; for the Christian reader, relief comes only in the remembrance of the love of God in Christ.

what about the twentieth century?

If our contemporaries are writing the greatest literature the world has seen, this fact will be known certainly only when other generations and other trials to the human spirit have tested its teaching and delighting capability. Talking our language and illustrating with our lives, writers of our century see man's baseness clearly. Many—Woolf, Hemingway, Fitzgerald, Lawrence, Joyce, Faulkner, and Tennessee Williams among them—write of a world peopled with the depressed, the indecisive, the animalistic. Others, influenced by existentialism and including Camus and Kafka, deal with individual man—inadequate, alienated, hopeless. Though all are clear on man's baseness and many on guilt and impending judgment, they do not suggest what can be recognized as Christian solutions.

There are, however, writers of our century who continue the Christian tradition: Eliot, Auden, Alan Paton, Graham Green, C. S. Lewis, Dorothy Sayers, Flannery O'Connor, J. R. R. Tolkien, Charles Williams, and others who thus far remain not often enough read in general literature courses.

what about language?

In reading modern literature and in creative writing, the student is faced at once with the complex matter of "dirty" language. Some Christians have fought hard in their local communities to remove, from libraries and stores, books using swearing or Anglo-Saxon words for bodily functions; other Christians have fought historic battles for complete freedom of speech and publication. The student should consider many facts before he makes his decision, among them these: that genuine Christians are likely to be in the minority even in a "Christian" democracy; that laws do not change men's hearts; that one spelling for an idea can hardly be "more Christian" than another; that, indeed, certain arrangements of alphabetical symbols can hardly be called sinful per se; that language communicates thought and emotion and influences thought, emotion and action; that a recent study showed factory-workers using one "dirty" word in four, and the student average may be as high.

He should remember further that meaningful words can be lost to a language if not used; that overuse of a word tends to make its meaning vague; that speech habits show personal character in fiction or in life ("from the abundance of the heart the mouth speaketh"); that misrepresenting a character's language is in effect lying about him; that Christianity includes an obligation to tell the gospel to one's contemporaries—presumably in a language they can understand; that meaningless (vain, empty) use of the names of God is forbidden in the Ten Commandments; that one does not use lightly the name of one he loves—much less reveres, and so on. Here again there are no pat answers.

Another language problem faces any writer who often deals with a single subject: a tendency to use the same words until they become meaningless. Christians often use a language which is both unclear and offensive to people outside their sector of Christianity. The Christian student, therefore, if he would teach and delight, must be sure that his writing represents his own vivid experience or something he has observed and thought about carefully so that he does not let accustomed words flow without meaning.

So where does English lead? Courses in literature lead to learning that is delightful in content and form; courses in writing lead one to teach delightfully by content and form. What better combination can any college department offer the thinking and feeling student, perhaps especially the Christian student?

Douglas D. Feaver

Classical Languages

Latin? Greek? A major in classics for a Christian? What relevance can the classics have for a university student whose ultimate commitment is to serve his own generation in the name of his Lord? Are not resources of credits, time, and intellectual energies so precious that the Christian, as a prudent steward, dare not waste them on such dusty bypaths?

No doubt the cynical pagan might remark that the Christian student would do well to avoid the classics, if he wishes to retain his faith. The New Testament will seem bland and tame beside the rich sophistications of classical literature, he might argue; studies in classical religion might show him that "Christianity was just another Hellenistic mystery religion," and the brilliant insights of classical philosophy might erode his faith in Christian doctrines. Finally, the critical study of language, statistical linguistics, and *Quellengeschichte* will provide him with a whole battery of weapons with which to carve up the New Testament to a point beyond recognition or utility. Ought the Christian student, then, to take the risk?

utility in the classics

Most who ask such questions about the classics—for that matter about any university subject—look for answers in a very narrow area. Will this or that course or major train them for some future occupation? Or are they at least prerequisites mysteriously placed as hurdles on the road to one's chosen profession? Will they "pay off" in accreditation, status, or money?

This kind of an answer can be very quickly given for the classics. Their "pay off" value is limited. It is not nil; after all, I am earning a comfortable, if not opulent, living as a classicist; moreover, in so doing I am convinced that I am, for the moment, fulfilling the purposes of God in my life. Furthermore, the classics are, in my opinion, one of the most valuable courses of study for pre-theological students. Though you can get into seminary without any Greek, a grounding in classical Greek language and thought will make the mastery of the very similar New Testament language far easier, and in addition the student will have obtained a priceless appreciation for the background of ancient philosophy, history, art, and religion against which the Christian revelation first appeared.

Nor need the Christian fear for his faith. Christianity won the day in the first place with people who knew far better than the most erudite classicists of today what classical culture was really like. Augustine, who once despised the New Testament because it seemed too simple beside the rich complexity of Cicero, was converted from a life of sophisticated despair by a simple verse of the once-despised Scripture.

Classics have had and continue to have a valuable role in pre-professional training, not only for teaching and the ministry, but also other professions such as law, medicine, and library science.

the foundation of western culture

But the greatest relevance of the classics to the Christian student has little to do with pre-vocational training. The fact that he as a Christian is in the university at all means that he has entered one of the basic tensions of Western civilization, summarized neatly by the famous diatribe of Tertullian: "What has Athens to do with Jerusalem? What has the Academy to do with the Ecclesia?" For the university, more than any other single institution, is a child of ancient Greece and Rome.

Christians are fond of saying that in the West the universities were the children of the church, founded, in most cases, for the glory of God. True, but one should remember that the universities were the adopted, not the natural, children of the church. On every hand its basic ideology and characteristic modes of thought betray the lineaments of its natural parents. The Christian in the university must come to terms with Tertullians's question. For him, the answer was unequivocal: Jerusalem had nothing to do with Athens; the Christian must repudiate classical culture in its entirety. There has always been an important strand of Christian thought which has been anti-intellectual, and the force of its convictions must be weighed carefully. Obscurantism was not invented by the "Bible Belt" in the nineteenth century.

What does Athens stand for? For Tertullian, it was classical culture in its entirety; for us today, it is that culture particularly as expressed in the modern university. Both show similar dominating conceptions and modes of thought.

three dominant ideas

The first controlling concept is that of the autonomy of inquiry. The books of truth are open for the student to inspect at all times; he may ask questions of all authority, sacred or otherwise. So it is that the instinctive attitude of the Athenian is to question. A university is a place where one asks questions. What the Christian must settle is the query, "Does God mind us asking him questions?" But is not the questioning mood the precise opposite of the fundamental attitude of the Christian, faith? This is what Tertullian thought, expressing his defiance of classical norms by his famous dictum: "I believe because it is absurd." Now if faith precludes inquiry, or if doubt is the antithesis of saving faith, no Christian has a right to be in a university, not even a Christian university.

The issue is vital and cannot be evaded by the Christian without fatal schizophrenia. Yet I believe that Tertullian was wrong, as his own personal history demonstrated, and that Augustine was right that the classical search for truth could be a *präeparatio evangelii,* a preparation for the gospel. Why?

For one thing, saving faith in the New Testament is not "faith that . . ." but "faith in. . . ." In other words, it is not a matter of propositions but of commitment. Now the apprehension of propositional truth is highly important ("faith that . . ."), but it is subsequent to "faith in . . .", which is a commitment to a Person. As the writer to the Hebrews puts it (chap. 11), it is by faith (as defined by the personal experiences of the men of God related in the chapter) that "we have faith *that* the worlds were created. . . ." The patron saint of the scholar is the disciple Thomas, who finds answers and acceptance even as he asks his questions. Though as Jesus said, those who have not seen and yet have believed have a happier lot, yet Thomas' vocation is both valid and necessary. The Christian is not afraid to ask questions of truth because of his personal experience of Incarnate Truth. He knows the kind of person Truth is.

The second controlling concept is that of the ultimate unity of the universe. Autonomous inquiry is both legitimate and directed by a belief in the ultimate unity by which all experience can be explained. As the Christian believes that it is worth one's while to seek God (Heb. 11:6), the scholar believes it is worth one's while to seek truth. This is the uni of the uni-versity. In the name of this faith arises the community (koinonia) of scholars; this explains why teaching takes second place to the search for truth, but it is a search in which both teacher and student alike participate. Its characteristic procedure is the dialogue, not the lesson.

In antiquity several mutations of the species of the university had already occurred—the philosophical and humanistic schools in Athens, and the scientific and mathematical schools in Alexandria—but all were committed to the ideal that physics, mathematics, the mind and imagination of man, and moral and aesthetic values were all related to one another. So there is more connection between the professor of physics and the professor of classics than the fact that their salaries are paid by the same administration.

Now it is true that precisely at this point the modern university community is suffering an acute erosion of its basic controlling concepts. Some are saying that there are no longer universities, only multiversities. Certainly there are signs on every hand that Athens has been experiencing urban sprawl as more and more suburbs are being built further and further from the center; communications are becoming more and more choked, and a suffocating smog of the fumes of the waste materials of its processes threaten to smother its life. Academe, like New York, is threatened with being overwhelmed with its own garbage. To abandon the metaphor, the very nature, purpose, and even procedures of the universities are threatened by circumstances, seemingly out of control, driving everyone to narrower specializations and discontinuity. A new tower of Babel is arising, and we all are finding that we can no longer talk to one another.

What has happened? Certainly the university cannot accept the breakup of the academic community, the fragmentation of life and the abandonment to intellectual nihilism as the wave of the future. The hunger for unity, continuity, and meaning which drove the Greeks to invent the university cannot simply be choked off by a petulant spasm of despair. They are the university's raison d' être.

Yet it is abundantly clear that the university lacks the power to generate from within itself the unifying vision. This was where the ancients failed; this is the point where the Christian scholar can speak. Even amid today's explosion of knowledge, when its borders seem to be expanding no less swiftly than novae slipping over the edge of the visible universe, a commitment to God as revealed in Jesus Christ gives one not merely an emotional, or spiritual, but also an intellectual reference point from which to chart the journey of understanding, as well as a moral certitude in the continuing explicability and beauty of the universe. Having begun to make God's acquaintance, and beginning to sense the infinitude of his capacities, and even personally experiencing powers beyond the categories of nature, we confidently proceed in a faith in ultimate unity, derived from a glimpse of the Creator, as well as a study of his creation.

The third controlling concept of Athens is the centrality of man. "Man," declared Protagoras, "is the measure of all things." Now, the ancients were rarely atheists, though it is significant that it was in Greece that a doctrine of atheism did arise. Nor were they on the other hand materialists, though here too a doctrine of materialism did arise. Man held center stage between the material and the divine. Whatever place religion might have had in their scheme of things it was never first place. The divine was conceived in human terms, subjected to criticism by human values, and only important in serving human ends. Prayer was a bargain struck with a god, wheedling a concession in exchange for a promise of some ritual act. Mystery cults promised salvation in the other world in exchange for the scrupulous observance of some secret sacrament.

This concept, too, continues to control the Athens of the modern university. The citizens of academe see religion, if admitted at all, in an ancillary role only. Man is the center of focus, the arbiter of value, and the end of knowledge. Humanism is the normative religion of academe; historically it arose as a rebellious espousal of classical culture over against Mediaeval Christianity.

Can the Christian make any peace with this religion? Considered as an absolute faith, No. It is simply not true that in the material universe man is the measure of all things; nor is it true in the world of values. For the Christian, humanism as a faith is idolatry, a worship of the less than Ultimate. Moreover, the humanist is perpetually vulnerable to disillusionment when faced with the dark side of man.

On the other hand, the Christian, freed from the idolatry of man, is free to accept man unconditionally as a creature of God, fully cognizant of the evil and the good. The Christian, then, can wholeheartedly admire every achievement, treasure every insight, listen without fear to any thought of man, because his security is higher than man. More important still, he can be delivered, too, from the special sin of the humanist, who worships man but does not love men. For the Christian every individual man is of inestimable value, because he is loved by God. Every treasure of the humanist—man's artistic, scientific, or social achievements—the Christian claims (in Augustine's image) as treasure rightly belonging to the King, no matter on whose property it is found.

concluding observations

It may seem that I have talked about the university in general, and not about the classics. It should be clear now that I find them inseparable. Not that I have the slightest illusions about the centrality of departments of classics in current university situations. They have long since lost their once leading position in the university world. But classics are no longer the exclusive possession of classics departments. A major portion of the offerings of departments of English, art, political science, history, or philosophy is concerned with classical matters directly; and the dominant concepts of the classics still shape the thought of the rest of the university. Whether or not the Christian student is called to a vocation in the classics will depend on matters of guidance, through prayerful consideration of interests, talents, and opportunities. But the problems, challenges, and possibilities which the Christian classicist faces are, in essence, no different from those faced by a Christian in any academic discipline.

When Paul came to Athens (Acts 17) he neither shunned the intellectuals nor capitulated to them. Instead, boldly expropriating a whole series of philosophic doctrines, mainly from the Epicureans and Stoics, he declared Christ to them, announcing a revelation from the God whom the intellectuals unwittingly worshipped, and finishing with the truth (so unwelcome to intellectuals) that we as individuals are judged by the man, Jesus. Though some mocked, and others temporized, some (we must never forget) did believe. Like Paul's, the modern Christian's sojourn in Athens can be a time of reaffirmation of truth, from whatever source, together with a witness to the Truth from whom all blessings flow.

Athens, then, has a great deal to do with Jerusalem. The latter, in fact, claims jurisdiction over the former, but only in the name of the King. His ambassadors, if assigned to duty in Athens by their Sovereign, may well take up rightful and fruitful residence at its very center.

Dale D. Rott

Drama

"Spectators learn how to commit adultery by watching a play."
"Plays can be the handmaiden of religion." "Play-going is like
swimming on the brink of a whirlpool." "Drama can be used for
instruction in morals and language."

These representative contradictory statements have been verbalized and recorded throughout history by church fathers,
monks, bishops, ministers, and laymen, as the institutional
church, like a blade of grass in the changing winds, condemned
and condoned drama.

condemnation and praise

Through official decrees, sermons, tracts, and books, the
"church," so a student will learn, has condemned drama at one
period or another for a host of reasons: (1) Dramatic elements
were inherent in the pagan rituals. Drama's birth from these
spontaneous and organized expressions caused a guilt-by-associ-
ation reasoning. (2) Representational arts were considered forbidden by the second commandment, "Thou shalt not make
unto thee any graven images." (3) Plays dealt with earthly
affairs, hence they opposed spiritual aspirations. A Christian

Platonism (based on 1 Jn. 2:15-17), influential during the
Church Fathers and Puritan periods, fostered a conflict between
the world (flesh) and heaven (spirit), which approved only
future hopes, not daily duties. (4) Drama, as an illusion of
reality, overtly and intentionally deceived viewers into con-
fusing reality and illusion. (5) Plays denounced the Bible and
profaned Bible stories by bawdy humor and distorted scripture
truths. (6) Immoral lives of actors and actresses undermined
church-dictated moral standards. (7) Some governments cen-
sored plays and imprisoned actors, therefore the church should
not accept drama. (8) Plays, presented for mere entertainment,
encouraged idleness. (9) Plays portrayed, discussed, or hinted
at all seven deadly sins in an alluring manner, seducing the
innocent or naive into a life of sin. (10) Playhouses sheltered
vagrants, thieves, horsestealers, whoremongers, contrivers of
treason, and other idle and dangerous people. (11) Plays caused
plagues and other physical sickness. And (12) drama precipitated violent storms and catastrophes. These representative
statements reflect religious people's rational and superstitious
reasons for rejecting drama.

Conversely, the church has condoned drama, for drama could
(1) be used for instruction in morals by presenting plays with
good examples, (2) aid congregations in worship, (3) educate
congregations in church dogma, (4) teach literature through
reading plays in their original language, (5) edify by a moderate
use of humor, necessary for relaxation, and (6) engage children
and young people in wholesome activity.[1] In short, if drama
could be utilized as a means to a religiously sanctioned end,
church officials would then consider drama a valid activity.

Playwrights and producers have varied in their attitudes
toward the church as much as the church has varied its opinion
about drama. Dramatists have proclaimed the church's message
in scripts and productions but they have also satirized the
church and ridiculed its ministers. Ignorance of each other's
mission and methods, inconsistencies in each other's attitudes
and policies, and fear of each other's ability has continually
caused conflicts and schisms. Each must understand the other's

legitimate critical approach to eliminate a major conflict: Church criticism is ethically and theologically based; dramatic criticism is technically and artistically based.[2] Drama, therefore, can be a coworker with theology in the educational, worship, and social areas of the church, but the church *must* recognize drama as master in the artistic/aesthetic realm. If the church is to fulfill Christ's command, drama must be as accepted in the church as lectures and music are now.

At a Christian Writers Workshop session entitled "Why I Write," a recognized woman writer exclaimed, "I write because I must pay the grocery bill." During her speech she never implied Holy Spirit aid or receiving a divine calling. But Christ's "self-denial" statements include a calling to a divine vocation, and thus the dramatist should not be motivated to achieve artistic recognition from his audience, to develop loyal disciples, or financial profit, but rather to aid in establishing a personal relationship between God and man. The Christian dramatist's goal is art for Christ's sake and not art for art's sake. Art for Christ's sake does not demand didactic propaganda but requires a recognition of theistic eternal values, sacrificial devotion, perfection in technique, and a God/Christ/man relationship in content.[3] The content focuses on such God/man relationships as alienation, redemption, and service. Art for Christ's sake provides an incisive creative wisdom through the Holy Spirit. The Christian dramatist does not write, act, direct, or design alone. His reliance upon the Spirit's inspiration benefits mankind and keeps his own selfish desires from becoming paramount.

difficult questions
Every generation has researched the church/drama relationships and attempted an eternal productive marriage, but questions constantly recur. Inevitably, there is the question, "How can a believer in Christ portray a drunkard or prostitute?"[4] The issue is whether a Christian ought to portray a personality inherently alien to his own new Adam nature and to enact a scene which seemingly involves committing a sin. Some hold that the "abstain from the appearance of evil" rule (1 Thess. 5:22) and

the Pauline meat controversy (1 Cor. 10:25-32) negate any participation which produces questions.[5]

But if one examines the context of these verses and understands the conventions of drama, he may come to a different conclusion. For example, when Roy Fluth, human being, portrays an historical or fictional character, Henry VIII, the audience is expected to *see* Henry VIII and not mainly Roy Fluth. With costume, make-up, and directed actions he no longer "exists" on stage as Roy Fluth but is the representation of Henry VIII. The play is a representation of reality and *not* reality itself. When Roy dresses and portrays Henry VIII, he is imitating the stage character's reality and not the life reality of Roy on stage. He enacts, to the best of his talent, a representation of a character, and the audience must, to the best of its ability, imagine Roy as Henry.

Specific theater conventions govern every aspect of the play. When the final curtain drops and costume and make-up are removed, Roy reappears and with the audience returns to the different rules which govern real life.[6] During the play's action real life rules are suspended and dramatic conventions are enacted. Although real life rules are sometimes used in a play, they are considered only a representation of life's rules and are subject to the dramatic conventions for the performance time-span.[7] Some people do not understand the play as a representation of reality. They "see" the actor as the *person* they know and not as the *character* he is portraying, and, because they cannot divorce stage actions from life actions or because they are ignorant of the dramatic conventions, they confuse life reality with theater's representation of reality.

Other actors answer the problem of portraying a "sinner" by claiming that the end justifies the means. For example, the plot of a non-believer becoming a believer in Christ could involve portraying the seven deadly sins prior to his conversion. The believer in this situation portrays any or all of the "sins" without feeling guilt because the salvation end redeems the "sinful" actions in the preceding acts. The critic of the ends-means standard claims that some actors desire to enact the unbeliever to have vicarious experiences and thus, subtly, yet wilfully, commit sin.

A third answer to the problem involves the audience's criteria of judgment. Audiences disagree on which stage actions are "sins." One individual may rise in righteous indignation against an actor holding hands with a woman on stage, whereas another viewer may see an actor making delicate caressing advances on parts of a female body and think absolutely nothing is "sinful" in this character portrayal context. This positive reactor considers the actor's motivation, the scene's ultimate meaning and the theater's conventions. The negative reactor emphasizes that the actor's body is incapable of knowing that it is on stage and not on the street thus requiring it to "turn off" normal physical reactions usually reserved for wedlock. The rebuttal claims the mind governs the body and knows when it is "on stage" thus governing body reactions accordingly.[8] Each actor is responsible for his actions before God and thus the believer in Christ should be extremely sensitive to possible compromises of his convictions and offending a weaker brother.

Also at issue here is how realistic must words and movements on stage need to be in order to convey the meaning of an emotion or an action. The "realistic" problem begins with the playwright. How overtly realistic or subtly suggestive should a playwright be in his choice of words, actions, and attitudes? What criteria can be used to weigh his script as a potential stumbling block for a weaker brother against his script being an instrument for the salvation of a person? Some people hold that "drama mirrors life" and thus requires the playwright to give an objective presentation of reality. But no playwright can be wholly objective since he is conditioned by his environment and reflects his *subjective* opinions concerning life in his scripts. The playwright as a man is susceptible to old Adam influences. Thus his motivation is the crux to realistic writings. If the playwright's dialogue and action aims at sensationalism or gimmickry, then he is committing a spiritual/aesthetic sin; but if he feels the realistic action or word develops character or plot which in turn clarifies the God/man relationship, then it is difficult to criticize the realism.

Next, the director takes the script, with its "realism" problem, and either attempts an exact stage representation of the playwright's intentions or molds the script into his directorial image. There have been numerous productions of *Hamlet* and in each production viewers have heard Shakespeare's script but have never seen two identical Hamlets. The director is artistically obliged to create the essence of the playwright's script, but the director as creator can determine which realistic actions he desires to highlight by specific blocking or which actions he desires to underplay by subtle nuances.[9] During these decisions, the Christian director must consider the "art for Christ's sake" principle.

Although the actor is submissive to directorial concepts, he can rehearse to create such realism that the audience forgets it is watching a representation of reality and becomes consciously or unconsciously involved in the action. With this potential influence the actor must enact his role according to the "art for Christ's sake" principle.[10]

The lighting craftsman can highlight or subdue scenes, moods, persons, etc. through color, movement, intensity, spotting, etc. The costume designer, through color, texture, and lines can design a costume with subtle or obvious meanings. The make-up artist can mold lines, shapes, and colors to overtly or covertly convey meaning. All must analyze their contribution to the "realism" according to the "art for Christ's sake" principle.

matters of language

Swear words, profane phrases, and blasphemous expressions verbalized on stage take us into another problem area. "Swearing" in Scripture indicates mainly a legal oath on a life or a debt and is not to be confused with contemporary words considered "profanity." The problem today lies more in the area the Bible calls "blasphemy." Such words as *God!, God damn!, Jesus Christ!,* and *Holy Spirit!* are scripturally blasphemous words when used irreverently, but Scripture does not claim *hell, devil, bitch,* or *bastard* as blasphemous words.[11] Some Christians use the very reverent word *heaven* within a mundane expression, "Oh, for heaven's sakes!" Which is the greater profanity, *Hell!* expressed by an actor in the midst of a spiritual struggle, or *Heavens!* used in a flippant manner by a frustrated Christian? When a preacher uses *Hell, damn,* or *Christ* as an illustrative word or within a story in his sermon, the congregation may blink their eyes but they seldom censure. But, when these words are verbalized or even visualized on stage, some people react sharply, forgetting drama's special frame. Yet the sermon, like the play, occurs within a special frame, and both forms can highlight positive concepts by visualizing and/or verbalizing negative aspects.

under pressure

The dramatic art form seems to be criticized more frequently than other art forms except for sex in movies and paintings. Music and painting, in many instances, can blaspheme or relate sins without the audience's knowledge because a symphony and a canvas can be more abstract than drama, and people do not realize that a specific note, stanza, line, or color condemns the Christ life. A thunderous minor chord with dissonance may abstractly connotate, in the tactual sense, a fist in the face, but the drama's concrete visual portrayal activates the auditory, olfactory, and tactual senses in the viewer. This immediate confrontation, visualization, or concreteness of actions, so lifelike, causes questions not asked of art and music.

The arts tend to bring out the egotistical self of a human personality more than other vocations because the artist's skill—whether playwright, director, or actor—is on exhibit and achievement/recognition is predicated upon critical acclaim and audience applause. The resounding applause which is clapped upon the actor because of recognized excellence may echo in his ears as he exits the boards to walk the concrete. He may feel as though everyone recognizes him as the performer, encouraging a continuing of the stage character or development of an "effect" which masks his real personality. One may easily become enamored by his own toil and achievement rather than express thanks to God who granted and guided the talent. Too often when an individual considers the dramatic arts he looks toward national fame on the illuminated screen. The "star" system is anathema to Christ-like humility. When a Christian artist's path leads to commercial success or to accomplishments as a director of a community theater or a college players troupe, he is also under pressure to take glory rather than to give it.

The Christian dramatist must observe, dissect, and integrate with the world, yet be selective by pruning and judging. One of the most difficult aspects of the dramatist's life is to divorce himself from the trends and traditions of his time in order to stand apart for an objective observation and differentiation between appearance and reality. Inevitably, critics will misinterpret, condemn, and reject him, but during these lonely moments he must remember his work in that special puzzle whose ultimate solution God alone knows.

The Christian dramatist's life contrasts with the bulk of passive humanity. He enters the field as a pioneer and may become a martyr. God may force him to be a Jonah resisting the journey to Ninevah, yet going. He may cry out like Amos, or live as God directed Hosea. At other times he may resemble Samuel, tossed between God's will and the people's rejection. He must have the preaching fervor of a Peter and the poetic sensitivity of a psalmist and, in every instance, the theological capabilities of a Paul.[12]

The Christian dramatist as artist cherishes the theistic eternal values of the universe and a Christ-pivoting life as he deciphers, vindicates, and celebrates these values on a spiritual/aesthetic plane. As preacher, priest, and prophet—secure only in God—he ministers to an exploding, polluted world secure in nothing.

Notes

[1] Space here does not allow my listing of the numerous primary sources. The pro and con reasons are paraphrased from the following secondary works: Philip A. Coggin, *Uses of Drama* (New York, 1956); Fred Eastman and Louis Wilson, *Drama in the Church*, rev. ed. (New York, 1942), see particularly chaps. 1-2; Harold Ehrensperger, *Religious Drama: Ends and Means* (New York, 1962), Part 2; Tom F. Driver, "Church, the Theatre, and the World," *Dialog*, LI (1962), 48-54; and John Gassner, *Masters of the Drama*, 3rd rev. ed. (New York, 1954).

[2] Harry Farra, *Theology and Theatre: The Religious Critical Hierarchy* (unpublished manuscript).

[3] Alfred R. Edyvean, *This Dramatic World* (New York, 1970), chaps. 1-2, 12.

[4] People seldom question portraying greed or hate, indicating a truncated Old Testament mentality that omits Christ's "thinking-can-be-sin" concept (Mt. 5:21 f, 27 f—NEB and Charles Williams trans.). Such people seem concerned with overt actions and words and seldom request clarification of anti-Christian attitudes prevalent in subtle movements or vocal intonations.

[5] If the strong and weak Christians could agree on texts to prove their respective viewpoints (1 Thess. 5:22) and agree to accept whichever solution matches scriptural exhortations (1 Cor. 10:30 ff; Col. 3:16 ff; Mt. 7:1 ff; Phil. 4:8; Rom. 14:1—15:6), we would then have answers to problems posed in this essay.

[6] Toby Cole and Helen K. Chinoy, eds., *Actors on Acting* (New York, 1964).

[7] Of course, happenings, improvisations, absurd, or guerilla theater styles allow an intermingling of life-reality and an imitation of reality through interaction with the audience, script notations, and adaptations in actions and dialogue from performance to performance.

[8] Directors work with both types of personalities and attempt to discover during auditions whether an actor is able to control himself or if he only wants the role for a vicarious experience. Most directors and actors refuse plays and scenes involving actions or thoughts contrary to their convictions. Most scenes or dialogue which suggest compromising acts sometimes are cut or replaced with substitutions. In a "cut" or "doctored" play, censorship or shift of responsibility is involved, and this opens another controversy for debate.

[9] Another question arises as one views a scene or listens to a vocal inflection which suggests to him an immoral act or thought but was never intended by the director. Do we then censor the director's art, or do we stone the viewer's imagination (Mk. 7:15 ff)?

[10] A difficult problem for the Christian centers around the learning process, for all critics agree that drama can powerfully teach ideas and produce—and desirably so—an emphatic response from the audience. If man, then, like all primates, learns by observing, does the Christian cast in a particular role with a compromising part actually teach viewers certain ideas or acts growing out of the demands placed on that part? Or to take another example, does one's use of certain profane language create any basically compromising situations? As Aristotle said of the fictional character portrayed in the play (*Poetics*, 1461[a] 3 ff), so may the Christian of the role he takes: One must consider the intrinsic quality of the word or deed, for both carry a moral dimension. As yet no studies have been undertaken which indicate to what extent audiences in fact discriminate satisfactorily between stage situations and those of real life. Thus the Christian student at this juncture lacks empirical data to help in his decisions, and hence will need to decide each role on his interpretation of scriptural principles, guided by the Holy Spirit.—Ed.

[11] *Interpreter's Dictionary* (New York, 1962), I, 445 f, and III, 575 f. It is not the word that denotes profanity, but the emotion or intention given to the word as used in the real life context. The personal name "Joe" could suggest blasphemy if used derogatorily or the word "and" could replace any current four-letter swear word if society thus dictated.

[12] Finley Eversole, ed., *Christian Faith and the Contemporary Arts* (New York, 1962), Part 1; and Roger Hazelton, *Theological Approach to Art* (New York, 1967).

Robert W. Smith

Speech

At 9:45 A.M. Jim Steiner gulps his last bit of coffee in the Union, gathers his notebooks, and shuffles off to Old Main and his 10:00 Speech 241 class. It's the first session. Ambivalent about it—he wants to learn to speak to audiences but has heard stories that the instructor is some kind of nut, and a demanding one at that—he settles into his seat among twenty-five or so others who seem to represent a cross section of underclassmen.

Jim's reading of contemporary newspapers and certain popular literature has led him to conclude that speech centers on success—"putting oneself across," becoming the top salesman for the company, or developing a more buoyant personality. He has seen little that suggests any sort of relationship between oral discourse and moral issues,[1] except that the quacks he has heard—including some in the pulpit—wasted his time! It never occurs to him that speech, in the sense of public speaking,[2] can intersect with Christianity at various points.[3]

He soon finds, however, as do others in the class, that the speaker, whether in public or private speech, wrestles with problems of truth, values, and morals. Theorists from Plato to the present have agreed that responsible speaking necessarily involves a moral posture, because every rhetorical effort has a moral effect. On the other hand, if speech has no moral dimension, if it is as one ancient declared, "to make the worse case appear the better cause," if it displays superficiality or pseudointelligence, then it merits all the scorn Plato and his modern progeny have heaped upon it. Augustine, an important rhetorical theorist as well as Church Father, warned his followers to "beware of the man who abounds in eloquent nonsense, and so much the more if the hearer is pleased with what is not worth listening to, and thinks that because the speaker is eloquent what he says must be true."[4]

One cannot insist too strongly that truth should have the most effective, clear, and persuasive spokesmen possible. While, ultimately, veracity will prevail, society has no assurance it will do so in a particular span of time—for example, one's lifetime. The genocide of twelve million Jews at the hand of Hitler testifies to this. Error and sophistry too often own the clever spokesmen as their standard-bearers, leaving truth and accountable discourse hanging on the gallows. Edmund Burke expressed the point rightly, particularly for the Christian, when he stated that all we need for evil to triumph is for good men to keep silent long enough.

We cannot idolize oral discourse. Ethical speakers cannot affirm Thoreau's declaration that "we love eloquence for its own sake, and not for any truth which it may utter, or any heroism it may inspire."[5] Rather, they learn to speak well because God delights in expressed truth, and people need that truth to better their own lives.[6] Wise interpreters of ideas, like genuine friends, will spread knowledge and healing (Prov. 15:7; 12:18).

The Christian speaker, unlike his pagan colleague, looks to God for help, insight, and the preparation of his listeners' minds. But such dependence does not obviate hard work on his part. "Whatsoever your hand finds to do, do it with your might," he is reminded (Eccles. 9:10). One could as soon justify the surgeon's neglect of his studies and craft because all life rests in God's hands as he could defend the speaker who refuses to acquire speaking skills on the grounds that only the Holy Spirit can move men. When Jesus counseled his disciples not to prepare their speeches "on that day" (Mt. 10:19-20) of political and religious persecution, he was not thinking of speaking generally. The Christian speaker, as elsewhere in God's creation, is a colaborer with Christ.

Before examining four important elements in speech, we should raise one essential point. Customarily, textbook authors assume that speech is an overlaid function; that is, all organs used in speaking—tongue, lips, teeth, breathing mechanism, etc.—are primarily biological organs which have been adapted for phonatory use. Hence vocalizing is secondary to the organs' primary use in survival. But note the assumption: Man's basic purpose in life is survival. Suppose for sake of argument that man's basic purpose is to be in fellowship with his Creator and fellow creatures. Then the reverse would hold: Breathing, eating, swallowing, and the like would function secondarily to the organs' chief mission of aiding communion. Few authors acknowledge either their arbitrary premise or that speech may be a primary and not secondary fulfillment of man.[7]

One can discern Christian implications for each of the four components of the speech juncture: speaker, speech, audience, and occasion.[8]

the speaker

While Aristotle saw three chief means of persuasion—the logical, emotional, and ethical—the latter outweighed the other two.[9] By ethical persuasion—Greek, *êthos*—he meant what the audience thinks of the speaker when he is speaking. It includes character,[10] sincerity, thoroughness of preparation, and goodwill. This element carries special import for the Christian because God has entrusted him as spokesman—when he espouses the right—for a particular cause. Unless the audience views the speaker as trustworthy, his message will strike the ears like a clanging cymbal. Understandably, the Bible has much to say concerning character: honesty, purity, diligence, and respect for others.

Other sources, too, have emphasized it. Emerson stated what is now a cliché: "What you are ... thunders so that I cannot hear what you say to the contrary."[11] Quintilian, the Roman contemporary of St. Paul, felt that a speaker's moral character was so important that he defined the orator as "a good man skilled in speaking" (*vir bonus dicendi peritus*).[12] A nineteenth-century German scholar, Franz Theremin, so closely related speaking and integrity that he devoted an entire book to the ethical dimensions of speech, entitling it, *Eloquence, A Virtue.*[13]

One can enjoy Byron's "Childe Harold's Pilgrimage" despite knowing about his promiscuous life, or Poe's "Raven" recalling his psychosis, but who will listen to another speak on important matters unless he has confidence in him? Such reticence likely stems from the fact that the spoken word complicates adequate reflection prior to desired action, whereas the printed page allows more time to deliberate upon the ideas. The speaker should strive for that attitude expressed of Jesus: "No man ever spoke like this man!"

Not only is personal character essential to the speaker, but also is his handling of stagefright. St. Paul knew its feeling,[14] yet he not only learned to control it but went on to speak before some of the most sophisticated audiences of the ancient world. That God stands on the side of truth, justice, and mercy should strengthen the legs of the fainthearted. Virtually all stagefright springs from fear of making a fool of oneself in a given platform situation. Therefore, when the speaker's confidence lies not in himself, but in (1) the goodwill of the audience and his creator, (2) the truth he has examined and prepared, and (3) his desire to help his listeners become better people, much of the trauma can be resolved.

Juxtaposing these items, one can see beauty, art, and wholeness not readily perceived otherwise. Why? Because the speaker, whether student or not, more fully realizes his niche in life: an honest and creative spokesman for what is right and good.

the speech

Five purposes (ends) of speaking constitute practically all the types of speeches one finds: to inform, actuate, secure belief, entertain, and inspire. In each of these, four important parts or tasks (canons) have strong moral overtones.

The first—invention—historically has dealt with ideas, arguments, and their proofs. It has always stood at the heart of speech content, for without important and useful ideas with acceptable evidence, a speech will fall on annoyed listeners and waste valuable time. One black circuit rider of the last century, when asked about his secret to preaching, replied, "It's simple: I read myself full; I think myself clear; I pray myself hot; and then I let go." The oral communicator, whether Christian or non-Christian, must study to show himself approved by God and man, conscious of the implications of his position.

Another dimension one sees in speech is content. The use of arguments substantiated by evidence is far more humane (and Christian) than ignoring content and living at the gut-level of existence. The latter maintains one's antagonist is not important, or at least that he is quite incapable of using rational processes to arrive at a given end. Emotional appeals, not complemented by facts, not only demean the listener but imply that God did not make man in his image so much as he did in the likeness of the lower animals who operate at a stimulus-response level. Sound arguments, cogent reasoning, and strong evidence dignify man, elevating him to a level not shared by other living creatures. They both bestow personhood on others and maintain it for oneself. They posit that men are not to be manipulated as objects but to be treated as persons—God's highest creation. The speaker who declines to bolster his oral remarks with appropriate content, as well as the listener who treats it indifferently, is something less than a full person, at least at that moment.

Should the speaker stress truth even when it hurts? Yes, but he must do so in love (respect) for others, genuinely desiring their betterment. He must at times pick subjects even if they hurt speaker and audience, as the prophet Nathan and Abraham Lincoln found—speaking as a dying man to dying men. But like the young man born blind whom Jesus healed (Jn. 9), he will want to argue about the known, and not the unknown: "This one thing I know. . . ." Moreover, truth will fulfill us creatively and subjectively by giving us a sense of well-being.

The second canon—arrangement or organization of one's ideas—dictates the order in which to couch one's thoughts. Theophrastus, famous Greek literary critic and student of Aristotle, stated that "an unbridled horse ought to be trusted sooner than a badly arranged discourse." Experimental evidence has not established the retentive or persuasive effect which clear arrangement of ideas has on audiences—though rambling, disjointed discourse often irritates—but one can confidently assert that when a speaker respects his audience, he will help them to grasp ideas by making them as clear as possible.

The third canon of speech—style—includes language, syntax, vocabulary, and grammar. If a student believes speaking is significant enough to ask divine help in his choice of topics, he should also express his thoughts "in that form of language in which alone it can appear to the audience to be truth in its particular bearings and applications."[15] The words we choose may well determine the degree of retention and persuasion we achieve.

Words can easily mislead audiences, as Paul counseled the Corinthians 2,000 years ago (1 Cor. 14:9), and therefore violate respect due them. Unfortunately, some practitioners of oral discourse deliberately confuse audiences by employing well-known words while attaching new meanings to them. One finds this in some contemporary pulpits and on the political hustings when the speaker implies a familiar idea, though in fact intends something quite different. Carlo Bucher has observed that contemporary theology "does not use other words to say the same thing [that traditional theology says], but uses the same words to say something different."[16] A speaker who is guilty of such verbal behavior only confuses and ensnares, but is at least as culpable as those who use emotional appeals which cannot be substantiated by evidence.[17]

Not only is clarity important, but so is economy and simplicity. Some speakers encumber their speeches with excessive words and either obscure their intention, or deliberately beguile audiences (Prov. 10:19). Jesus noted that on the day of judgment, men will be held accountable for every careless word they utter (Mt. 12:36). Imagine the docket facing some of us! Oddly enough, we tend to verbalize more the less we have prepared our speeches, striving, it seems, to cover up our shoddiness. Just as in music, the fewer the notes the more the ideas stand out, so in speech the fewer the words (within limits) the more prominent the ideas. The beginning student should alert himself particularly to excessive use of meaningless phrases like "you know ... you know ... you know... ," and "I mean ... I mean ... I mean. . . ."

At the same time one should strip away high-sounding phrases which add nothing to the content or impact. St. Paul's desire to accentuate ideas drove him to preach "not with the wisdom of words lest the cross of Christ should be made ineffective" (1 Cor. 1:17). He had observed or knew of the rhetorical schools of Alexandria, Athens, and Rome and determined not to vitiate the gospel by such verbal display.[18]

The final canon[19] of speech is delivery. "Truth alone," noted Yale's Chauncey A. Goodrich over a century ago, "has comparatively little power over the mind. It is the manner of exhibiting that truth, of making it press with irresistible force on the understanding" that commands attention.[20] Thus, the speaker will wish to speak as vitally, animatedly, and directly as possible. Indifference to delivery borders on sin because (1) an incomprehensible speech wastes the audience's time and (2) poor delivery undermines the audience's respect for the speaker and his topic. Mumbling, speaking too fast, or establishing poor audience-contact appreciably decreases the audience's positive reaction and complicates one's rhetorical task.

the audience

As the third element, the listener occupies an essential role in the total milieu of public discourse, not only because without him no communication takes place, not only because people are worthwhile as people, but also because God says people are important (Ps. 8:5). He proved their immense worth through his creative act eons ago, and supremely at Calvary. To treat them as anything less than God's esteem merits calls into question his values in creation and redemption.

The speaker must, then, know those to whom he speaks. He cannot just love ideas and truth in the abstract, but must love (respect) in the concrete situation. Such knowledge and respect do not demand that he cowtow to the audience, but they do necessitate, as Paul showed before the Areopagus (Acts 17) or William Wilberforce to his nineteenth-century English audiences, that the oral communicator should fashion his message to particular people. A proper attitude toward others can build trust between speaker and audience—always an important ingredient in public discourse.[21]

How the student looks at people will largely determine how he will view the speech situation. If he conceives the latter as an opportunity for public display, as did students in the sophistic schools of the ancient world and as elocutionists and other speakers have in our time, his speech will seek to parade himself and his ability. Any classroom or commercial agency which stresses "selling oneself" at the expense of truth or the betterment of one's audience prostitutes to that degree a discipline and medium of instruction whose raison d' être stands at the font of liberty.

Frequently audiences may believe a speaker said something when in fact he never did. How is this possible? While the impression may stem from the speaker's ambiguity and possible dereliction, it may also result from the Holy Spirit's interpreting the content in a manner quite different from that intended by the speaker, bringing home truth more forcibly. One should learn to expect unusual factors in all discourse, for God may operate in unanticipated ways to establish truth.

Not only may speakers affect an audience, but by the audience's reaction (feedback)[22] to the words, ideas, gestures, and the like, the latter may influence the communicator. Votes, comments, and applause encourage most speakers in their rhetorical efforts, but wise speakers will not depend on effect, realizing they have a higher calling. Their task: to be faithful spokesmen for worthwhile causes, irrespective of the audience's reaction. Strong, polarized stands may alienate audiences, but when speakers have cast in their lot for the right cause, they must stand square to the front, conscious that but for God's grace they would have the same blind spots. This posture merits no egotism, no messianic complex, no disdain for others, but rather humility of spirit and speech.

What course should the student speaker plot in or out of the classroom when his persuasive efforts have failed? May he justifiably disrupt society to achieve ends? A quick answer we cannot give. Perhaps the speaker has been indolent in analyzing the total situation and in preparing his speech, or has deliberately sought to antagonize those in decision-making capacities—such tactics frequently occur today—thus vitiating all possibility of success. Perhaps also his audience (whether one or one hundred) simply does not wish to move at this point. In any case, the speaker has failed to produce the desired effect, for his arguments (ultimately too weak) have not moved his listener(s) to action.

Should he wish to take other and more decisive action, he faces responsibility along several fronts. First, he cannot bemoan the disappearance of a free society, for the democratic structure with its free speech has not failed, but rather the speaker himself has proved unequal to the task. Second, he must prepare himself for possible consequences to any infraction of the law. One can hardly circumvent legal requirements placed on society and then responsibly demand amnesty for his act. To ask such a price suggests a childish mentality: One wants for himself what he is unprepared to grant to others. Rather, like Martin Luther King, Jr., such a speaker must be willing to sit out his punishment in jail. Third, he must realize that if he chooses the route of coercion, having failed in his rhetorical efforts, someone else may come along (with a bigger mob) and remove his rights when those speakers fail in their speaking. What is gained by force is just as easily lost by force. The Golden Rule would seem to apply with particular force here.

the occasion

"The final component," and now Jim Steiner's ears prick up, for the professor has seemed to approach the end of his journey, "the final component dictates in part how much one can say and how far he can go whether in the home, church, classrooms, on the stump, or in a tavern."[23] How long one should speak, whether inside or outside the classroom, his choice of dress, topic, and evidence will all be partially determined by the occasion. Some communist speakers, like Castro or Brezhnev, frequently speak three hours or more. St. Paul's all-night discourse at Troas may not have been too long, even though a lad fell asleep, dropped from a window, and was picked up for dead (Acts 20:6 ff). Perhaps the total situation demanded this length. Some professional speakers err when they believe they must limit themselves to twenty minutes. Others fault when they keep an audience half that long! In any given case one must analyze the circumstances to determine the optimum length of time.

To sum up: The student will do well to recall St. Paul's admonition, "Let your speech always be gracious, seasoned with salt" (Col. 4:6), as well as to remember, "as a man speaks, so is he."

These and related principles will allow one to create an artistic product with his own unique stamp on it. It is his much as a newborn baby belongs to its mother, and for similar reasons.

As Jim Steiner wanders back to his room, he ponders the lecture and, while a little surprised at the religious overtones, he admits to himself that the discipline may have more possibilities than he has anticipated. "Maybe I ought to give it a try," he mutters.

Notes

[1] Dale Carnegie's courses, and those similarly success oriented, view speech differently than the type largely described in this essay.

[2] By public speaking I mean oral discourse, theoretically or potentially for the masses.

[3] Since more students are exposed to speech in the sense of public speaking than to any other, this essay will focus on that aspect of the field. It should be remembered, however, that radio-television, speech correction, phonetics, oral interpretation of literature, oral communication, rhetorical criticism—all these and more fall under the canopy of speech.

[4] Augustine, *De Doctrina Christiana*, IV, 5 in *Select Library of the Nicene and Post-Nicene Fathers*, ed. Philip Schaff and trans. J. F. Shaw (Grand Rapids, 1956), II, 576; Paul had earlier warned the Ephesians, "Let no one deceive you with empty words" (Eph. 5:6).

[5] Henry D. Thoreau, "Civil Disobedience," *Miscellanies. Writings of Henry David Thoreau*, X (Boston, 1893), p. 168.

[6] Did Tacitus (*Dialogus de Oratoribus*, 40 f) correctly argue that great orators appear during times of greatest excitement and chaos? Will hell, then, have better speakers than heaven? Cf. Henry P. Tappan, "Philosophy of Expression in Oratory," *Biblical Repository and Classical Review*, IV (1848), 706. See the entire article for various implications.

[7] An exception is Georges Gusdorf, *La Parole*, trans. Paul T. Brockelman (Evanston, 1965). Gusdorf sees the tongue as primarily for speaking and not biological purposes (p. 62).

[8] This treatment will follow the approach of classical rhetoric, that type of oral discourse devised and amplified by the ancient Greeks and Romans, and since practiced for two thousand years. More recently a communication approach, alluded to here and there in this essay, has found increasing acceptance. Two books treating the subject from the latter angle are David K. Berlo, *Process of Communication* (New York, 1960); and Gordon Wiseman and Larry Barker, *Speech—Interpersonal Communication* (San Francisco, 1967).

[9] Aristotle, *Art of Rhetoric*, $1356^a 10$ ff.

[10] One recent experiment has found character one of the two important ingredients of ethos; see James C. McCoskey, "Scales for the Measurement of Ethos," *Speech Monographs*, XXXII (1965), 65-72, cited in Wayne N. Thompson, *Quantitative Research in Public Address and Communication* (New York, 1967), p. 56.

[11] Ralph W. Emerson, *Social Aims*, rev. ed. (Boston, 1888), p. 95.

[12] Quintilian, *Institutio Oratoria*, XII, i. 1. If the Roman writer here had expediency and accommodation in mind for his *vir bonus*, George Campbell (*Philosophy of Rhetoric*, 7th ed., [London, 1850], p. 97)

certainly did not.

[13] *Die Beredsamkeit eine Tugend, oder Grundlinien einer systematischen Rhetorik* (Berlin, 1814). For a contemporary account, perceptively treating ethics in public address, see Virgil L. Baker and Ralph T. Eubanks, "Toward an Axiology of Rhetoric," *Quarterly Journal of Speech*, XLVIII (1962), 757-68.

[14] "And I was with you in weakness and in much fear and trembling" (1 Cor. 2:3).

[15] See Henry R. Day, "Ideal of a Perfect Pulpit Discourse," *American Biblical Repository*, 2nd ser., XII (1844), 85-111 for observations on preaching in particular and implications for public speaking in general.

[16] Cited in *Christianity Today*, 13 Oct. 1967, p. 18.

[17] If Georges Buffon was right (*Discours sur Le Style* [Paris, 1926], p. 16), and I think he was, when he told his French audience 200 years ago, "Le style est l'homme même," a speaker's deliberate double talk reveals his character most deeply. Jesus alerted us to the same idea with "out of the abundance of the heart the mouth speaks" (Mt. 12:34).

[18] Yet great preachers profited by this sophistic training. One thinks of Basil the Great, Gregory Nazianzen, John Chrysostom, and Augustine—to name four. One can find further data on the influence of Greek rhetoric on Christian preaching and oral discourse generally in Edwin Hatch, *Influence of Greek Ideas on Christianity* (New York, 1957), pp. 86-115.

[19] I am omitting memory, treated in considerable detail by the ancients, because as a classical doctrine it has fallen into disuse in modern times.

[20] See the impressive evidence on the importance of delivery cited in Thompson, *Quantitative Research,* pp. 82 ff.

[21] Kim Giffin, "Interpersonal Trust in Small-Group Communication," *Quarterly Journal of Speech*, LIII (1967), 224-34 provides a summary of studies in interpersonal trust.

[22] "Feedback" does not formally occur in classical rhetoric, but clearly Demosthenes and other Greek orators in the boule were conscious of it, as was Cicero in the Roman senate and courtroom—so their speeches abundantly indicate.

[23] Dwight L. Moody held forth in taverns a century ago, and Bob Harrington still does today in New Orleans and elsewhere.

Kenneth L. Pike

Language

Of all the academic disciplines in the United States, it is probably in linguistics that groups of Christian scholars, known and specifically labeled as such by their peers, have had the greatest impact on its theoretical outlook and practical techniques. The centers of this influence have been principally three: The Summer Institute of Linguistics (and the Wycliffe Bible Translators with which it is associated), the American Bible Society, and the Kennedy School of Missions of the Hartford Seminary Foundation. The first of these is most extensively engaged in analyzing the structure of preliterate languages and translating the Scriptures into them; the second in the publishing of Scriptures; and the third in training missionaries.

It is peculiarly fitting, therefore, that a student might ask, Does the Christian engaging in linguistics bring to bear upon it a special outlook and belief which determines his approach to the discipline?

An empirical answer: Christian scholars are utilizing every major theoretical framework current in the USA and Great Britain. No known restriction prevents the similar utilization of any theory from other parts of the world. The implication is therefore clear: Christian presuppositions do not *determine* the actual linguistic framework which he utilizes.

Since there is no such determining relation, we must then ask whether Christianity makes more probable the adoption of one theory or another. Science seeks observable regularities—tested, repeatable results under constant conditions. The expectation of same-result-under-same-condition may be called a "law." An interlocked pattern of such laws, within a consistent—preferably mathematically stated—explanatory framework may be called a "theory."[1]

Yet a problem enters the search for any empirical law: Conditions are never exactly constant for repeating any experiment. We cannot step into the same river twice; in this sense we cannot step into "the" river twice, or even name "it." Somehow, nevertheless, we must pretend that we can do so, or ignore—*as if* they did not occur—the changing parts of the environment. We hope—without guarantee—that what we have left out will make no difference to us in the future for understanding the event.

models of reality

Sometimes we are wrong. The data left out proves to have been relevant. We are reminded of this danger a little better if we call our tentative, human results a "model" of reality rather than full "truth" itself. All science, in this sense, deals with models of reality; and these models (not the reality) are changed from time to time in order to get a better matching of description to the reality. Such a model can be called a theory of the phase of reality it attempts to describe; and a theory may likewise be called a model.

We must emphasize, then, that science operates through theoretical models; but a model—or a theory—is useful to the scholar only if it deliberately *leaves out* some *relevant* data. Since the world is vast, and the potential data to be studied infinite, a model which included all the data would be no more intelligible than unanalyzed reality itself. Science, therefore, in order to be able to study the world leaves out some data so as to get a simplified description of a small part of the remainder under unreal, idealized conditions. The law of gravity, as a model of falling bodies, does not mention problems of air friction or of the wind.

When the scholar does not wisely choose material to omit, then that absent material may prove to have been so essential to his immediate interest that the resulting model will be useless to him. On the other hand, relevant material will always be omitted. Why? Here I make another assumption: The nature of any part of reality can be fully understood only if its relation to its containing environment is fully known. Yet the environment can be viewed as made up of concentric, ever enlarging circles of relationships. In that case, relevance of containing environment eventually goes out to infinity—beyond the capacity of man to trace it. At *some* point the scholar must cut off his study of the expanding circles; but every such conceivable cut-off is arbitrary; and the next expanding circle would continue to be relevant.

Another assumption: Any theoretical model which in integrity attempts to deal with some abstracted phase of reality can be useful to the scholar. This will be true for the Christian scholar even if the chosen model does not go out to infinity—or does not include the nature of God. Again and again the Christian scholar utilizes such models whether or not the one proposing them personally believes that the next expanding circle—or one far in the distance—will include God in it. The Christian scholar, therefore, may differ as to his beliefs about the ultimate relationships of a model, even while agreeing with his non-Christian colleagues as to the usefulness and limited fruitfulness of the particular abstracted viewpoint.

The Christian scholar, however, in spite of his ultimate commitment, is chained by the same restriction: He, like all others, must abstract from reality in order to operate at all. The non-Christian, viewing the Christian's abstractions, therefore, can similarly utilize the Christian's model of observable reality, precisely to the extent that the Christian has not at that particular moment built into his restricted model the theistic ultimate enclosing circle.

Note, furthermore, that the very nature of essential restrictions on all conceivable models leaves room for sharp disagreement among Christians in their preference for use of particular models for their work. Since all models are incomplete, and all of them attempt to lay a groundwork for dealing with some facet of reality, three of them, say, may be equally true (or equally false) but cover sharply different or overlapping parts of experience. In the following diagram, for example, we suggest three theories, A, B, and C, each represented by a circle in the rectangle of total reality. Since each of them deals adequately

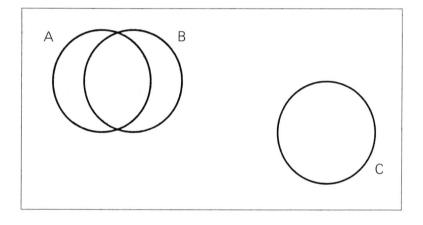

with some phase of reality, we can consider it "true" to that extent. Proponents of one view, however, may be tempted to assume that the others are "false"—yet truth or falsehood here is irrelevant to the fruitful description of their interrelations. Holders of both A and B may sharply reject view C as irrelevant since it does not deal with problems *of interest* to them. Yet adherents to A and B may in turn quarrel fiercely with each other if they fail to understand the nature of theoretical models. To one scholar the other seems blind and stubborn, refusing to see some "obvious" elements necessary to reality, and "stubbornly" holding to statements which "make no sense."

Does this mean, then, that the Christian's assumptions are likely to have no impact on his choice of models? By no means. Sometimes the items of interest to the particular investigator may very well impinge upon theological commitment. One will then want to use a model which leaves room for the theological commitment rather than either omitting it or clashing with it.

One place where this is likely to occur would be precisely in the choice of the relations of expanding circles of the kind I suggested above. The very definition of a model as having relevance going out to infinity may in principle suggest to the theist—whether Christian, Jew, or Moslem—that eventually "in him we live and move and have our being," and that no model is acceptable which does not leave room for this. It has theological overtones, implicitly, by suggesting that we cannot be happy without leaving room for God in our *ultimate* view.

In any case, a scholar uses a model of linguistic theory as he uses an automobile—to get him where he wants to go. But his choice of destination, and his point of origin, are not determined by the automobile.

linguistic theories

Various theories of linguistics are currently available. They employ a variety of concepts and differ in their goals. A careful description of each would require hundreds of pages. Perhaps my academic colleagues will allow a gross oversimplification (will permit me, that is, to suggest a model of these theories in which I deliberately leave out relevant data in order to make a certain point expressible to the beginning reader!).

The generative-transformation model, whose chief proponent is Noam Chomsky of the Massachusetts Institute of Technology, is currently the most widely discussed linguistic theory in the United States. It attempts to understand the competence of human beings to learn a language, by showing through a machine-like set of rules that the kind of sentences which people make can be represented in an abstract form. The end product of this quasi-mathematical process is a string of symbols ready to be pronounced as sentences. The starting point for its chain of rules is a symbol representing sentence-in-general. Then this starting symbol is replaced by a pair or string of symbols, and each of these by further symbols, and so on, until the entire ultimate symbol string is there.

A second approach is being developed by Sydney Lamb of Yale, and others. They wish to prove that language can be decomposed into a sequence of layers, or strata (hence the label of the approach as "stratificational") which are interlocked with one another. A unit of a lower level (a sound, for example) serves as a relevant part of units of the stratum directly above it in the system (a suffix, for example). As one climbs from sound through word and sentence, one eventually ends up with meaning. And the whole finally becomes a network with multiple links in various directions within the system of units.

A third view, the "prosodic" one, was developed by the late J. R. Firth of London's School of African and Oriental Studies, for the discussion of sounds. He attempted to compensate for the over-segmentation of work done a generation ago which cut a sentence into separate sounds. He wished, instead, to describe elements of pronunciation which extended over whole words or syllables. More recently Michael Halliday of the University of London has expanded the approach to include more grammatical problems. He wishes, for example, to rank units in various ways, so that degrees of refinement in detail can be clearly specified in all grammatical areas.

Tagmemic theory, toward whose development members of the Summer Institute of Linguistics have played the primary role, grew out of an attempt to analyze a wide variety of languages.[2] The empirical need for a useful description of languages forced the development of this system. Its basic unit is the tagmeme, derived from a Greek word implying arrangement, and illustrated by the subject or object of a sentence.

These units of language, and any others such as sounds, sonnets, clauses, or words, are by tagmemic theory assumed to be well described only when certain conditions are met: Specified properties of a unit must allow us not only to recognize what it is, but also exclude what it is not; they must indicate how the unit can vary in detail while remaining constant in principle (cf. the river and its molecules, above, or note that the survival of social structure requires that if I am engaged to a girl today I must be able to recognize her tomorrow after a hair-do); and the relevant properties must include a statement as to the appropriateness of the unit to occur under a variety of circumstances.[3]

All these views compete with the dominant view of a couple of decades ago, initiated by Bloomfield[4] of Yale and currently championed by Charles Hockett of Cornell. The Bloomfieldian development emphasized heavily the phoneme—a unit of sound like "s" or "o"—as the crucial, central theoretical construct of the system. The approach demanded that analysis precede directly from this phonological unit to grammar, with no influence of the latter on the former.

beyond the theories

The theist may now ask: Where does truth enter such discussion? The reply: Each of the theories deals with a phase of truth. The theistic scholar can use any or all of them provided that he gives to none of them commitment as being the *whole* of truth, undistorted. They are abstractions from reality, a crude representation of only a part of that reality. He must realize there are multiple perspectives on reality. (See tagmemics with its complementarity.)[5] The clash comes, therefore, when scholars become exclusivist in their belief about their grasp on total truth through a limited model.

The Scriptures do not allow such a claim. Rather they affirm that he who thinks he knows anything, does not yet know it as he ought to know it; we know only in part (1 Cor. 8:2; 13:12). By embracing in humility such warnings, one can happily encourage all science to grow. In addition, however, we must affirm our belief that beyond discovery by the scientific method lie those concentric circles of truth which include the relevance of the nature of God, believed in as a personal commitment on the basis of his revelation through the Scriptures. Yet, one might ask, is it possible to have any true statements at all? If science works through models, and if all models are incomplete, do we have any statements which are trustworthy? Here, again, we must ask: "trustworthy relative to what?" Models, with (ideally) a built-in modesty as to their limitations, are relative to their area of abstraction and may be true within that limit. On the other hand, an excessive commitment to a theological presuppostion that demands that the nature of God always be explicitly present in every scientific model (that is, which denies to the non-Christian or to the non-theist the capacity to make any statement of true fact) would deny to science, in this extreme instance, the possibility of recognizing any truth.[6]

A number of our problems in understanding truth involve the nature of language. This, perhaps, is no surprise since we all get in trouble trying to say what we mean. Perhaps, however, it would illuminate our difficulty a bit if we could see that in some sense every sentence is itself a "model" of "what we want to say," just as theories are models of reality which we want to represent.

Every sentence must leave out something. The whole world of knowledge cannot be put into a single phrase! Nor can one book contain a formula relating every molecule of every hair of Napoleon's head to each atom in the feather of a sparrow fallen in New Guinea (if there are any there!). Yet full knowledge, and complete description of the "flower in a crannied wall," would require that sort of detail. God alone possesses that kind of knowledge. We must get by with our restricted substitutes—just as he also has chosen to do when he speaks to us (in the Scriptures) in our languages.

As we have complementary theories, we have complementary sentences, paraphrases, reports—or gospels. Each, well done, contributes another adequate part toward the whole. Only later on will we know fully as we are known (with a different symbolic device, perhaps, or with deeper and more direct experience of Christ).

Meanwhile, we know both truth and *Truth*. "I love you" tells us something of how to act in both spheres. Language is designed to do this efficiently. For that it is adequate. It is not planned to make us proudly omniscient.

Notes

[1] But many different implicit definitions of the term "theory" are in use and confuse discussion when inconsistently used; see an unabridged dictionary.

[2] The Institute is currently studying and translating in some 400 languages and hopes to work in hundreds more.

[3] Other characteristics of the tagmemic view emphasize hierarchical relations (of lexicon, phonology, and grammar; language viewed as part of behavior (rather than as merely an abstracted code); the need for a multiple perspective on all units and events (complementarity of particle, wave, and field); and an insistance on keeping always in view the relation of form to meaning as a composite (rather than the abstracting of the one from the other for separate treatment).

[4] For a general introduction to the nature of language, including the Bloomfieldian and generative viewpoints, see Henry A. Gleason, Jr., *Introduction to Descriptive Linguistics*, 2nd ed. (New York, 1961). For a more formal introduction, now outdated but still useful, to generative grammar, see Noam Chomsky, *Syntactic Structures* (s'Gravenhage, 1957). For recent developments in the scale and category view of Britain see Michael Halliday, "Categories of the Theory of Grammar," *Word*, XVII (1961), 241-92. For the stratificational view see Sydney Lamb, *Outline of Stratificational Grammar* (Washington, D. C., 1966). For the tagmemic view, the basic theoretical volume is my *Language in Relation to a Unified Theory of the Structure of Human Behavior*, 2nd ed., (The Hague, 1967); nonspecialists might enjoy more a list of the concepts in "Beyond the Sentence," *College Composition and Communication*, XV (1964), 129-35.

[5] See footnote 3 above.

[6] I have written elsewhere—see *With Heart and Mind* (Grand Rapids, 1962), pp. 46-53—that truth should not be equated with degree of detail. Degree of magnification has no direct reference to the nature of a true statement even though often confused with it. The possibility of true statements *must* be assumed if human nature is to survive either in its ordinary or in its scientific aspects.

Pauline B. Johnson

Art

The fine arts generally include painting, drawing, sculpture, and architecture; however, poetry, music, the dance, and dramatic arts are sometimes included in this category. These areas all have one thing in common that distinguishes them from the other subjects in the curricula: They are the means by which man expresses his feelings and thoughts and the uniqueness of his personality, in an ordered and pleasing form. The products of these expressions and the conditions that produce them become the academic subject matter of the discipline.

Significantly the arts preceded most of the other fields of study, for they have occupied an important place in the life of man since the beginning of time. In fact, according to Otto Klineberg, aesthetic drives are parallel in importance to hunger, thirst, and sleep. He states that "sooner or later every human being will show hunger for food, water and aesthetic delight. The hunger for lasting values feeds the inner man as food feeds the physical man."[1] Even the most crude and archaic weapons, utensils, and tools of early periods were embellished, indicating a need for more than just functional satisfaction.

That the visual arts are meant to provide pleasure and fulfill a need for beauty in all forms of existence is obvious from the uses to which they have been put. Primitive man tattooed decorative patterns on his body in order to achieve distinction and probably to satisfy the "desire to be fine." Personal adornment continues as a major form of expression and one which has been carried to all sorts of extremes. With many young people who defy conventional standards of dress, it has become a symbol of rebellion and a defiance of an ordered society. Thus art has been channeled to serve various purposes.

In earlier periods the arts were closely identified with religious functions and objects of worship, and it was from such forceful motivations that monumental works were produced. The results are revealed in magnificent temples and cathedrals and in the inspired paintings of the Renaissance in subjects such as the "Annunciation," the "Crucifixion," and the "Ascension" of Christ. The ancient Hebrews considered the worship of Jehovah-God the highest function of life and related the arts to holiness, as in the building of the Tabernacle and the Ark of the Covenant. These works expressed the height of man's aspirations, bringing delight to the spirit and glory to God.

In spite of the fact that the arts have occupied a significant place in all cultures and periods, they have not been recognized as a branch of knowledge as extensively as the sciences and social sciences in the college and university curricula. This is due in part to the fact that they do not fit the pattern of objective realism or rationalization generally attributed to academic subjects nor can their final product be measured by the scientific method. The arts are concerned with intuitive and imaginative factors that operate in addition to the logic of reason. By their nature they are elusive and difficult to categorize, yet they are based on fundamental principles requiring developed judgments.

creativity

A liberal arts curriculum includes a study of historic material for cultural and informational purposes along with the theory and practice of art, with an academic education based on both traditional and empirical methods. Unfortunately, few students today have as much opportunity for personal participation in the arts as they had in former periods of world history. There is not as much encouragement to bring into being something of aesthetic worth that is uniquely and distinctly their own—a play or a poem, a drawing or painting, a pot or textile, or a piece of music. The thrill of creation is something that all can experience under suitable instruction through the development of expressive and appropriate skills. In this particular process we find the human personality linked to the Creator of the universe in a special way, for man experiences in a limited scope the creation of a miniature world of his own that is ordered and complete. According to Clyde Kilby, "artistic creativity is perhaps the highest attainment of man"[2] for in his aesthetic involvements he reveals himself as made in the image of God.

The origin of all creativity is recorded in Genesis where we read that "in the beginning God created" for the "earth was without form and void." Just as God brought form to a formless world, creating order out of chaos, so man as artist, in a relative way, experiences the making of something new in which he produces order out of the confusion abounding. We see that the creative process occurred "in the beginning," with God the artist creating a beautiful world filled with aesthetic objects expressed in sculptured rocks and mountain forms, colorful flowers and sunsets, and in the perfect symmetry of the human body. Man, as a designer and creator, is sensitively and acutely aware of what it means to produce even a simple structure from already available material. All his talents, senses, and intellect are employed. He sees art as a recreation of the existing world, not as an imitation of nature, but operating on the same principles and possessing a life of its own. Paul Weiss of Yale University has said, "If man is a creature of God he evidently was created to create. In nothing else does [he] so closely resemble the Creator in whose image he is supposed to have been made, than in an artistic enterprise, making a world which never was before."[3]

Modern thinkers believe that the creative imagination in man simulates in operation and activity the creative forces in nature, but in diverse media. There is a design at both the macro and micro levels showing a plan of order from which man derives his order and is able to understand more fully the universe with which he identifies. This order, revealing a perfect mathematical structure, is the greatest discovery of science, and from this organization in all living things, the arts have derived their form. According to Archipenko, a modern sculptor, animals and insects use the same constructive laws instinctively that man has learned and applied to his constructions. An example is the spiral staircase which resembles the structure of the spiral shell.[4]

René Dubos, bacteriologist, claims that "despite the immense diversity of creation, we all accept that there exists in nature a profound underlying unity."[5] The unity of which the scientist is aware is also known to the artist who seeks the principles upon which relationships are established. This unity underlies the whole and is the framework for musical harmony, architecture, and all the other arts. It results from an orderly cosmos whose origin goes back to the God whose divine intelligence and creativity are manifested throughout the universe and through the creativity of man.

The means for structuring a work of art are derived from and allied with all creative phenomena of nature. These include various modes of experiencing through a medium, the organization of line, color, light, sound, form, and all the resources of the arts which the artist manipulates to achieve a unity of composition. The principles of rhythm, repetition, balance, contrast, and dominance which he employs operate as fundamental truths throughout the universe. Each art has its own language through which it communicates, and like any language it must be learned.

contemporary trends

In contrast to former periods, the arts of today are abandoning traditional forms and creating new orders. Technological standards have largely replaced earlier concepts of beauty, resulting in the loss of the humanizing effects once provided by the arts.

Yet man's desire to create and to express his individuality in personal ways still exists where he can make use of his inner resources and reveal what he is. But his work tends to reflect the materialism and worldliness of the present culture, and since it no longer serves the state or the church, is apt to become more egocentric. He is no longer working for the glory of God, but for self or a social cause. He sees himself as portraying the truth as he knows it, though by nature remaining blind to spiritual values. There is no real search for truth nor concern with moral aspects of right and wrong. When the artist disregards order and the structural relationships upon which a unified personal statement is projected, he destroys the means for a basic criterion. For the theory that man originated as a result of chance or accident, that life is meaningless or nothing, has invaded the artistic world where almost anything that strikes the eye is apt to be accepted.

The gradual decline of the arts from an emphasis on the supernatural to an emphasis on man, precipitated the naturalistic trend which flowed through the Graeco-Roman tradition and provided the direction for our Western culture. Thus the humanistic trend began with human reasoning replacing divine wisdom, and man focusing more on himself and his own sufficiency. The movement downward from a God-centered universe to a man-centered world reveals the alienation from God that has led to the present period.

One can see that the present condition of the arts reveals the present state of man, and such has been true from the beginning of time. A philosophy of despair extends from anxiety and guilt to the problem of coping with the evil abounding. Instead of looking to God, man strives to save himself through a form of secular salvation based on a liberal humanism. He attempts to turn evil into art as a substitute and form of religion, for unregenerate man seeks to remake himself and his world without outside help. He is his own god and responsible for his own destiny, or so he believes.

In the changing pattern of aesthetic modes, the Christian may encounter problems that are seemingly contradictory to his

principles and belief. When confronted with material that is
offensive or contrary to his faith, he will have to decide what
position to take in the light of his ultimate objectives, or, as a
Christian, to what extent he will be influenced by arty literature
that borders on the pornographic, by the new mannerisms in
the dance and theater, or by the obscenity in the visual arts. As
he becomes aware of the great invasion from without and the
attacks on his moral and ethical standards, he should realize
that he has a responsibility to live up to the scriptural knowledge he possesses, for Christ said that as a man thinks in his
heart, so is he.

the nude in art

Sometimes the student faces problems, however, which require
impersonal attitudes but personal solutions. For instance, there
is the matter of posing in the nude, or sketching a figure in the
nude, a common practice in professional classes in many
schools. The serious student of art is trained to view the body
objectively as a perfect form that serves as a point of departure
for the creation of a work of art. He learns that this is not done
by a direct transcription of the subject but by the organization
of aesthetic factors. Nevertheless, the Christian student has an
obligation to perform in such a manner that he does not become an offense to others. Anything he does that contributes to
physical excitement or causes others to question his Christian
commitment should be considered undesirable or inappropriate.
He has a responsibility to conduct himself in a way that his
appearance is not suggestive of sensual overtones. The matter of
posing in the nude is something he must realize could provide
wrong connotations and lead to retrogradation. Although we
are told that "nothing is unclean in itself" (Rom. 14:14), the
apostle Paul also admonishes "that no man put a stumbling-
block or an occasion to fall in his brother's way" (Rom.
14:13–KJV).

The English art historian, Kenneth Clark, explains the concept of the figure by distinguishing between "the naked" and
"the nude." He says, "To be naked is to be deprived of our

clothes, and the word implies some of the embarrassment most of us feel in that condition. The word 'nude,' on the other hand, carries, in educated usage, no uncomfortable overtone." He refers to the nude as being "the most complete example of the transmission of matter into form" and that "as a means of expression it is of universal and eternal value."[6]

The nude has figured prominently as a major subject of art for many centuries, especially during the period of Greek sculpture and the great painting of the Renaissance. The Greeks expressed their philosophy in "human wholeness" and according to Clark "this serious awareness of how much was implied in physical beauty saved them from the two evils of sensuality and aestheticism."[7] They saw the body as composed of ideal proportions that fitted perfectly into the geometric forms of the circle and the square. The proportions derived geometrically became the basis of their architectural structures, with the form of the body itself compared to an architectural column, of monumental quality.

Clark refers to the human figure as a vehicle for the expression of all kinds of concepts—extending from Michelangelo's "Last Judgement" (in which the figures have been referred to as containing nothing that is not spiritual), to such things as door knockers and handles on objects of use. He continues:

Nor are we likely once more to cut ourselves off from the body, as in the ascetic experiment of medieval Christianity. We may no longer worship it, but we have come to terms with it. We are reconciled to the fact that it is our lifelong companion, and since art is concerned with sensory images the scale and rhythm of the body is not easily ignored . . . and it is no accident that the formalized body of the "perfect man" [Christ] became the supreme symbol of European belief. Before the Crucifixion [by] Michelangelo we remember that the nude is, after all, the most serious of all subjects of art; and that it was not an advocate of paganism who wrote, "The Word was made flesh, and dwelt among us . . . full of grace and truth."[8]

secular art

The artist commonly draws upon life as he sees it in order to convey a social message or to present a political commentary. In this way art becomes a vehicle for the communication of ideas or a story-telling medium. The literary content does not, however, constitute the aesthetic criteria by which the work is judged. It serves only as the motivation and point of departure and helps determine the form the work will take. An example is the dramatic use of dark-light employed by Daumier in his lithographs of the French Revolution. Picasso used art symbolism in his painting of "Guernica," produced as a strong protest and condemnation of the terrible bombing of an innocent Basque village that was used as target practice by the Nazis in order to see how quickly and effectively they could wipe it out. According to Wendell Mathews of Carthage College, "Such a work [as this] can have great meaning for the church. It does not give the Christian answer, but it is a strong artistic expression of the human predicament of our time. Works such as 'Guernica' serve to illuminate the human situation, corrupted by evil and under the judgment of God. They do not proclaim redemption in Christ but show man's need for redemption."[9]

The artist today enjoys unlimited latitude and freedom in determining the nature of his message or subject, and is free from censorship to express life as he knows and sees it, however offensive. Complete freedom in a meaningful society, of course, implies responsibility. Yet some egocentric individuals take advantage of certain aspects of a degenerate and confused society to express their own sick minds. Their attempts to be free and autonomous, achieving ultimate release, have led to lewd expressions masking as social and political protest. This new reality and new morality in art results from a rationalistic humanism untempered by divine revelation and redemption. It is but another indication of the downward trend of man.

christian art

In light of the direction of the arts and their reflection of a secular society, the question arises whether there is a Christian art today of any great spiritual and artistic significance. Is anything being produced that can be compared to the poetry of the Psalms in the Old Testament, the great and inspired hymns of the church, or the magnificent cathedrals of the past? The answer lies somewhat in the conflicting interests of society and lack of motivation.

The Christian, too, is concerned about society and the world but sees the problems and their solution in a different perspective and in the light of eternity. He is aware that the condition of the arts is indicative of man's degeneracy and spiritual state, but he uses this as a barometer to determine the needs and his responsibility to meet these needs. He does not condemn the arts because they are at odds with established belief but sees them as a means of communication through which he can channel his ideas to serve his purpose. Like the apostle Paul, he can say that "all things are lawful unto me, but all things are not expedient: all things are lawful for me, but I will not be brought under the power of any" (1 Cor. 6:12—KJV).

In judging art from a Christian viewpoint, it is important to determine whether the art possesses significance and values in keeping with Christian principles and whether it can lay claim to the qualities of excellence that place it within the artistic tradition. This eliminates much of the "pretty" and sentimental pictorial painting used only because it portrays religious themes. High standards must prevail in all aspects of aesthetic concern.

The extension of God toward man is revealed through the arts from the beginning of history by means of the Holy Scriptures and various other records as well as by the preservation of objects. This large body of evidence is significant, but the greatest revelation is the fact that God can become personal and real to each individual, for the one who brought order out of chaos stands ready to repeat the act in the lives of men. The creativity of God continues on in each human being who seeks to know his divine will and plan for his life. This is the most important disclosure that any one could receive.

Notes

[1] Otto Klineberg, *Social Psychology* (New York, 1954), p. 68.

[2] Clyde S. Kilby, *Christianity and Aesthetics* (Chicago, 1961), p. 10.

[3] Although I am unable to locate the exact source of this statement, Professor Weiss assures me in a letter dated February 2, 1969, that it represents his view.

[4] Alexander Archipenko, *Archipenko: Fifty Creative Years, 1908-1958* (New York, 1960), p. 34.

[5] René Dubos, "Science and Man's Nature," *Daedalus*, XCIV (Winter 1965), p. 227.

[6] Kenneth Clark, *Nude—A Study in Ideal Form*, A. W. Mellon Lectures, 1953 (New York, 1956), pp. 3, 9.

[7] Clark, p. 15.

[8] Clark, pp. 27, 29.

[9] Wendell Mathews, *World of Painting*, Christian Encounters Series (St. Louis, 1968), p. 96.

James Paul Kennedy

Music

program notes *(by Edward A. Cording)*
This "composition," cast by the composer into four movements, prelude, theme, three variations, *and* coda, *was written for college students who may have either of two kinds of interest in music: as one of the important fields of knowledge which reaps rewards throughout life or as a vocation to serve God in community, church, and school.*

The prelude tells what music is, who creates it, who recreates it, and who consumes it. The theme states that music is one of God's great gifts. The three variations portray goodness, truth, and beauty, indispensable for successful living. The coda suggests that music is one of the great disciplines through which we serve God and our fellow men.

As for its purpose, the composer writes, "Americans are basically uninformed about music since the subject is rarely referred to in social histories. Often the best educated express little serious interest in music since, in college, few involved themselves in artistic affairs. Since the next generation, who will mold educational and spiritual philosophies, is now filtering through college curricula, this is presented in the hope of stimulating more involvement with the best music."

prelude

Maestoso: Ralph Vaughan-Williams, the English composer, once said,"Music is the most useless thing in the world; you can't eat it, sit on it, or make love to it. Consider the humble brick and compare it to a Schubert song. I can think of a thousand uses for the brick including hitting my enemy on the head with it, for which purpose the Schubert song is totally inefficient."

Although music may make an inefficient brick, it is certainly deeply woven into the fabric of society. Its uses are both subtle and obvious, both direct and indirect. In our everyday speech, for example, we find ourselves borrowing from music vocabulary to make our meanings more clear and vivid. We speak of "sharp" cheese, a "flat" tire, a "composed" person, and a "dissonant" attitude.

Beyond providing us with a language which helps us in our everyday conversation, we find that music has a long history of therapeutic values. Four thousand years ago the ancient Greeks used "musico therapy" prescribing scales (instead of aspirin) to reduce a fever. Today we use music to increase metabolism, improve circulation, influence glandular secretion and induce sleep. It is well known that playing musical instruments and singing strengthen the throat, lungs, and abdominal muscles; they increase oxidation of tissue through deep breathing; they aid digestion; and, as a substitute for anesthestics, they leave no unpleasant after-effects. Dairy- and poultry-men have discovered that music increases milk and egg production up to 20 percent. Those ancient shepherd songs may have fattened lambs as well as soothed fears. These few functional aspects of music thus belie the idea that "music is useless."

Cantabile: While music tends to defy verbal concepts, it is still important here to attempt a definition of it in order to better understand it and its relationships to God and the world. Music is more than sound. It is motion, embodying energy, speed, patterns, alternations of tension and release. Through the manipulation of these elements, our imaginations are evoked and our emotions are stirred. While this may serve as a simple definition, it is still far from indicating the mystery of melody

or music's communicative powers. It does not explain the supernatural forces for evil and good which primitive man ascribed to
it, nor the impelling force which drives modern man to experience it.

Music is experienced in three ways: in composing, perform-
ing, and listening. The composing of music is a part of man's
endless movement of creation and recreation. As such it is a
means of spiritual renewal. If composers stopped composing,
orchestras and opera houses might soon become obsolete, and
music would soon decline into a historical curiosity. In performance pianists, vocalists, instrumentalists, and conductors become midwives to composers by bringing ideas to life which lie
submerged on the printed page. These ideas are activated
through live performances which provide indescribable pleasure
both to the amateur and the professional. In listening, the
efforts of the composers and the performers is received and
experienced. Fortunately, modern technology, which has
brought us tapes and disk recordings, has multiplied the potential for pleasure in one performance.

Religioso: Music is a window through which we may view
cultures in their many aspects, for all men have sought to express the meaning and joy of life through music. This means, of
course, that the very foundation of all cultures—man's relationship to his God—has been a primary impulse for music throughout history. From earliest times, singing and instrumental playing have been part of religious rites.

In the Bible, we find many references to music. David played
his harp to soothe Saul (music therapy); trumpets blew down
the wall of Jericho (the first marching band); Elisha called upon
a musician to create the mood for prophesying (blues music);
Saul, when anointed king, surrounded himself with a group of
prophets, each with a musical instrument (a combo); a heavenly
chorus proclaimed the "good news" to the shepherds the night
Jesus Christ was born ("Eine Kleine Nacht Music"); and Paul
and Silas rattled the prison walls with hymns of joy (stereo-
phonic sound).

This last mentioned—hymn singing—is an especially rich

thread of musical heritage as reflected in our Christian religion. Matthew notes that "when they had sung a hymn, they went out to the Mount of Olives," suggesting the musical interests of even the unlettered. Hymns, referred to as "an ecclesiastical seventh-inning stretch with sound effects," carried much of Luther's message as he preached throughout central Europe. The thousand hymns of Charles Wesley figured prominently in the spread of Methodism in modern Britain and America. It was the fervent hymn singing which enhanced the great Welsh revival of the nineteenth century, and the Welsh are still noted for their singing today.

While the melodies of hymns underscore inspired words, instrumental music can also turn our minds and hearts into altars. The symphonies of Schubert and the string quartets of Beethoven testify to this. In Bach's time churches had both orchestras and choirs, and each was expected to kindle holy flames.

During music's classical period (1750-1830), composers were most often educated in schools attached to churches, and their masterpieces reflected spiritual motivations. Music was considered an expression of the soul, a glorification of God. Often we see on scores, "Soli Deo Gloria" (To God Alone be the Glory!).

Unfortunately such spiritual concerns are not the predominant impulse for much of the music of our present times. Each generation decides which traditions to perpetuate or neglect, and our twentieth century is witnessing the dissolving of many conventional sounds. Beginning with jazz, changes have occurred "molto accelerando" through the many forms of pop, serial, chance, electronic, and folk music. Many of today's folk songs, lamenting the loss of love and personal identity, and psychedelic music, exposing and promoting the baser nature of man, reflect the unrest, violence, and breaking of restraints which stir a large segment of today's youth. While the Christian message of reconciliation and renewal may also be found in folk songs, the total experience of psychedelic music—words, music, and performance—calls forth an immediate, irrational, and glandular gratification of self. Thus, only a small portion of our modern forms of music reflect the religious heritage which is such a vital part of music.

theme

While we can exist without music, since speech would suffice, seldom are we satisfied with only the utilitarian approach to life. Music possesses special powers, lifting us beyond mere existence, enabling us to unite with a force higher than ourselves, confronting us with God's gifts of goodness, truth, and beauty.

three variations

Variation I: Goodness satisfies: "And God saw that all he had made was good." Qualities of goodness in music are both illusive and subject to debate. But one of the more consistent tests is time. Masterpieces, for example, possess strikingly original qualities in contrast to hit tunes which are lucky to make the top ten list for two successive weeks before falling into oblivion. Time, the great tranquilizer, cools off original successes and renders tributes of goodness to later arrivals. For instance, the works of Anton Rubinstein were considered immortal in his day, but today are rarely heard. On the other hand, the first symphony of Brahms bitterly disappointed even his most ardent admirers; today it is a standard classic.

Variation II: Truth is found in music when it is true to itself; that is, when it expresses reason and logic through its form (structure). Like any language, music is based on ideas and concepts involving units of thought—phrases (sentences), periods (paragraphs), and movements (chapters). To understand this methodology, of course, requires arduous study. This understanding is the goal for college courses optimistically called Music Appreciation.

Martin Luther wrote, "When music is heightened by art, there man first beholds with great wonder and can examine the great and perfect wisdom of God." To capture and experience what Luther is referring to requires a discipline which weds the mind and the heart. Acquisition of listening and/or performance skills through such difficult and continuing discipline gives one the freedom to partake more deeply of the truth of music. It is the bondage of discipline which allows the freedom of experience.

Having disciplined oneself to a level of understanding music that is true to itself, one is in a position to benefit from a listening experience with music of substance. Among other things he may receive a glimpse of the eternal. Again the parallel between music and man's relationship to God is clear. A great symphony remains constant in its symmetry of form, beauty of melodies, warmth of harmonies, and complexity of rhythms, and yet our response to the symphony varies according to the level of our perception.

Variation III: Beauty, the primary intent of music, involves line, proportion, and texture. A superb performance of a great masterpiece may prompt us to examine our lives in the light of eternity. Henry David Thoreau once remarked, "Ah, if I could put into words the music that I hear, that which brings tears to the eyes of marble statues!" Music may become a means of man's instinctive search for beauty, enabling him to convey ideas and emotions about beauty to others. The great French painter, Pierre Auguste Renoir, suffering from severe arthritis, agonized even to hold his brush. When asked why he persisted in painting, he replied, "The pain passes, but the beauty remains."

No branch of science has yet surpassed music in healing severed relationships. Richard Nixon, as former vice-president, was mobbed during his South American tour (1958). Soon afterwards the New York Philharmonic moved into the same explosive area and was wildly acclaimed. Our soloists and orchestras behind the Iron Curtain have had similar experiences after diplomats had utterly failed to establish good will.

The healing balm of music speaks to the intuitive spirit of all men. A Red Chinese scientist, Ma Yen Sheng, confessed to his superior, "Having listened too much to Western bourgeois classical music, I gradually had a blurred class viewpoint when looking at problems. After enjoying Beethoven's *Ninth Symphony* many times, I began to have strange illusions about the idea of 'universal love'—of bourgeois humanitarianism which was praised in the choral section of the symphony. I asked myself, if the world is really filled with friendly love among nations, then will the world not permanently rid itself of war and will there not be everlasting peace?"

One word of caution—if art is purely aesthetic pleasure, it can become a shell without a soul. If we idolize music, we can succumb to the temptation of striving to save the world through good works or worshipping the creation rather than the creator. The ultimate mission of beautiful music must be to point beyond itself—to God's great glory.

coda

The impulse to create, recreate, or respond to music is derived in some mysterious process from the great composer, God. The reader has undoubtedly realized by now that goodness, truth, and beauty are interlocking segments of music. As the poet's song and the prophet's word are given the grace of melody, as the thoughts of a great mind are clothed with instrumental colors, music can be a source of goodness, a spring of truth, a fountain of beauty.

God has diversified his gifts "as he wills," but we all have natural talents regardless of various backgrounds. We are more musical than mathematical. Our heartbeat, breathing, and walking have rhythmic reoccurrences; our speech is refined by pitch variations. We were created to articulate God's cadences and harmonize with his purposes. We must not only discover, develop, and dedicate our natural gifts, we also must orient them toward the uplifting of others. God gave man music to illuminate his way, to widen the meaning of his life, and to give him "spiccato" of spirit.

We can do no better than conclude on the note sounded by the psalmist ages ago (Ps. 150:3-6):

Praise him with trumpet sound;
   praise him with lute and harp!

Praise him with timbrel and dance;
    praise him with strings and pipe!
Praise him with sounding cymbals;
    praise him with loud clashing cymbals!
Let everything that breathes praise the Lord!
Praise the Lord!

Robert D. Baird

Religion

Religion as a field of study within the university does not aim at
producing religious persons or Christian character. While the
founding of Harvard College had its transcendent justification,
the modern university is justified on a humanistic base. Although the study of religion is included with increasing frequency in the curricula of state universities, this does not indicate a return to a transcendent justification for education or a
desire to stem the tide of a rising secularism.[1] Rather, such a
phenomenon indicates that religion, too, has come to be justified on humanistic terms as necessary for an understanding of
the human heritage.[2]

This secularization of the field of religion is merely part of
the secularization of the university, without which religion
probably would not find a place in the modern university.[3]
Leaving aside whether or not it would be more desirable for the
modern university to be based on Christian principles, the fact
remains that no modern university is moving in that direction.
The Christian, therefore, is faced with the alternative of leaving
the secular university for the Christian institution or of recon-
ciling the apparently irreconcilable goals of humanistic education with a Christian view of life.[4]

the secular study of religion

The secular study of religion, when taught as one way of deepening one's understanding of man, can be affirmed by the Christian as penultimate while being rejected as ultimate. To make humanistic education an end in itself is idolatrous from a Christian perspective, but it still remains a legitimate, though partial, endeavor for the Christian. To demand that secular education become Christian to be legitimate or that the study of religion be done under avowedly Christian assumptions is like demanding that the modern corporation, including its advertising and sales departments, become Christian before the Christian can be part of it. Quite legitimately one can affirm the humanistic study of religion as a part of the Christian's total responsibility before God.

Although the study of religion may either strengthen or weaken a student's faith, generally the purpose of such study is far more limited. Since the goal is a deepened understanding of the human experience, it is not surprising to find the curriculum retaining courses which fit into the more traditional division of Bible, church history, and theology. Such a division of courses grew up under the influence of Protestant seminaries, and since the Scriptures and tradition of Christianity have been a dominant force in Western culture, they are seen as a prerequisite for understanding that culture. Because human heritage is broader than Western culture (a fact that some departments and institutions are slow to acknowledge), it is no surprise to find a growing list of offerings in Asian religions and the phenomenology of religion.[5] Justifying the study of religion as a part of human culture has also added to a growing number of courses which relate religion to art, music, politics, and social issues: for example, "Religion in Human Culture" and "Religion and Literature."

The study of religion does not possess a distinct methodology. It utilizes the methodologies of history, literary criticism, philosophy, sociology, or phenomenology when they seem appropriate, avoiding reductionism only to various degrees.[6] More than that, other disciplines sometimes present religion with some of its most pressing problems and significant insights. The concern of philosophers with the nature of language has made it imperative that students of religion formulate a view of the nature of religious language.[7] The twentieth-century emphasis on history has presented theologians with the inquiry into the nature of historical knowledge and how this relates both to theology and to the study of the Scriptures.[8] Social problems and changing ethical standards have given those who work in the area of ethics much to consider.[9] A shrinking world, plagued with political strife, coupled with the rapid growth and self-assertion of nations in Asia, Africa, and the Middle East, is forcing those who work in the field of religion to make a careful study of the dominant religions of these areas, particularly "Hinduism," "Buddhism," and "Islam." Not infrequently such studies are part of the growing number of area studies programs.

The significant feature about the last mentioned development is that it is the universities which are on the forefront of this endeavor. This simply underlines the fact that the university considers religion a humanistic field. If it were the theological problem of the relationship of Christianity to non-Christian religions that put the study of world religions at the fore, one would expect seminaries to add faculty in this area. But we see no immediate trend in this direction.

historical implications

Having described the goals and general structure of the study of religion in the university, we turn, then, to certain implications for the Christian as he encounters the academic study of religion.

Even religion courses which are not titled historically (for example, "Historical Background of the Bible") are frequently handled in a historical manner. A course in "World Religions" may deal with the religions of the world in historical sequence, while a course in "Religion and Culture" may deal with the various ways that religion has related to culture in history.

The historical method searches for sources and dependencies.

Such a quest is historically significant but cannot be pressed to indicate either the truth or value of a concept or practice. It is a fruitful approach until it clothes itself in the form of "historical argument." For example, the argument that Arminianism is a dangerous doctrine since it led to liberal theology may seem probable in its historical dimension. But the historical connection between Arminianism and Liberalism does not prove that either the one or the other is either true or false. Such a judgment must depend on more careful theological reasoning. Perhaps a person inclined to make history bear too much freight in this instance (if liberalism is false, Arminianism is dangerous), should be reminded that Calvinism and orthodoxy were the antecedents of Arminianism.

One must realize that, in the final analysis, according to the historical method there is no origin or starting point. There are historical dependencies, and the only thing that hinders one from penetrating further into the past is the lack of source materials. It is a genetic fallacy to suggest that since an idea is "Greek" rather than "Hebrew," it cannot be part of the Christian message, or that because a notion is Hindu in "origin," it cannot be true. Were the historian of ancient Greece to have sufficient sources, he would show that the notion was not "Greek" at all. The realization that the search for historical dependencies does not involve the question of truth should free the Christian to admit the apparent sources upon which even the biblical material rests.

Historically-oriented courses may lead the student to assume that since there are so many conflicting views, and since they can all be seen in a certain historical and cultural context, then all views are relative to the historical and cultural contexts in which they are found. But this is the historical illusion of relativity.[10] Historical description can never settle the question of truth. The existence of conflicting truth claims can lead to the logical conclusion that they all cannot be simultaneously true, but it does not lead to the conclusion that none of them is true. The question of truth is settled in a quite different manner.[11] To further illustrate, a historical study of American democracy is not sufficient to prove that it is superior to Russian communism. And a historical study which reveals that a certain thinker had no social concern or was mentally ill is inadequate to refute the position of that thinker. Truth questions are not determined in this way. One must give cogent arguments as to a thinker's inadequacy.

normative implications

A study of the human heritage leads inevitably to an estimate of conflicting human values. The humanities are concerned with the question of truth and hence involve normative judgments. The Christian is no different from others when he approaches the material with a given premise. Only his premise is different —for him it is the biblical interpretation of the self-revelation of God in Christ.[12] In his evaluation he uses the commonly accepted canons of logic.

Furthermore, it is not being bigoted to expect that when one examines various religious expressions, he will find some of them to be erroneous. If two thinkers affirm opposing views or engage in cult practices which imply conflicting viewpoints, it is clear that both cannot be true. One cannot logically affirm every point of view. Any statement limits the possibility of making certain other statements. For example, if I say a certain course was interesting, I cannot say it was uninteresting without thereby denying that it was interesting. Therefore, if one affirms anything, he may expect that it may be necessary to deny something else. One should not feel intimidated when he finds it necessary to negate a position presented to him.

While one must expect the presence of error, he should also recognize the possibility of truth. One need not agree on everything to agree on something. If, as a Christian, one makes an affirmation which he considers true and then finds its counterpart in another religious tradition or in modern literature, he is not only justified but also responsible to recognize and affirm the truth there as well.

It is true that the systems contained in the *Tipitaka* of Theravada Buddhism and in John Calvin's *Institutes of the Christian*

Religion are poles apart. But that does not mean that the Christian will find no truth in the *Tipitaka.*[13] Both Christians and Theravada Buddhists agree that this shifting world is not worthy of ultimate trust. While further analysis may reveal only more diverging ideas, there is no reason not to affirm points of agreement. If the Bible had not anticipated this in its doctrine of general revelation (Rom. 1–3; Jn. 1), mere observation would probably have driven us to the same conclusion.

Christians have at times implied that to admit similarities between Christianity and other traditions is to destroy Christianity's uniqueness and therefore its truth. Nothing could be more erroneous. All traditions have elements that are unique, but not therefore true. To describe the unique is not necessarily to describe the true. The differences between Christianity and other religious expressions do not make Christianity true any more than the similarities between them make it false. The Christian message is the gospel of grace through Jesus Christ, and the truth of this proclamation is neither strengthened nor weakened by the points of difference with other religions or the points of contact in even the most unusual places—Indian religion or modern literature. The inability to accept truth where it is found points more to a defensive person unconvinced of the truth of his Christian faith than to a defender of that faith.

human implications

If the study of religion in the university is a humanistic enterprise, granting the wide range of professorial types, the ultimate concern and commitment of the professor is not necessarily a major factor in the student's effort to understand the religious factor in the human heritage, nor should it detain him. Increasingly, professors of religion are hired on the basis of scholarly competence rather than religious commitment. And professors of religion who have deep commitments of an ultimate nature realize the nature of the university (and particularly the state university) and do not confuse the classroom with an evangelistic crusade.

All professors, however, have a human streak which makes

indoctrination a real problem. Indoctrination attempts to by-pass the critical judgment of the student in order to gain the acceptance of a certain point of view. Although this type of brainwashing seldom goes unnoticed by the alert student, it can have certain subtle manifestations. (And indoctrination is not limited to a church-controlled institution, or to the study of religion.[14]) One of the most cherished methods is the use of humor or ridicule to "refute" an opposing argument. It can be accomplished by assigning books which present only one or a limited number of positions which are congenial to the professor. It can also be effected by showing a certain enthusiasm (or lack of it) for certain points of view or movements when they occur in the material. Such pitfalls are difficult to avoid completely in any field.

Another pitfall which the student must avoid is the inclination to accept unhesitatingly a new and compelling point of view. It is always well to remember that no matter how much has been said or read, there is always another argument or point of view to be considered. While one can never wait until *all* the facts are in before making a decision, many decisions are made with inadequate evidence and before the alternatives are clearly seen.

The Christian can expect varying degrees of assistance in relating the humanistic study of religion to his Christian faith. Sometimes that assistance is slight. But then, we do not expect the university to supplant the church.

Notes

[1] Robert Michaelsen, *Study of Religion in American Universities* (New Haven, 1965).

[2] Clyde A. Holbrook, *Religion, A Humanistic Field* (Englewood Cliffs, 1963).

[3] Harvey Cox, *Secular City* (New York, 1965), pp. 217-37.

[4] Such seems to be the assumed solution of Frank Gaebelein in his essay on "Education" in *Contemporary Evangelical Thought,* ed. Carl F. H. Henry (Great Neck, 1957).

[5] The phenomenology of religion involves a search for the structures which are manifested in the religious phenomena as observed. This method proceeds on neutral, and hence not avowedly Christian, grounds. For an example of what this might entail one may read *Sacred and Profane* or *Patterns in Comparative Religion,* two among the many publications of Mircea Eliade. While phenomenology of religion does not proceed on Christian assumptions, the Christian has every right to relate the results of this method to his Christian faith. For one such effort see Edward J. Jurji, *Christian Interpretation of Religion* (New York, 1952). A brief but incisive essay, "Other Religions," can be found in Donald Walhout, *Interpreting Religion* (Englewood Cliffs, 1963), pp. 430-42.

[6] Reductionism refers to the methodological practice of seeing religion in terms of psychology (as Freud), social function (as Malinowsky in *Magic, Science, and Religion*), or some other discipline.

[7] As an example see Frederick Ferre, *Language, Logic, and God* (New York, 1961).

[8] See Van A. Harvey, *Historian and the Believer: The Morality of Historical Knowledge and Christian Belief* (New York, 1966).

[9] Carl F. H. Henry, *Christian Personal Ethics* (Grand Rapids, 1957); Paul Ramsey, *Basic Christian Ethics* (New York, 1950); and also Carl F. H. Henry, *Aspects of Christian Social Ethics* (Grand Rapids, 1964).

[10] For a different view of the nature of history see R. G. Collingwood, *Idea of History* (New York, 1946) and Sidney Mead, "Church History Explained," *Church History,* XXXII (1963), 21. For the logical fallacies in historical relativism see Maurice E. Mandelbaum, *Problem of Historical Knowledge* (New York, 1938). See also Robert D. Baird, *Category Formation and the History of Religions* (The Hague, 1971), esp. chap. 3.

[11] Cf. Edward John Carnell, *Introduction to Christian Apologetics* (Grand Rapids, 1956), pp. 45-64, 103-21.

[12] For a discussion of the problem of authority see Bernard Ramm's two books, *Pattern of Authority* (Grand Rapids, 1957) and *Special Revelation and the Word of God* (Grand Rapids, 1961). Robert Clyde John-

son, *Authority in Protestant Theology* (Philadelphia, 1948) and Dallas M. Roark, "Authority in Protestantism: 1890-1930," *Journal of Religious Thought*, XXII (1965-66), 3-22, also provide helpful insights.

[13] For a more categorical rejection of non-Christian religions see two of Hendrick Kraemer's books, *Christian Message in a Non-Christian World* (Grand Rapids, 1963) and *Religion and the Christian Faith* (Philadelphia, 1956).

[14] For the possibility of indoctrination across departmental lines see Holbrook, pp. 86-112.

George I. Mavrodes

Philosophy

It is not easy to explain just what philosophy is, nor is it easy
for the beginner to get an idea of what it is by looking at a
number of samples. This is because both the proper methods
and the results of philosophy have been matters of dispute
among philosophers themselves from the beginning. As a result,
philosophy has been and is now being carried on in a great
variety of ways, and many different results have been claimed
for it. We shall try to develop here one way in which a large part
of philosophy can be understood. At the same time this may
help us understand some of the ways in which Christians may
find philosophy to be related to their own faith and witness,
and to see why some of them may adopt it, or may be called by
God to adopt it, as their own field of professional interest.[1]

linguistic meaning
Put as briefly as possible, philosophy can be understood as a
concern with *meaning*. But this short statement can only be a
beginning. Probably anyone who must read term papers in the
humanities will be struck by the frequency with which students
use such terms as "meaningful" and "meaningless." Anyone

who must read such papers critically, however, will also be struck by the vagueness and ambiguity of these terms. Perhaps such deficiencies are related to the variety of approaches exhibited in the pursuit of philosophy! At any rate, we should distinguish two broad senses of "meaning." Then, we need to relate each of these senses to philosophical interests and methods, and finally connect these senses, and the corresponding philosophical interest, to each other.

The first of these senses we might call "linguistic meaning." We are using this sense when we say that a random collection of words, strung together like a sentence, has no meaning, or when we speak of an unclear or ambiguous word, phrase, or sentence. A large proportion of current philosophical work, especially that being done in England and the United States, is explicitly concerned either with general questions about meaning—such as What is meaning? Under what conditions is a sentence meaningful? What sorts of meaning are there?—or with the meaning of particular expressions. Work of this sort is often now called "analytic" philosophy. It is, however, by no means confined to modern philosophy. For example, a large part (though not all) of what Plato was doing can be construed as an inquiry into the meaning of moral expressions, such as *good, justice, courage,* etc.

Let me develop the importance of linguistic meaning by means of an analogy. Much, if not all, of our thinking is done by means of words and sentences, and so is a large part of our communication with each other.[2] I suggest that our linguistic equipment can be thought of as a sort of tool, or better, a very complex and interrelated *set* of tools, for thought and communication. Now, to be useful for a complex and extensive task, every tool in a set should have some function different from other functions, but still related to them. We dare not underestimate the importance of difference. A carpenter whose tool box is filled with a dozen copies of one type of hammer is not much better prepared for driving nails than the man who has just one; after all, he can use only one hammer at a time. And he is totally unprepared to do many of the other tasks which belong to carpentry.

But one cannot listen to college discussions for long without hearing someone who seems to use the same meaning for half his words—if indeed they have any meaning at all. He may, for example, use the words *true, rational, logical, known, verified,* and *objective* interchangeably. At least, he slides from one to the other with no indication that he notices any change. Since the person apparently recognizes no distinctions here, he naturally cannot recognize any useful relations either. So he cannot progress from one idea to another. We may well suspect that he seems to use all of these terms with the same meaning because, in fact, he uses them with practically no meaning whatever! One of the tasks of philosophy, then, is to clarify, distinguish, and relate our conceptual and communicative tools.

This brings us to a second useful analogy—a map. A large part (perhaps all) of what is involved in knowing where a place is consists of knowing how it relates to other places, how you can get there from other places (and vice versa), as well as which ways are blocked. Similarly, a large part of knowing or specifying what a given expression means consists of knowing or specifying how it relates to other expressions. A road map indicates the mutual relations of cities. We can think of philosophy, at least in part, as mapping out the relations between the various things we want to say (or think). This aspect of philosophy is perhaps identical with *logic,* in the broadest sense of that term, as the study of the relations between expressions.[3] A conceptual map of· this sort, then, helps us to find our way around in our own thinking, as well as in our talking with other people.

For example, someone may say in a discussion, "But if there is a God, why does he allow such-and-such an evil to continue?" Is that a question? Perhaps. We shall refer to it as "Q." How about, "Can you lend me your pen for a minute?" Both of these have the grammatical form, intonation, and punctuation of a question. But the second is probably not a question, but a disguised request. It would be inappropriate to respond merely by saying, "Yes." So, too, the "question" about God may not really be a question, but a disguised objection—equivalent to, "If there were a God, then he wouldn't allow such-and-such an evil to continue." But this is not a question at all; it is a statement. We shall refer to it as "O."

Now if the original expression is to be understood as a question—"Q"—it requires an answer of the form, "The reason for God's allowing such-and-such to continue is _____." In many cases, however, the Christian may not know what the true answer is; that is, he doesn't know what goes in the blank. And he may as well admit he doesn't know, for no consequence of much interest follows from his ignorance. There is no more reason to expect him to know all of God's reasons any more than to know all of his neighbor's reasons. (Notice this has nothing to do with any special "religious" type of faith.) But from the fact that I do not know God's reason, it does not follow that there is no God, nor that he has no reason, nor anything else of theological interest. All that follows is that I do not know everything, something one might have guessed anyway. In other words, on the logical map neither "Q" nor my failure to know the answer to "Q" is closely related to any statement of theological importance. In particular, there is no plausible way of going from either of them to "Therefore, there is no God."

If, however, the original expression is understood as equivalent to an objection—"O"—then it is quite another matter. From "O" plus the statement that such-and-such an evil continues, it does follow logically that there is no God! And presumably, if he is speaking in good faith, the "questioner" has expressed this objection because he believes "O." And perhaps "O" is one of his reasons for not believing in God. Now "O" being a statement, is quite different from "Q," even though they both might be expressed in the same words. We have already seen that the Christian's failure to answer "Q" is irrelevant to the objection. Similarly, his success in answering "Q" may also be irrelevant. For the objector may not believe the answer, and hence may continue to believe "O" just as before. What the Christian must set himself to do is convince the objector that "O" is false. I know of no guaranteed way of doing this.[4] But once we have distinguished "Q" from "O," and determined that he is really interested in "O," we at least know what we have to do to be of any aid to him. We have our work cut out for us.

This is, of course, only a single example. But since Christianity includes such a large intellectual element, and since it puts so much emphasis on communicating our faith, clearly we should use any help we can get in improving the intellectual tools with which we work.

significant meaning

We turn now to the second sense of *meaning*. It is closely connected with notions like insight, illumination, importance, "the key which opens up a new world," etc. We use it, I think, when we speak of some experience as being "full of meaning," or of some novel as being "meaningless." We sense here that the world is not all surface, that some things conceal (or perhaps *reveal*) a depth into which we might penetrate. And often there is also the suggestion that in this depth, if we could plunge into it, we would find the key to the understanding of the world of our own lives—we would get to what is fundamental and primordial.

Traditionally, this sense has functioned mostly in the branch of philosophy called *metaphysics,* now somewhat unpopular in England and the United States. We can understand some of the traditional metaphysical controversies reflecting differences over which features of the world had this depth, or, perhaps, where it was most easily penetrable. Idealists held that matter was superficial, but mind ran deep in the nature of reality and, consequently, reflecting on the nature of mind led to the profoundest insights. The materialists reversed this order, making matter fundamental and mind superficial. Other controversies, such as that between monism and pluralism, reflect differences over what clue is found in these experiences of depth. (This is due in part, but perhaps only in part, to differences over which experiences really touch the depths.)

Many modern philosophers, of course, seem merely to ignore significance; their work, if it has value at all, belongs to our first category. Among the major current schools the existentialists deal with significance most openly, though, unfortunately, often in obscure terminology. Some, in the end, deny that it applies to the world or to our lives. These are, they say, ultimately "meaningless" and "absurd."

the christian encounter

With this aspect of philosophy—its concern with significance—the Christian faith comes most immediately into contact. For the Christian, too, believes there is something behind the surface. He believes that behind the world—behind its structure and existence and history—stands God the almighty. And he believes that in his experience with Jesus Christ the way opens for him to touch God and the depths of life.

The Christian, then, shares immediately with the philosopher this concern for the significance of the world and of our life and experience. Naturally, he will differ with some philosophers, as they do with each other, over what that meaning is and where it is to be found. But, he will share with the philosopher an interest in putting the significance of the world into words that are intelligible and believable to his contemporaries. In this attempt he may be able to make good use of some philosophers' attempts to read the significance of life, if not by accepting them completely, then by expanding, comparing, or contrasting them with a view more Christian.

Some readers will have noticed that in the last paragraph I have brought together again the notions of linguistic meaning and significance. Indeed, Christianity seems always to have emphasized the importance of verbal formulation and communication of the faith on the one hand, and of each individual's direct contact with God on the other. This may suggest these two sorts of meaning are not entirely distinct; they seem to be inter-translatable, at least in part, and the conversion of significance into linguistic meaning may be an important aspect of the understanding of the significance of our experience. In fact, one of these sorts of meaning may be only a special form of the other. For example, if one were to ask for a paradigm case of a surface/depth phenomenon, we could perhaps do no better than to show him a printed page. In one sense an illiterate man may see all there is on the page. But in another sense he does not see the most important thing—he cannot see what it says. Only the man who can read can penetrate to what lies behind the pattern of marks. Here, then, we seem to have a case in which significance and linguistic meaning run together. It may be that they always do, and that understanding something of the meaning of the world and of the events of my own life is not entirely different from understanding a speech or a poem. Perhaps the world is, at its own deepest level, the speech of God with man.

In this connection several biblical passages are very suggestive. In Genesis God is represented as creating the world by *speaking*. Thus at the very beginning the account suggests there is a profound link between the existence and nature of the world and a divine activity which is construed on the model of speech, a linguistic act. In Psalm 19 the world itself is described as speaking, "telling the glory of God," "pouring forth speech," and "declaring knowledge." Here again the linkage between the significance of the world and the meaning of linguistic entities seems to come to the surface. In the first chapter of the Gospel of John, Jesus Christ is said to be the Logos, the "Word" of God, who creates and maintains the world and who "enlightens every man." I find it very suggestive that John, writing here of Christ's place in the eternity of the Godhead and of this relation to the cosmos and to man, finds it appropriate to use for him the linguistic term "Word."

What we have here is no fully elaborated philosophical doctrine. Nor do I know just how to expand these suggestions fully and to develop their consequences.[5] But I suspect that this is a point at which the current of much modern philosophy, with its emphasis on the analysis of linguistic meaning, runs very close to the age-long Christian interest in *revelation,* in the reality and the mode of God's speech with man. Perhaps here philosophical interests and techniques will play a part in leading all of us into a deeper understanding of, and participation in, the fellowship of God whose speech is a word of life.

Notes

[1] For another brief attempt at this same project see Arthur F. Holmes, *Christianity and Philosophy* (Chicago, 1960).

[2] We sometimes communicate in ways which do not *seem* to involve linguistic entities; for example, we may beckon with our hand or blow a horn. Just how these methods differ from linguistic methods, however, is a difficult and interesting question. (It is, perhaps, equivalent to the question of just what a linguistic act or entity is.) It is probably related to the topic which I discuss in the last few paragraphs of this paper.

[3] Logic in the narrower sense, in which it is usually encountered in introductory courses, is concerned with the *truth-relevant* relations of expression; that is, those relations which focus on truth and falsity. Consequently, it deals mostly with declarative sentences, statements, etc., since it is these which can be true or false. However, we can also speak, in the broader sense, of the logic of questions, commands, etc.

[4] Perhaps we might begin by asking the objector whether he has any reason for believing "O." He probably doesn't. And we might go on to point out that there are some evils which human beings ought not to prevent, even if they can do so; for example, perhaps a mother ought not always to prevent the children from losing their toys even if she can do so. So it may not be that God ought to prevent every evil. But if not, then "O" is false.

For an excellent, though technical, discussion of the problem of evil see Alvin Plantinga, "Free Will Defense," *Philosophy in America*, ed. Max Black (Ithaca, 1965).

[5] Edwin Lewis attempted to develop a notion something like this in his *Philosophy of the Christian Revelation* (New York, 1940).

II. The Social Sciences

David O. Moberg

The Social Sciences

An eminent paleobotanist walking to his work at Smithsonian Institute in Washington, D. C., noticed a tiny plant beside his path. To his consternation he, an expert on plant life, was unable to identify this specimen of the local flora. Day after day he observed it and puzzled over it. Only when it sent up a miniature seed spike did he realize that it was common wheat, stunted in its growth and sickly in its development because of its adverse environment.

This incident contributed to Lester Frank Ward's pondering over the nature of and solution for man's social problems. If a plant can be so distorted by its environment that a botanist cannot recognize it, is it not possible also that warped human lives have been twisted by an unfavorable social milieu? If so, the improvement of social conditions should raise the quality of mankind and promote societal progress.[1]

Ward's theoretical work relevant to social problems led him into the social sciences. He became one of the American pioneers in the development of sociology and was elected the first president of the American Sociological Society in 1906. While he was on the faculty of Brown University (1906-1912), his rich background in law, geology, botany, and medicine, besides his personal studies in philosophy, religion, and the social sciences, made it possible for this "American Aristotle" to offer a course on "A Survey of All Knowledge." Encyclopedic approaches of that kind were common in the middle ages and well into the nineteenth century. Among the ancient Greek philosophers, who in many respects are the intellectual ancestors of modern Western education, there was no sharp differentiation between the various fields of knowledge; their insights apply in many ways to the historical legacy of all of them. Except for a few Great Books programs, such broad approaches to human knowledge are totally unheard of in the current educational system, despite the implication from the derivation of the word *university* that such an institution is concerned with totality, the universe.

All academic disciplines, to say nothing of the specific subjects with which each deals, represent abstractions from reality. The universe is so vast and complex that man's mind and senses can comprehend but a small portion of its totality. What is known has been divided into rational compartments within which specialists work. Within each of these, in turn, sub-specialties have arisen, and the accumulation of knowledge in many of them has led to the demarcation of sub-sub-specialties.

The need to integrate the diverse perspectives of the discrete disciplines may lead to renewed attempts to gain a holistic perspective on man and his universe. Interdisciplinary seminars invariably have a limited focus, however, for even when they draw upon data and insights from many academic areas of specialization, man's finite condition necessitates narrowness of other kinds, such as focusing upon but one or a few of his practical or philosophical problems.

some characteristics of the social sciences

The social sciences deal with one of the vast segments of human knowledge, that which pertains to society and man's social behavior. They arose historically out of social philosophy, with which they are still closely related. They are "sciences" insofar as they depend upon the scientific method of investigation. The specific orientation of each is evident from the respective chapters which follow. Not all will agree that certain of the fields included here are social sciences. Several areas of geography are more validly considered as part of the physical sciences. Psychology focuses upon man as an individual, with special emphasis upon his mind; more validly classified as a "behavioral" than a social science, it is sometimes grouped academically with the biological sciences. Most historians would prefer to have their field of investigation known as a humanity rather than a science, yet all of the social sciences are validly classified as humanities insofar as they focus upon human nature and are concerned implicitly, if not explicitly, with man's humane qualities. Health and education are not "sciences," but professional people in those fields draw upon social science insights, theories, and research findings (as well as those of other academic disciplines) in their development of principles for action and methods of reaching their goals, so they often are grouped administratively with the social sciences in college divisions and curricula. All the other professions similarly draw upon the social sciences. This is especially obvious in preparation for social work, politics, law, the ministry, business, and research occupations like public opinion polling and marketing research, but it is increasingly recognized in regard to occupations like journalism, medicine, nursing, dentistry, and even engineering.

Growing recognition of the social factors that are among the major causal roots of all human problems will make the social sciences even more significant in the future than they have been in the past. The applied aspects of the disciplines are irrevocably linked with their theoretical developments, but the pressures of urgent social problems today are leading social scientists toward more emphasis upon the practical than the "pure" areas of their research efforts. They are called upon more and more to lead in the evaluation of programs to meet man's social needs. Their careful, systematic scrutiny using scientific methods and techniques of investigation eventually may replace the casual appraisals that still prevail in most areas of education, government, religion, and social welfare. These studies include viewing each specific subject in the larger context of the total social system of which it is a part. At the same time, however, the call for "relevance" and the demand of the "new sociologists" and other activists for a clear commitment to the solutions of social problems which they propose may involve social scientists in more political struggles than is presently the case.

The applied emphasis leads to an increasing number of special institutes, centers, and programs which focus around specified problem areas and draws upon numerous academic disciplines instead of but one or two. Interdisciplinary centers to study human development and aging, suicide, death, disasters, mass communications, population control, urban affairs, race relations, law enforcement, family life, Afro-American studies, and a multitude of other specialized subjects are springing up at a rapid rate on college and university campuses, as well as independently in other institutions or autonomous contexts.

No problem of man in society can be fully analyzed with the perspectives and techniques of only one discipline. A phenomenon like religious conversion may be interpreted in part from the perspectives of psychology, sociology, education, anthropology, history, biochemistry, and physiology. The analysis within each necessarily involves separating the phenomenon into its component parts. Yet even the totality of all scientific findings still falls short of a total and holistic understanding of that experience. Furthermore, even if all scientific perspectives and methods are applied to the investigation of any subject or problem, some aspects of reality related to it will still evade analysis. The restriction of scientific investigation to empirical data precludes a holistic approach.

The waggish evaluation of college humorists bears an important element of truth: "Academic progress involves learning more and more about less and less until one knows everything about nothing." Similarly, the more one knows he knows, the more he knows he does not know. The person who professes to know all things, or even almost all, is highly suspect in academic circles, for none is so aware of the limitations in any area of human knowledge as the person who is a specialist in it, and institutional centers of higher education are filled with such specialists. While arrogance may result from a sophomoric education, intensive study of any social science promotes humility with respect to man's social behavior.

A student need not be alarmed by the constant changes occurring in all the social sciences. The accumulation of knowledge and alterations in the values and interests of men as a result of modifications in their condition are major reasons for those changes. As a result, even history, one of the most stable of the social sciences, must be rewritten for each generation because new problems and hence new questions emerge which lead to new perspectives on events of the past.

Using the same methods and viewing the same events as the "secular" historian, the Christian has a different frame of reference for his interpretations. The history taught in the typical Sunday church school has a different purpose from that taught in the high school or college history class; one is oriented toward progressive events in Judaism and Christianity that led to the present Christian church, while the other is oriented toward events that culminated in the present socio-political situation of the nation. One historical approach totally ignores events emphasized in the other, just as the history of India taught in New Delhi has a considerably different focus from the history of India taught in Oslo, Norway, or Atlanta, Georgia. Variations in perspective among the social sciences or between them and a Christian interpretation of any phenomena do not ipso facto indicate either the "truth" or the "falsity" of the respective positions.

problems for christians in the social sciences

There is a wide range of reactions among Christians when first exposed to social science subjects in college. Some have developed a philosophy of life with principles that adequately cover every situation, so they do not even recognize that there are any special problems. Others have been sheltered from "the world" and acculturated into a compartmentalized faith that is antagonistic toward "the wisdom of this evil age." If they also have been given an inflexible world view, based on interpretations of the Bible alleged to be "the only Christian perspective" on human evolution, the course of world history, or the nature of government, social welfare, and other social relationships, they are very vulnerable to apparent discrepancies between their academic subjects and their faith. The majority of students presumably fall between the two extremes, experiencing occasional problems but generally adjusting well to academic life.

Comments on many aspects of the problems of Christian social science students appear in the following chapters. Each is oriented primarily to one discipline, but all present perspectives which are relevant to the other academic specialties. Even the student who is committed to a major field of study will therefore benefit from chapters dealing with other subjects as well as his own. I shall resist the temptation to discuss the subjects covered in one or another of the specific chapters, such as cultural and moral relativism, spiritual illiteracy among scientists, the anti-religious operational stance of the "cult of objectivity," anti-Christian presuppositions of social scientists and professors, and theological-psychological tensions related to guilt, anxiety, pride, aggression, and morality among Christians.

The models of man prevalent in the social sciences are diverse, as the chapters on history, political science, economics, education, anthropology, and psychology indicate. No single model suffices to cover the complex totality of man. The various, relatively deterministic images of man that predominate in the social sciences may be necessitated by the very nature of scientific investigation, but there is, in my opinion, a growing recognition among social scientists of the high degree of autonomy that still resides in men within the context of their limited determinative social environments. The scholar who treats man as if he were completely determined usually thinks quite differently when he himself must make a significant personal decision!

The fact that human choices are limited by such factors as

the level of economic development of one's culture, emphases and deficiencies of its educational institutions, value orientations linked with one's racial or ethnic and religious subculture, his social class position, and a multitude of other identifiable elements that place restrictions upon the scope and nature of decision-making does not negate the exercise of man's will. Behind his decisions lies ultimately a philosophy of life that provides the guiding values on the basis of which specific choices are made. This fact has led some philosophers, theologians, and social science theorists to say that every man has a religion or pseudo-religion of some kind.

Some Christians are tempted to conclude that there can be but one Christian perspective to any given social problem. The past errors of Christians holding that viewpoint, the finiteness of man in his confrontation with an extremely complicated universe, the limited scope of knowledge about social relationships, the diversity of Christian values that bear upon any given complex situation (some of which contradict other equally Christian values), the fact that current scientific knowledge is always based upon past observations and deals with the future only by extrapolations from them, and the controversies about politics among devout Christians all serve as warnings against the facile adoption of any one viewpoint as if it were the only one consistent with biblical revelation.

Every action-orientation is imperfect, so no political, economic, or social position with regard to social problems is completely pure; all have various shades of sinfulness. This means that the practical choices facing Christians in the civic, social, and political sphere of life seldom, if ever, are choices between complete good and complete evil. Rather, various degrees of justice and injustice, love and hatred, kindness and harshness, mercy and cruelty, selfishness and selflessness, and other competing values are present in the typical situation. What obviously harms some people benefits others. Short-range advantages to society may produce long-range impairments. Implementing one humanistic and Christian virtue may obstruct the fulfillment of another. Study of the social sciences will make this increasingly clear to the alert student.

As a result of these facts, as well as of certain schemes of biblical interpretation which relate Christian values only to personal piety and an eternal life beyond the confines of the present world-age, many Christians have succumbed to the heresy that they can be neutral with reference to political issues. They fail to recognize that a stance of neutrality is in effect siding with whichever side has the greater power, giving it their implicit blessing. In a democratic society none can be neutral. Inaction is a form of action. It contributes to far greater evils than taking sides with and working for whatever seems to be "the lesser of two evils" if not a clearly righteous position in political and social conflict. Even more ironic, some of the most politically inactive Christians are among the most vocal in condemning injustices and inequities in political and social institutions. Their failure to work actively for righteousness on a level that supplements and transcends "winning souls to Christ" has contributed to the very evils they reprehend.

One of the chief functions of the social sciences is to reveal the latent (that is, unintended, generally unrecognized) consequences of man's social institutions and activities. This unmasking role is most easily fulfilled when social scientists are outside the seats of power in society. It is often linked with a debunking orientation that divests the falsehoods, misleading impressions, and pretentious claims of vested interests. A common effect of social science investigation therefore is the revelation of hypocrisies in which groups pretend to pursue certain goals but in fact fail to do so or even unknowingly promote contrary positions. As a result, members of the power structure of society and its institutions tend to fear the exposure that social science research may bring. To a considerable extent, the social sciences are in this regard like Jesus Christ who so often said to his contemporaries, "You have heard it said . . . , but I say unto you. . . ."

When the insights of social science theory and research are brought to bear upon religious institutions and behavior, the results may appear to clash with Christian faith. Usually such efforts are responsible reflections and interpretations of the actual situation. If evil is revealed, it was not produced by social scientists but only disclosed or documented by them. One should interpret such revelations as an aspect of discovering truth and fulfilling the virtue of honesty, in contrast to the dishonest proclivity of all men to avoid or cover up the unpleasant.

The orientation of the social sciences toward seeking the truth is evident even in the language they use. They typically do not refer to research findings as good, bad, evil, or desirable in a value-laden fashion, but wish, rather, to find the facts related to an area of investigation, whether these make people happy or not. As soon as a social scientist sets out to *prove* his hypothesis is true instead of to *test* it to find out whether it is or is not supported by observable facts, he has ceased being scientific and has departed from the virtue of honesty.

Interpretations of scientific data are based upon numerous unstated presuppositions as well as upon explicitly stated theories and reported facts. When conclusions contradict Christian values, either the scientific or the Christian interpretations may have flaws of logic or problems traceable to hidden assumptions. Limitations of social research are evident in the technical problems of sampling and statistical inference, the need to define concepts operationally, and difficulties in constructing measuring instruments, collecting data, and linking facts and hypotheses with theory. These add to the possibilities for misinterpretation. Certain aspects of human life may never become susceptible to strictly empirical research procedures, their analysis resting instead upon *Verstehen,* the introspective and intuitive approach to human experience used by some social scientists.

problems related to social change

Social scientists tend to hold socioeconomic and political perspectives that are relatively "liberal." They see the problems and inconsistencies in present institutional arrangements and desire to promote the basic values of the Bill of Rights in the

American Constitution. They therefore desire change instead of adherence to the status quo or reversion to some alleged "golden age" of the past. (Radicals who wish to overthrow the entire social system interpret that position as one of "conservatism," for it calls for relatively gradual changes within the framework of present institutional arrangements and values instead of sudden revolution.) Seeing the ways in which injustice is perpetuated under local and state governments, many social scientists promote the federalizing of public educational, welfare, and health services. Desiring peace on earth and realizing that the welfare of people in any one nation is closely linked with that of all others in the modern world, they tend to support internationalism and to oppose chauvinistic patriotism.

Many social scientists have assumed falsely that a conservative theological position inevitably and irrevocably necessitates the holding of conservative socioeconomic and political views, and vice versa. Supported by many Christians who hold similar views, their position contributes to mutual antagonism with respect to local, state, and national politics. Each sees the other as one of its opponents. When, in addition, social scientists reveal the ways in which decision-making is in fact shifting away from the individual to the collective level (as governmental agencies add more and more regulations to control business, communications, transportation, and other aspects of social life, and as power shifts from local to regional and state levels and from them in turn to the federal government and its administrative agencies), the relationships between Christians and social scientists are even more strained. Fears of political dominance and control are especially great among those whose eschatological interpretations of the Bible foresee a world dictatorship that will suppress Christian churches and persecute Christians. Seeking evidence of the "end times," such persons interpret any shift from local to national and international power or allegiance as a portent of ominous events soon to come. This blinds them to other biblical teachings which lend support to current events and political movements that have a wholesome impact upon man's treatment of man.

To be sure, the Christian perspective recognizes that no economic, political, psychological, or social improvements can settle the ultimate questions of man's nature and his relationship with God. This has led some devout people to the false conclusion that the amelioration of social problems is at worst an anti-Christian activity and at best a waste of time. A balanced approach keeps both the immediate, mundane needs of man and his ultimate, eternal destiny in a healthy relationship to each other. Just as conversion as a personal act of Christian commitment is followed by changed attitudes, behavior, and self-conceptions, so truly Christian living in a rapidly changing world necessitates continual personal and social adjustments. Evangelism and an active social concern are both needed in the Christian church.

Social change need not frighten Christians if that change, like most recent developments related to race relations, criminal law, and social welfare, involves increased protection of civil rights. Whatever enhances the dignity of man is consistent with the Judeo-Christian doctrine that man is made in the image of God and is accountable to him. Similarly, God's love is for the entire world, not only for Americans. Christians who sincerely wish to imitate his love should be happy with the goal of promoting the dignity and rights of man over the entire world, trying to reduce human suffering and squalor wherever it may be. They, above all others, should be glad to give up a portion of their own wealth through taxes that help serve the needs of others. Since they realize that they have here on earth "no continuing city" (Heb. 13:14) and are instructed not to be "conformed to this world" (Rom. 12:2), they can afford to advocate changes that enhance the educational and socioeconomic opportunities of neglected minorities. Since their Bible has dozens of passages that instruct its followers to remember the poor, they can rejoice at all honorable efforts to promote the dignity and well-being of disadvantaged groups. To oppose social change categorically is the equivalent of idolatrous worldliness, the features of which are outlined in a non-religious context by the social sciences.

social science contributions to christianity

The social sciences can make significant contributions to the intellectual life, spiritual growth, and effective service of Christians. As the respective chapters indicate, they can help one develop Christian perspectives on economic policies, educational goals, teaching methods, health, government, other social institutions, stewardship of possessions, self-understanding, social problems, and interpersonal relationships. They throw light upon various teachings of the Bible. They thrust new perspectives about society upon the Christian, driving him to the Bible for reanalysis of stereotyped interpretations of man's social world and scrutiny of the alleged foundations of clichés about social behavior. They have the liberating qualities of the liberal arts, enriching man's understanding of himself, others, and his social environment.

The social sciences can be instrumental in promoting the goal of loving one's neighbor as he loves himself, for they reveal the indirect as well as direct consequences of alternative forms of action. They make it possible to know how others perceive and experience acts related to them, and in general they furnish a clearer basis for serving others. They distinctly indicate that the results of individualistic loving of persons may be negated by failures to love men collectively as members of anonymous masses. They reveal ways in which injustice may be perpetrated even by efforts intended to promote justice. They disclose the unmerciful results of poorly administered "deeds of mercy." The sensitivity of the Christian to his fellowman and his wisdom about the virtues of compassion and reconciliation can be improved greatly through the marriage of social science and Christian values.

Social scientists tend to see religious faith and perspectives as dependent rather than independent variables; that is, as if they were effects of other causes, not causes of other conditions in society. Most religious leaders, on the contrary, hold the opposite. In the scientific context only research to test the roles of religious beliefs and commitments as consequences of change and as change-producing forces can indicate which is more common. Scientific research hence is a potential corrective of a narrow approach, but so is biblical study. Jesus taught that "the heart" is the source of human action (Mt. 15:10 ff), and many biblical passages refer to the corrupting influence of social conditions upon the individual. Reciprocal relationships prevail between man's social condition and his faith commitments.

A parallel phenomenon is the tendency of some social scientists to view religious activities and institutions instrumentally, that is, only as tools to promote social values, or as means to serve the goals of society and other non-religious ends. Religious leaders who view their programs and institutions solely from the perspective of their values for human health and welfare, social interaction, economic well-being, general education, or artistic, literary, and musical appreciation implicitly support the same instrumental approach to religion.

Since ultimate values cannot originate in the sciences, it is not anti-scientific to seek them in one's religious faith. Of course, the student should not confuse those values with the data, concepts, and theories of his academic disciplines by failing to recognize the distinctions between them. *What is* rarely coincides with *what ought to be.*

summary and conclusions

All the social sciences are concerned with human society and social behavior. They share the application of the scientific method of investigation, although their concepts and techniques vary with their respective areas of study. They reveal the unity of mankind, the fact that all men on earth are interrelated as beneficiaries of common blessings and victims of problems that cannot be confined to the boundaries of their communities, states, and nations. They clearly indicate the inequalities of weal and woe that prevail among men, making the suffering of some a source of benefit for others. Both their theoretical and applied fields have significant implications for Christendom. They are especially helpful in clarifying Christian social ethics— what men and women who have faith in Christ can do to implement and disseminate love and justice in the world.

Christian students who face problems in their social science classes usually can resolve them by having a clear understanding of the nature and limits of the social sciences as well as a firm faith that is capable of distinguishing human traditions, folklore, and interpretations of the Bible from what the Bible itself teaches. While there can be no compartmentalization of religious commitment because one either is or is not a Christian, it is always necessary to divide up the totality of reality in order to cope with it. At times it may be necessary to learn perspectives in which one does not believe, but knowledge is not the same as personal commitment.

Problems in the relationships between the social sciences and Christianity reside as often in the flaws among representatives of the latter as among the former. With a mental and spiritual orientation that tests all things and holds fast to that which is proven to be good while abstaining from even the appearance of whatever is evil (1 Thess. 5:21-22) a Christian will honestly hold an open mind until adequate evidence has been obtained. Social science tools can be of great help in all aspects of this, even providing many aids for interpreting the Bible.

Because "the only human thing that is permanent is change," the structures and institutionalized behavior associated with Christianity are changing along with the social sciences and everything else. Only God the Creator, who revealed himself to man in the person of Jesus Christ, remains unchanged from generation to generation and from age to age (Heb. 13:8). Sorting out timeless truth from culture-bound and time-limited elements of society, including their own religious groups, is a major challenge for all students, Christian or not.

Notes

[1] This incident was narrated to me by Dr. Thomas D. Eliot, Professor Emeritus of Sociology, Northwestern University, while traveling to the American Sociological Society convention, August, 1955.

John Scanzoni

Sociology

Christian perspectives of sociology are just that—a set of perspectives, not an attempt to delineate a "Christian sociology." In fact, a "Christian sociology" does not exist any more than a "Christian psychology" or a "Christian biology." Sociology, ever since its inception in early nineteenth-century France, represents an attempt to apply scientific methodology to the study of *relationships* between individuals and between groups ranging in size from two persons all the way up to entire societies.[1]

We must insist on a distinction between Christianity and various disciplines, not that we fear lest a particular discipline be clouded by Christianity, but lest Christianity become too closely identified with the vagaries of scholarship within that discipline. Some who have argued for a "Christian psychology," for example, have done so out of fear that "atheists" within this field would subvert unsuspecting minds if certain conclusions went unchallenged. Such efforts have resulted in an emasculation of both the discipline and of Christianity. In short, any science is a set of generalizations induced from observations about empirical phenomena. Christianity, on the other hand, is a set of deductive propositions, many of which are simply beyond the ken of empirical verification. It is therefore fatuous to try to congeal them in the fashion of some enthusiasts.

Yet, many Christians—including some scholars—have over-reacted to this travesty by failing to search out *any* linkages between a particular discipline and Christianity.[2] Linkages there are, and to explore them one must first proceed from a clear definition of New Testament Christianity; that is, that God, the unmade maker of the universe, the unruled ruler, revealed himself in the person of Jesus Christ, that through his death and resurrection, wayward man can be brought into the family of God, and that now every man must decide for himself whether or not he will submit to Jesus Christ as Savior and Lord. Second, Christ as maker and sustainer of the universe called himself the *Truth* (Jn. 14:6). Whatever province of knowledge a particular discipline carves out for itself, it is in fact investigating one small part of the infinite Truth, Jesus Christ. Thus, the twentieth-century social scientist who is a Christian finds his motivation to be the same as many of the earliest English scientists who sought to "subdue nature for the glory of God." Like Kepler, he may conceive of his scientific investigations as "thinking God's thoughts after him."[3]

perspectives of the discipline

Sociology desires to be a "basic" or "pure" science in that it seeks knowledge about human interaction apart from any prior concern as to its specific application. It is true, however, that much sociological knowledge is applied by social workers, urban planners, and government policy makers interested in social betterment, reform, and progress.[4] Nonetheless, sociology per se is not to be confused with any of the foregoing, since sociology is concerned with research and investigation, whereas social work deals with application and amelioration. Many otherwise informed Christians fail to make this crucial distinction, and some go so far as to equate what they call "godless sociology" with socialism and even communism![5]

In short, sociology is one way to gain knowledge about human relationships. For the Christian, this means he is gaining further knowledge about what is the most vital segment of God's universe. Our first perspective on sociology, therefore, is based on a clear understanding of what the field is and, more specifically, on the motivation which impels a Christian to study in it.

A second perspective lies in the nature of the scientific method as it is applied to human relationships. Some have argued that many assumptions inherent in scientific methodology impose a type of determinism on the individual that tends to preclude human free will and responsibility as well as the untrammeled action of the Holy Spirit.[6] Consider, for instance, individuals who participated in the looting and violence that have swept many American cities in past summers. Almost all sociologists agree that these behaviors are due to the frustration, powerlessness, and despair of the ghetto. The ghetto is, in turn, a social system imposed by whites on blacks basically because their skin is dark. Whites systematically relegate blacks in the ghetto to the poorest housing, schools, and jobs.

For the social scientist, therefore, the following general proposition (among others) might emerge: If X (systematic deprivation by a dominant group), then Y (violence by a subordinate group). Questions of original sin, the power of Christ to transform lives and to help resist temptation—these questions and others like them which are central to Christianity are not considered because they are outside the realm of empirical verification.[7] By the same token, of course, no one can argue empirically for their invalidity. Christian assumptions and explanations regarding the *ultimate* causes, cures, and consequences of riot behavior (or any behavior) are grounded in the revelation of God, Jesus Christ. But science is not (and should not be) concerned with untestable ultimates, only with verifiable immediates. The Christian believes that these immediates (hatred, violence, etc.) flow from the ultimates, but this by no means implies that the immediates can be fully understood merely by referring to the ultimates in a superficial and simplistic manner, as do some Christians who think, for example, that violence is explained by pointing *only* to man's sinfulness.

To use a biological analogy, the Christian believes that God existed before all matter, that he maintains an active role in the creative process, and that the grand purpose of all life—especially human life—is to glorify and adore him. These ultimate issues are distinct from the *how* of God's activity, which is the task of the biologist to explore, as seen, for instance, in the formation of a human embryo.

Likewise, the sociologist telling us how riots occur, how families dissolve, how political parties cohere, is simply describing immediate human activity, not speculating on its ultimate linkages. It is apparent, however, that some nontheistic sociologists stumble into *scientism,* which is the obverse of the Christian trying to explain immediate happenings by a superficial resort to ultimate questions. The scientist, flushed with his success in analyzing the immediate, proceeds to dismiss the ultimate on the grounds that no verifiable linkage is apparent. Since this remarkable deduction regarding ultimates cannot be verified empirically, it actually takes on the status of a religion, defined as a set of nonverifiable ultimates, namely, scientism. From the Christian standpoint, this is worship of the creature more than the Creator, in other words, idolatry.

The Christian, while avidly avoiding scientism, just as avidly seeks for immediate explanations of human interaction which sociology can provide. These in no way undermine ultimate Christian assumptions, but instead *accentuate* them. In effect, sociology merely discovers patterns which already exist in human relationships. For the Christian, awareness of these patterns will help him to better understand the meaning of St. Paul's words, "Whatever a man sows, that he will also reap" (Gal. 6:7). Understanding of these processes in no way excuses or eliminates man's freedom and responsibility any more than does a belief in God's foreknowledge or his ordering of certain historical events (see Acts 2:23, 38). On the contrary, understanding the immediate "causes" of phenomena as diverse as race riots, political parties, or institutional religion, will enable us eventually to see more clearly their actual linkages to ultimate questions, and thus aid us in being more effective in the ongoing process of applying needed correctives.[8]

A final and related perspective pertains to the meaning of sociological knowledge for a Christian student. Our first theme concerned the *motivation* for seeking such knowledge, the second touched on some of the implications of the *method* whereby the knowledge is obtained. Now to the *meaning* of this kind of knowledge. Often the effect of studying sociology is to give a student a totally different picture of society and its arrangements from the one he held previously. This is especially true of the Christian student who has grown up in the typical middle-class home and church, surrounded by friends and relatives who continually reinforced certain ways of looking at society—ways which he learned from them in the first place. Over the years, through sermons and Sunday school, these merely cultural patterns tend to become unconsciously invested with almost ultimate sanctity. As a result, he tends to view the world through spectacles which are specially tinted "middle-class Christian." One of the first jolts that he gets in sociology is when he perceives the actual temporal nature of these arrangements—that they are merely relative to his own social background.[9]

social unrest
Consider once again the city riots. The typical analysis (of the riots) received by these students in their homes and churches focuses on those who riot. The student is told that arson, looting, sniping, etc., are crimes; and, what is more, they are sin. Thus, his image of what is happening in the cities is narrowed to include only the wrongs that are most apparent and obvious.

However, a sociologist, in seeking to explain the immediate reasons for deviant behavior, focuses not only on the rioters, but also on the whites that own substandard housing and charge exorbitant rents, the white store owners who exploit minority groups both in prices and credit charges, or who refuse them jobs, or who oppose tax-boosting educational innovations to free hapless ghetto children from the endless cycle of poverty. From the biblical standpoint, these also are sins—just as much as the looting and violence (see Amos 2, 5, and 8; James 2 and 5).

But how many churches, bound by affluent middle-class culture, emphasize these aspects of the gospel? Not many. And for the earnest Christian student exposed to these phenomena for the first time, the effect can indeed be jarring. However, if a Christian student keeps his wits about him, the sum of this exposure and similar experiences can be tremendously exhilarating and expansive, serving to emphasize the true comprehensiveness of Christianity.

For example, some students become disillusioned, perceiving that their parents and churches have presented only half the picture about the "other half" and that this failure is often due to their parents' identification of Christianity with the interests of the dominant middle class. As a result, some of them close their eyes to what they see, others become cynical, but increasingly, many see only the murky bathwater, and in their efforts to be rid of that, sometimes unconsciously rid themselves of the baby too. That is, if their study of sociology or other social sciences has led them to see how bound up institutional, middle-class Christianity is with cultural patterns that are patently evil and self-serving, then what is the sense of maintaining New Testament Christianity at all? In fact, many who "lose their faith" in college do so through this chronological sequence and not by questioning key doctrines. [10]

The tragedy of equating baby with bath water is that the two, in fact, are really not equivalent at all, and this is precisely where an exposure to sociology can have such a freeing effect on the spirit and mind of the Christian. For through such study, it can become exceedingly vivid to him that the essential elements of Christianity are supracultural—not bound to any institution, social class, nation, or political or social viewpoint.

sorting it out

Sociology has sometimes been attacked by Christians because these kinds of arguments may lead, they claim, to "cultural relativism"—the notion that nothing is absolute or applicable to all cultures at all times. But once again, we must be careful to sort out the immediate which is culturally relative, from the absolute which is not. [11] If the non-Christian errs by claiming too much to be relative, the Christian errs by claiming too much to be universal. One benefit for the Christian student in studying sociology, therefore, is to give him new perspectives on the social order(s). In turn, this should drive him to the Bible to discover for himself what it really says (or does not say) about human relationships of all sorts and on all levels.

An example of this sorting process can be noted briefly in the area of sex and marriage customs. The universal is the belief that the divine order is (1) leaving father and mother, (2) cleaving to each other, and then (3) becoming one flesh through sexual intercourse (Gen. 2:24; Mt. 19:4-6). In other words, sex follows marriage. [12] However, the customs and symbols surrounding these steps vary within each culture, and are relative to it. For instance, there is very little "Christian" about American middle-class "church wedding" customs. In fact, for ostentation and waste of substance, they are pagan; and Christians should be the first to sort this out and then point it out.

To take another example of this, recent sociological-type analyses (both popular and scientific) of the church as an organization lucidly reveal how much it is a product of society and not of supernatural forces. [13] The most striking instance is currently in the realm of racial integration. A recent film, "Time for Burning," presents an actual account of a situation which is becoming increasingly typical. [14] It describes a clergyman suggesting to his board and parishoners that they try to swap home visits with several selected black families from a nearby sister church of their own denomination. The upshot of these mild efforts to experiment on New Testament bases was to empty the pews of his church and eventually to force his resignation. In other words, the organization resisted an attempt to carry out its own basic values, so much so that had the minister insisted on the values, the organization would have collapsed. Thus, the church as human organization took precedence over the church as suprahuman organism—or people related in a vital, living, and dynamic fashion.

Nevertheless, awareness of the selfishness of church as organization should not therefore cause the student (as is increasingly the case) to reject the validity and vitality of church as organism. Here also sociological insights can serve as a basis for sorting out the immediate from the absolute. The "absolute" is that Christians must assemble together in some way. The "immediate" is that Christians continually adopt the way best suited to the social conditions in which they live. Thus, these kinds of insights can contribute toward the growing trend to experiment with new and vital patterns ("new wineskins"—Mt. 9:17) of church as organism.[15]

In these brief perspectives for Christians on sociology, we have attempted to touch on aspects of motivation, method, and meaning. Of necessity many specific questions could not be dealt with due to limitations of space.[16]   It is felt, however, that these three general issues subsume a good deal of the waterfront; and if a student has further specific problems, he is encouraged to begin to think them through within this initial framework.

The motivation for the study of human interaction is the same as for all other activity, to learn more of God's truth in order to glorify him more ably. The scientific methodology of sociological research, while stressing order and determinism in its search for immediate explanations, in no way vitiates the ultimate nature of Christian postulates regarding human relationships. Instead, the immediate elucidates and amplifies the applicability of the ultimate. Finally, the meaning of sociological knowledge can have one of two effects for the Christian, depending on how actively he sorts out the ultimate from the immediate. If he confuses the two, he may repudiate or else become indifferent to the exciting whole of Christianity. If he sees the distinction, he will vigorously seek to cull out those culture-bound elements which hinder New Testament simplicity and dynamic, and at the same time seek more relevant application for those timeless truths embodied in the person of Jesus Christ.

Notes

[1] Two excellent introductory sociology texts are Ely Chinoy, *Society* (New York, 1967), and Everett K. Wilson, *Sociology: Rules, Roles, and Relationships* (Homewood, 1966).

[2] Among some of the writer's earlier efforts in this direction are: "Why Try to Keep Up with Those Joneses?" *Sunday School Times*, 21 July 1962, pp. 524-525; "The Man with the Gold-Ringed Finger," *Eternity*, Aug. 1963, pp. 11-13; "Is 'Going Steady' Going Wrong?" *Eternity*, Nov. 1963, pp. 20-22; "Who Is the Worldling?" *Sunday School Times*, 21 Aug. 1965, pp. 592-593; (with Letha Scanzoni) "Devotion or Service?" *Sunday School Times*, 26 Oct. 1963, pp. 768-769; (with Letha Scanzoni) "Sex and the Single Eye," *Eternity*, Mar. 1967, pp. 12-14, 46.

[3] For a classic description of the relationships of early science to Christianity, see Robert K. Merton, *Social Theory and Social Structure* (New York, 1949), chaps. 18—19. Also see Guy S. Metraux and Francois Crouzet, eds., *The Evolution of Science* (New York, 1963).

[4] For discussions of how sociology may be utilized in an applied fashion, see Arthur B. Shostak, ed., *Sociology in Action* (Homewood, 1966); John Scanzoni, *Readings in Social Problems* (Boston, 1967). Among sociologists who are Christians, Professor David O. Moberg has been a leader in specifically describing some of the practical applications of Christianity to social issues. See his (with Robert Gray) *The Church and the Older Person* (Grand Rapids, 1962); and his *Inasmuch: Christian Social Responsibility in the 20th Century* (Grand Rapids, 1965). There is also a formal organization of Christians who are social workers. Further information can be obtained from the National Association of Christians in Social Work, c/o Wheaton College, Wheaton, Illinois, 60187.

[5] "Godless Sociology" was the title of an article which appeared in an evangelical magazine a few years ago, condemning the welfare state and equating sociology with "creeping socialism."

[6] See Ian G. Barbour, *Issues in Science and Religion* (Englewood Cliffs, 1966), Part II, for a complete discussion of scientific method and Christianity.

[7] Changed behavior in the form of transformed lives is, of course, open to empirical test. What is not is the Christian assumption that the ultimate cause of the transformation is God's power.

[8] Regarding "application," in this brief essay, we cannot raise the complex issue of the Christian and social reform. There is no doubt that currently evangelicals are thoroughly rethinking this question. For some help in this area, see Professor Moberg's titles cited in footnote 4. For historical evidence that, previous to this century, evangelicals had been in the vanguard of reform, see Earle E. Cairns, *Saints and Society* (Chicago, 1960).

[9] A jarring autobiography of a Christian shaking off these tinted specta-cles is found in Thomas Howard, *Christ, the Tiger* (Philadelphia, 1967).

[10] In this connection, see John Scanzoni, "No Faith to Lose," *Eternity*, Dec. 1965, pp. 19-21, 44; also, "College: Time for Triumph," *Key*, Jan. 1968.

[11] A striking example of differences over the *immediate* emerges in differ-ing attitudes between British and American evangelicals toward eco-nomic issues. The following quotation is from a highly regarded English evangelical publication: "In these days of the Welfare State, the Gov-ernment and Local Authorities contribute a surprising amount to our pockets. . . . This legal distribution of income is according to, if not necessarily in the spirit of, the early Church, as mentioned in Acts 2:45. . . . There are Pensions, Family Allowances, University Grants and Grants for House Improvement, as well as sickness and unemployment benefits. All these are right and due to us, if applicable, and our only duty is to submit a true and correct claim—and be thankful. Some might feel that a claim for National Assistance shows lack of faith in God to provide, but this money is merely a payment out of a fund to which (in the past, at least) the receiver has contributed. What the receiver must do is to swallow his pride and accept what is offered on the basis of a truthful claim. It is as much God-provided as a salary or pension" (*Crusade*, Apr. 1967). See also David O. Moberg, "Cultural Relativity and Christian Faith," *Journal of the American Scientific Affiliation* (June 1962).

[12] Space does not permit us to go into the rationale for this sex ethic in the light of those who question its actual universality, those who adhere to "situation ethics," or the "new morality." For a definitive rationale, see Letha Scanzoni, *Sex and the Single Eye* (Grand Rapids, 1969).

[13] A few examples: Pierre Berton, *Comfortable Pew* (Philadelphia, 1965); Harvey Cox, *Secular City* (New York, 1965); Rev. James Kavanaugh, *Modern Priest Looks at His Outdated Church* (New York, 1967). One example from the evangelical viewpoint is Keith Miller, *Taste of New Wine* (Waco, 1966). A textbook in the sociology of religion by an evangelical is David O. Moberg, *Church as a Social Institution* (Engle-wood Cliffs, 1962).

[14] The most significant article known to this writer in which an evangelical deals with black-white relations is by sociologist Ivan J. Fahns, "Why Evangelicals Are Failing to Reach Negroes," *Sunday School Times*, 16 Nov. 1963, pp. 820-822. A recent award-winning article by James L. Johnson, "Take the Fear out of Integration," *Christian Herald*, Aug. 1967, pp. 16-17, 19, 46, suggested a plan for peacefully integrating local communities. Also see James O. Buswell III, *Slavery, Segregation, and Scripture* (Grand Rapids, 1963).

[15] See, for example, Elizabeth O'Connor, *Call to Commitment* (New York, 1963) in which she describes the unique Church of the Savior, Washington, D. C. Another illustration of experimental new patterns is the Circle Church of Chicago, Rev. David R. Mains, pastor. This church meets in a Teamsters Union Building, interacts in dialogue after the sermon, and frequently meets in scattered groups in various homes on Sunday evenings.

[16] Some other questions are dealt with in David O. Moberg's chapter in Richard Bube, ed., *The Encounter of Christianity and Science* (Grand Rapids, 1968).

Jacob A. Loewen

Anthropology

Augustine once observed: "Man wonders about the restless sea, the flowing waters, the sight of the sky, and forgets that of all wonders he himself is the most wonderful." This *man* and his works are the object of study of anthropology—as its name (Greek: *anthropos* "man") already implies. The overall field can be divided by orientation into two distinct areas: physical anthropology and cultural anthropology. (Archaeology stands as a hybrid between the two for it investigates both the human skeletal remains and the surviving material artifacts which such people made in their lifetime.)

Physical anthropology concerns itself with the physical man, his prehistory, and his modern racial representatives, and, as such, it operates as one of the physical sciences (hence its exclusion from this paper). Cultural anthropology, on the other hand, devotes its attention to the person, his relationships, customs, institutions, and patterns of social behavior, and therefore belongs among the social sciences. As a social science, cultural anthropology shares many of the interests and concerns of sociology. However, it is distinguished from the latter in that anthropology has traditionally concerned itself with the so-called "primitive" peoples of the world, while sociology emphasizes the study of the so-called "civilized" societies. As a result of this division in fields of research, the two have developed rather separate philosophies and methodologies.

The divergence between the two fields has grown to such proportions that on some larger campuses the two exhibit considerable psychological distance, if not actual professional antagonism. Recently, however, (possibly under European influence) the two sciences are undergoing rapprochement, for on the one hand, sociology has been extending its concerns into many of the larger societies that formerly were the exclusive domain of anthropology; and on the other hand, anthropologists have become increasingly interested in applying their insights to their own society. These developments, at least in North America,[2] are being labeled social anthropology.[3]

The greatest single contribution of anthropology to modern scientific thought has been the concept of culture, which a well-known anthropologist defines as "the sum total of integrated learned behavior patterns which are characteristic of members of a society and which are therefore not the result of biological inheritance."[4]

Like every area of scientific inquiry, anthropology has developed its own set of presuppositions and premises. Often these are so thoroughly accepted by the instructor that he may not even stop to verbalize them. If the beginning student, however, is to be able to evaluate his class exposure adequately, he needs to become aware of these assumptions. This essay proposes to highlight a few of these spoken or unspoken premises in order to call attention to their potential hazards and benefits, especially as they relate to the Christian faith.

cultural relativism

One of the first observations that will strike the student of cultural anthropology is the vast array of societies and the almost endless diversity of their cultures. This heterogeneity expresses itself not only in the inventory of novel culture traits but also in the distinctive relationships of these traits to each other, and even more, in the differing values which cultures attach to them. When we compare what appear to be identical traits in different cultures, we find that they can have completely different implications and entirely different value tags. Thus, for example, for a mature woman to uncover her breasts in public would be a sign of moral looseness in North America, but for the Waunana of Colombia, uncovered breasts is a sign of moral purity—only prostitutes cover their breasts. Or consider one's responsibility to aged parents. For a pioneer American to abandon his aged parents to exposure and death would have been a crime. (I use pioneer America as the example because modern America often "abandons" aged parents psychologically in retirement centers and commits them to "death" as surely as by exposure in a snowstorm, and it does so without any real feelings of responsibility or guilt.) However, this same act for an Eskimo could be the sign of highest respect and love.[5] The nomadic Lengua in the Paraguayan Chaco consider such an act definitely wrong; nevertheless they practice it, especially if the aged person is a shaman. The Lengua are so afraid that the soul of the dead will harm them, especially if the aged person should die at night, that the band often abandons a moribund elder by day and flees for safety. In so doing they are choosing the lesser of two evils, for the safety of the whole group is of higher value than loyalty to a dying elder.

The cultural panorama thus offers an almost endless variety of what is demanded, expected, permitted, or condemned. This diversity in turn provides the foundation for the doctrine of cultural relativity which anthropologists have espoused so thoroughly that they tend to see all truth as relative. If this obviously valid principle of relativity is not taken in proper perspective, however, it can have some very tragic repercussions. For the weakly rooted, it can crumble the foundations of faith; while for its proponents, it often serves as a convenient excuse to avoid personal commitment to any transcendent values.

I remember a coed who came to my office in tears. This freshman, from a fine Christian home, suddenly felt her world of Christian principles crumble as the case for relativity was being built successfully by an agnostic professor. Her value structure was so shaken that she found herself unable to face her parents for the weekend. What she had failed to see is that while there is no question of relativity when individual traits are taken out of the cultural context and studied comparatively, these same traits do in actual fact generally have "absolutist" functions within the cultural whole from which they have been abstracted. Thus while, for example, the attitudes toward sex can vary greatly from society to society, each group nevertheless has a definition of what is immoral. In this way, undergirding the diversity there are in each culture some "absolutes" which are often readily translatable into Christian precepts.

man is an animal

There is really no question about man's place as a part of the overall animal kingdom, but is he an animal and no more? This emphasis on the "animal" may, of course, be a carry-over from the physical science aspect of anthropology, for it is closely linked with certain mechanistic views of human origins. Our concern here is to show that even the most ardent mechanistically-oriented physical anthropologist will unhesitatingly affirm that human intelligence differs from that of animals not only in degree, but in kind.[6] This distinction is frequently not clearly established in introductory courses of general anthropology, however, and as a result man appears as an animal in at least several contexts:

(1) Man is a stimulus-response mechanism, and his weaning and toilet training are the basic determinants of his personality.[7] There is no question that man reacts to stimuli, but he certainly is no mere reactor. He alone among living creatures has abstract values by means of which he filters, classifies, and otherwise grades all impinging stimuli. Important social responses are seldom mere reflex reactions. Furthermore, there is also no question that early childhood experience can play an important part in shaping man's personality,[8] but as a rational creature, man is not merely imprinted with instinctive reactions like animals, for he can modify, change, and readjust almost at

will.[9] In fact, anthropological research has shown that both the individual and the society as a whole can be "converted"; that is, both man and his social structures can be radically changed and restructured in values.[10]

(2) Man is a sexual animal. This emphasis represents the influence of earlier Freudian psychoanalysis. Without doubt, sex plays a very vital part in human life. And in many of the so-called "primitive" societies, sexuality is very visible and highly developed. This extreme emphasis overlooks, however, that sex is only one of several physiological drives which in the total hierarchy of drives are actually subordinate to the "higher" social needs.[11] In fact, it is the presence of these physiological and social drives in the human makeup that appears to be vitally important for the functioning of religion. Eugene A. Nida has shown that man tends to be drawn between the mere selfish fulfillment of his drives and the highest and best; that is, values that transcend time,[12] so that he lives most of his life in perpetual tension of one degree or another.

religion is a primitive survival

Earlier anthropology with its evolutionary view of culture saw animistic religion as a truly primitive and inferior prelude to eighteenth-century European achievement.[13] Today, when most schools of anthropology have long abandoned the evolutionary view of culture, religion is, nevertheless, still being treated as a hangover of primitive superstition. I remember during an informal conversation, one of my anthropology professors, speaking about a given Christian school, wistfully said: "If we could only get a good anthropologist into that school, we could soon get them to shed their religious superstition." To be educated—so it seems—means to be agnostic. However, even in anthropology itself, there have been voices of dissent. Robert Lowie, the famous anthropologist from the University of California, has pointed out that many modern intellectuals are really poor judges of religion since it is so remote to their experience—they are, in actual fact, "spiritual illiterates." In recognition of this situation Lowie testifies:

It did not take long to discover that to the primitive mind religion was of paramount importance. If I wanted to understand the Indians of that period I simply had to study its values for them. Moreover, my constant field trips brought me into contact with dedicated men of all faiths who were certainly deriving neither money nor renown by being missionaries to a group of Indians on a remote reservation. They lived as other members of the community did, in poverty, and they remained with their charges through pestilence and famine. One day it occurred to me that both the Indians and the hardy souls who were trying to convert them to Christianity *had some inner strength that I lacked.* Nor was I unique in this lack.[14]

It is common therefore for an agnostic professor to consider himself objective and therefore qualified to discuss religion "neutrally," while the religious person in class is usually considered immature and biased.[15] Obviously complete objectivity in regard to religion is a myth. No one can rid himself completely of his prejudices, biases, unspoken and (possibly even more dangerous) unrecognized values. Furthermore, many "objective" anthropologists are quite inconsistent in their treatment of religion. They can be tolerant and sympathetic while discussing Eskimo, Ashanti, or Hopi religion, but the same individuals will deny Christianity the same kind of treatment.[16] In many schools known Christians should therefore be prepared for some discrimination in class. This may be very benign, as when a professor apologetically says: "I have no intentions of hurting anyone's faith," but then launches into a rather unsubtle ridicule of belief in the supernatural; but it can also take the form of sarcasm and personal ridicule.

the condition of primitives before christian missionaries spoiled everything

The romantic notion of the happy primitive is no longer enjoying its earlier popularity, but its effects are still with us. Even where the "happy" is no longer being emphasized, the "intrusion" and the "damage" caused by killjoy missionaries is still frequently being proclaimed by anthropologists. It would be foolish to deny that many missionaries have made mistakes and that some have even indulged in abuses. There is, further, no doubt that the introduction of Christianity has often resulted in serious cultural problems.[17] But in spite of all the short-comings, failures, and problems, missionaries have generally been on the helping rather than on the hurting side. Even their disputed message seems to have a relevance far beyond that which their critics allow. Thus, for example, present-day nativistic movements in Africa show that the majority of these groups have modified extensively, if not exchanged, their tribal beliefs for a basically Christian philosophy, because this approach to life and reality is seen as far more relevant to the times in which they find themselves.[18]

Further, such criticism often overlooks the fact that the missionary is neither the only nor even the first major outside influence to which tribal societies are exposed. Gold miners, diamond hunters, and rubber collectors have often beaten the missionary by a long lead, and their effect has surely not always been the best either.

new insights

If, on the one hand, anthropology involves some hazards for the believing student, on the other hand, it offers him some very worthwhile dividends. Of these we will highlight only three: recognizing the unique structure of each culture and its implication for ethnocentrism, appreciating the supracultural nature of God's message to men, and equipping people with the basis for effective cross-cultural service.

On the one hand, the study of anthropology will make the student aware of the ethnocentric limitations of his own culture. The phenomenon of ethnocentrism was first recognized and labeled by William Graham Sumner who defined it as the unquestioning acceptance of the culturally alike and the rejection of the culturally unlike.[19] Ethnocentrism is an affliction that is native to "primitive" and "civilized" alike. The Tarahumara in northern Mexico do not hesitate to classify themselves as "the sons of God" and to call everyone else in the world "the sons of the devil."[20]   By the same token, the Spanish crown and its church emissaries found it necessary to hold repeated conferences to determine whether the natives in the Americas were mere animals or whether they had immortal souls.[21]

Even "God's people" from the early Jews to latter-day Christians have had trouble with ethnocentrism. The Jews expected a Savior for their own people, and the inclusion of the Gentiles in God's plan came as somewhat of a shock even to the apostles. Anthropologist Ruth Benedict has underscored that Christian nations have for centuries abused native peoples on the basis of what she calls "the unbeliever theory of native inferiority."[22] Even missionaries have been heard to complain: "These people can never form an indigenous church for there isn't one of them who can even set the table correctly." Becoming conscious of this limitation will not only help the honest student develop a more positive outlook toward people of different cultures, but it will invest the program of God embracing people from all cultures with a new kind of dignity.

On the other hand, the student will also learn to recognize that all cultures, including his own, have a meaningful structure. No culture, no matter how "primitive," is a mere conglomeration of traits; all cultures organize their trait inventory into culturally meaningful "bundles." These trait bundles in turn are organized into institutions which form the larger visible segments of the cultural whole. Ruth Benedict has labeled this integrated structure of a culture its configuration. In fact she went so far as to suggest that at the core of this hierarchical structure there usually is some central unifying theme or complex of values.[23]   Furthermore each of the traits, trait bundles, and institutions have attached to them value tags which indicate their relative importance to the total configuration. These integrative patterns and the value structure combine to provide the socialized participant in the culture with a characteristic way of looking at reality called world view.

There is no question that both the Old and New Testaments were inspired within specific cultural contexts, and that the understanding of these contexts is often essential to an understanding of the fuller implications of the message. On the other hand, at least one of the purposes of the life and ministry of Christ was to point men to the fact that all the prohibitions and demands of Scripture can in essence be summed up in two supracultural commands: " 'Love the Lord your God with all your heart, with all your soul, with all your mind.' That is the greatest commandment. It comes first. The second is like it: 'Love your neighbour as yourself' " (Mt. 22:37-39—NEB). This double-edged commandment is obviously not bound to any culture, time, or space. A thorough grounding in the insights of anthropology will not only strengthen one's appreciation for the supracultural nature of the core of the divine message, but will make apparent its relevance to men in all cultures.

Several factors seem to be working together to distinguish our time as a period of the most widespread, the most rapid, and the most comprehensive culture change. In the first place, improved communication has made the isolation of any large group of people in this world virtually impossible. This increased contact with other cultures has not only made people aware of their differences, but it has, in the second place, also raised the expectations of millions of people in the world. These rising expectations often cause many people to borrow indiscriminately from their "superior" neighbors. If such borrowers are to be spared hurt, they will need mediators who will help them maximize the benefits and minimize negative side effects of cultural borrowing. Of course, such culture "brokers" will need adequate anthropological awareness, not only of the cultures concerned, but also of the processes of change and adjustment.

In the third place, possibly in response to the rising expectations in the so-called underdeveloped nations of the world, we find an increasing number of people going abroad to change cultures. Over and above the traditional agents of change—diplomats, colonial officers, and missionaries—we today see teachers, technicians, agriculturalists, literary specialists, Agency for International Development personnel of various kinds, Peace Corps, voluntary service, military advisers, etc. Adequate grounding in cultural anthropology may spell the difference between success and failure for the cultural change agent himself and the difference between hurt and help for the recipients.

What may be even more welcome to the student of cultural anthropology is the fact that departments of anthropology are becoming increasingly aware that they can no longer afford to remain purely descriptive and uninvolved, for they have realized that even the very presence of an anthropological investigator and his investigative program in a tribal culture often sets in motion wheels of change for which the researcher must assume some responsibility. This awareness has made the academic community more ready to become personally involved in planned change and has also provided a new respect for programs of applied anthropology.

Notes

[1] The following source is an excellent popular introduction to some of the important concepts of anthropology from a Christian point of view: Eugene A. Nida, *Customs and Cultures: Anthropology for Christian Missions* (New York, 1954). A serious and valuable source by a Roman Catholic scholar is Louis J. Luzbetak, *Church and Cultures: An Applied Anthropology for the Religious Worker* (Techny, Ill., 1963).

[2] Prior to the newer developments, social anthropology was usually considered to be the British equivalent of American cultural anthropology.

[3] Paul Bohannan, *Social Anthropology* (New York, 1963), pp. 4-7.

[4] Edward Adamson Hoebel, *Man in the Primitive World* (New York, 1958), p. 7.

[5] Peter Freuchen, *Book of the Eskimos* (Greenwich, Conn., 1961), pp. 146-48.

[6] Leslie A. White, *Science of Culture* (New York, 1949), passim; and Mischa Titiev, *Science of Man*, rev. ed. (New York, 1963), p. 190.

[7] Suggesting an influence of Watsonian behavioral psychology.

[8] See instinct imprinting in the very early life of animals in Bernard Berelson and Gary A. Steiner, *Human Behavior: An Inventory of Scientific Findings* (New York, 1964), p. 41.

[9] Margaret Mead, *New Lives for Old: Cultural Transformation—Manus, 1928-1953* (New York, 1956), p. 548.

[10] George A. Miller, E. Galanter, and K. H. Pribram, *Plans and the Structure of Behavior* (New York, 1960); see esp. chap. 4.

[11] Abraham H. Maslow, *Motivation and Personality* (New York, 1954), esp. chaps. 4—5.

[12] Eugene A. Nida, *Religion Across Cultures* (New York, 1968), pp. 1-19; Jacob A. Loewen, "Religion, Drives and the Place Where It Itches," *Practical Anthropology*, XIV (1967), pp. 49-72.

[13] Edward B. Tylor and Lewis Morgan were two typical proponents of the evolutionary view. See Felix M. Keesing, *Cultural Anthropology: The Science of Custom* (New York, 1958), pp. 139-43.

[14] Robert H. Lowie, "Religion in Human Life," *American Anthropologist*, LXV (1963), pp. 532-42, reprinted in *Reader in Comparative Religion*, William A. Lessa and Evon Z. Vogt, 2nd ed. (New York, 1965), p. 134. Italics mine.

[15] There are exceptions. I remember that my agnostic professor of primitive religion remarked to me: "Maybe you should be teaching this course because you have religious faith and experience. I guess I cannot really hide my skepticism and I am probably as biased against it as I consider you to be biased for it."

[16] Lowie, p. 134; also John Greenway, ed., *Anthropologist Looks at Myth* (Austin, 1966), pp. ix-xii.

[17] Jacob A. Loewen, "Anatomy of an Unfinished Crisis in Chulupi Culture Change," *Suplemento Antropologico de la Revista del Ateneo Paraguayo*, II (1966), pp. 231-34.

[18] David B. Barrett, *Schism and Renewal in Africa* (Nairobi, 1968), passim.

[19] William Graham Sumner, *Folkways* (Boston, 1906), quoted in Roger Brown, *Social Psychology* (New York, 1965), p. 484.

[20] Nida, *Customs*, p. 7.

[21] Bohannan, p. 201.

[22] Ruth Benedict, *Race: Science or Politics* (New York, 1940), quoted in Bohannan, pp. 200-01.

[23] Ruth Benedict, *Patterns of Culture* (Boston, 1934), p. 48.

Robert J. Willoughby

Health &
Physical Education

Health and physical education have been part of the school curriculum for a good long time. As far back as Homer, some three thousand years ago, education had such stated objectives as good health, physical and mental well-being, and the worthy use of leisure. Systematic exercise occupied a prominent place in the education of Greek youth and gave rise to sports spectacles such as the Olympic Games (776 B.C.). The Greek concept was transmitted to the Romans and continued through the Renaissance without much change. Early modern educators such as Jean Jacques Rousseau, Johann Basedow, Franz Nachtegall, and Pehr Henrik Ling gave support to physical education in the school curriculum. In more recent times the emphasis changed from education *of* the physical to education *through* the physical as the concept of the total unity of the individual's body, mind, and spirit became prominent.

Although the content of the physical education program has changed, the basic objectives still justify the inclusion of health and physical education in the school curriculum.

A student will find two types of courses in health and physical education at the college level. One type is intended to give knowledge and skill in activities which will enhance the well-being of the individual, while the other type is offered as preparation for careers in these fields. The non-major taking health and physical education activity courses can gain many physical benefits—improved health and an improved and maintained physical fitness level. Since physical fitness is a lifetime occupation, developing good habits of health and exercise is important.

the importance of physical fitness

Why should a person seek to be physically fit? Many forces will shape a young person's susceptibility to maladies such as heart attacks and strokes that may develop in later years. Physical inactivity, an over-rich diet, excessive body weight, smoking, drinking, and high blood pressure are among these forces. All of them are subject to modification by the individual and are basic to a person's physical fitness program.

Unlike the retention of motor skills, physical fitness can be retained only through frequent, regular exercise. Regular exercise, as strenuous as is consistent with one's physical condition, is a major factor in delaying or avoiding heart attacks and strokes. This has been well substantiated by several studies comparing people in sedentary jobs (such as a London bus driver) with those in more active positions (such as the conductor on a double-decker London bus). On the positive side muscular activity increases the efficiency of the organism, building up such factors as strength, endurance, and flexibility. There is a quality factor to life that demands energy expenditure. Merely existing for a specific number of years is a far cry from living an energetic life.

The process of acquiring and maintaining physical fitness helps to control weight throughout life. The control of body weight is rapidly becoming one of man's greatest health problems. It has been shown conclusively that overweight not only shortens life expectancy but also contributes to many diseases, particularly degenerative types. Then, too, the same person is physically more attractive when of normal weight and fit than when obese and unfit.

Medical research has shown the link between smoking and emphysema, lung cancer, and coronary heart disease. Alcohol is a major contributing cause to many physical diseases as well as mental illness, automobile accidents, and lost work days. Yet, despite the evidence against drinking alcoholic beverages and smoking, people continue to ignore the warnings.

High blood pressure, toxic goiter, migraine headaches, arthritis, apoplexy, heart trouble, and gastro-intestinal ulcers may result from worry, stress, and tension. In fact, medical science recognizes that emotions are responsible for the majority of our sicknesses.[1] Exercise can provide an outlet for these emotions, both by improving cardiac efficiency and by lowering the blood pressure.

A unique physical benefit is derived from learning to swim. As a preventive measure against drowning, everyone should have a basic proficiency in swimming. About 7,500 people lost their lives by drowning in 1970. Nearly 60% of these victims, based on previous trends, probably had not intended to go in the water but fell from boats, dams, docks, and pool decks. Therefore, even if a person does not intend to go swimming, it is certainly worth his while to learn to swim. About one out of every two persons cannot swim the 50 feet that would be necessary to save himself in a normal situation. Simply by taking care of this oversight in most students' education, we could prevent most drownings and preserve the life potential of many persons each year.

Physical education activities are not restricted to those who are "fit"; benefits and feasibility of physical education programs for the handicapped, both physically and mentally, are increasingly popular. Many activities can be adapted for various types of handicaps, as shown by the "Olympic Games" now held for paraplegics and the mentally retarded. Recent research in perceptual-motor development indicates that physical education can greatly help to alleviate problems of this type.

a christian view of the physical

The Greeks paid much attention to the care and development of the body, the ultimate purpose being for self-edification or preparation for conquest. And many people today make exercise, body development, and sports a god in their lives. Yet, neglect of the body is as bad as too much attention. What should be the Christian's attitude toward the body? The proper attitude is mentioned or implied in the sixth chapter of 1 Corinthians where Paul declares, "the body is not meant for immorality, but for the Lord" (1 Cor. 6:13) and "Do you not know that your bodies are members of Christ?" (1 Cor. 6:15) and "Do you not know that your body is a temple of the Holy Spirit within you, which you have from God? . . . So glorify God in your body" (1 Cor. 6:19-20).

In the first commandment[2] we are told to love the Lord our God with all our heart, soul, mind, and *strength.* Significantly, the apostle Paul partially describes the Cretans as "lazy gluttons" and tells Titus to "rebuke them sharply, that they may be sound in the faith" (Titus 1:12-13). If our bodies are so closely a part of Christ and we are to glorify God in our bodies, we should be interested in having as healthy and fit a body as possible. This should include keeping physically fit through regular physical activity, forming good dietary habits, maintaining weight control, getting proper rest, and abstaining from smoking and from drinking alcoholic beverages.

Not all of the benefits of health and physical education are physical—the benefits can be mental as well. In times of growing world tensions and increasing pressures brought on by the onrush of mechanization and automation, the need for ways in which human tensions can be released is becoming widely recognized. The stresses of living are responsible for a host of debilitating diseases, mainly through our faulty reactions to those stresses. Exercise and physical exertion can help us handle many mental stresses, by providing an outlet for the tensions that inevitably build up within us. Exercise encourages the release of built-up energy and induces natural muscular fatigue which results in relaxation.

Muscular activity also provides a means to express emotions. Some aspects of a person's personality, such as aggressiveness, self-discipline, perseverence, creativity and self-expression, may find a satisfactory outlet in a game or other exercise. Emotions are important in shaping our basic attitude toward other people and life itself. Faulty reactions to stresses may elicit emotions detrimental to Christian growth and effectiveness. Therefore, if we properly meet stress and tension our attitudes can be healthy, and we benefit from a clearer view of life and sounder inter-personal relationships.

Moreover, recreational activities may provide a Christian with the opportunity or climate setting for friendship evangelism. A wide range of activities and a reasonable degree of proficiency will increase the enjoyment and the possibilities for service. St. Paul urged, "Let each of you look not only to his own interests, but also to the interests of others" (Phil. 2:4). This implies, among other things, a repertoire of recreational activities.

What is to be done with leisure time, bound to increase in the future? Recreation of some form will absorb a large portion of it. The activities of an individual have an important effect upon his personal adjustment so it is important to use leisure time wisely. Even Aristotle saw the need for recreation in his day when he said, "Even for adults, play is a necessary aim in life, of which use should be made, especially during leisure time; for he who labors assiduously has need of recreation."[3] Most physical activities have recreational values and provide a worthy use of leisure time. John Dewey warned, "If education does not afford opportunity for wholesome recreation and train capacity for seeking and finding it, the suppressed instincts find all sorts of illicit outlets."[4] One of the things that must be practiced if one is to adapt to life's disease-producing stresses is to diversify the stressful agents.[5] Recreation does this.

Another social aspect of sports activities is the lessons they sometimes teach us about life. Many activities bring individuals together intimately, both competitively and cooperatively, and place them under the discipline of living up to established standards and rules. The famous miler Roger Bannister said, "Sport leads to the most remarkable self-discovery of our limitations as well as our abilities. It was sport that made it easier for me to think about the parallel stress that faces us in real life."[6] The apostle Paul found sport to be a good parallel to life and uses such activities as running, boxing, and wrestling to explain aspects of the Christian life. A sport has goals, boundaries, and rules of play which must be kept and respected. Excellence is attained only by a well-disciplined athlete. The Christian life must also be a disciplined life if one is to be victorious in the fight against spiritual powers. The point here is that the discipline and self-denial learned in sport may well transfer to living the Christian life.

professional opportunities

Several kinds of positions are available to the graduate who has majored in health, physical education, or recreation. These positions call for teachers; coaches; directors and supervisors of recreation programs in community centers, youth serving agencies, and industries; recreation therapists in hospitals or special education programs; camp directors; and outdoor recreation specialists. Normally these positions involve working with people in an informal, happy, social atmosphere. The relationship between student and teacher or coach can be close, with few barriers. As a result of this closeness, the teacher or coach often becomes a confidant or counselor. And because of the nature of the activities, the teacher is in a good position to arouse new interests, emphasize values, and form attitudes as games are played under conditions which parallel life itself. Jay B. Nash says, "Few activities outside of physical education offer more opportunities to guide the emotional drives, interests, and hungers of youth into approved channels."[7]

The Christian in these positions has an unusual opportunity to be a positive influence and to guide young people along Christian principles. However, such an influence is not automatic. Locker rooms and recreation centers can be filled with bad language and dirty stories, and games can be played amid cheating and unsportsmanlike conduct. The teacher or coach must actively promote sportsmanship and fair play by example and precept.

problems for the christian

Students considering physical education as a profession must face some possible problems. Many people regard physical education as unimportant, something for those with brawn but no brains. The attitude of the church (often reflected in the curricula of church-related schools) suggests that the intellect and the spirit of the person are far more important than his body. Educators, too, often look upon physical education as a frill instead of a basic subject.

Part of the blame for this attitude rests with some who have been teaching this subject. It is easier to "get by" with little planning and preparation in a physical education class than in most other subjects. The result is a meaningless play period, lacking goals and direction. However, to accomplish established goals requires much preparation and effort on the part of a conscientious teacher. One must take seriously the formulation of a sound philosophy of physical education, clearly setting forth its place and contributions to the total education of a child.

The proper relationship between physical education and athletics must be kept in mind, also. It is easy to devote much time, energy, and effort to the athletic program which deals with the better skilled students and to neglect the less glamorous physical education program which encompasses students of all skill levels.

Very little of the content of physical education is controversial for the Christian. For some Christians, however, the inclusion of social dancing might pose a problem. The broad area of rhythms usually is part of elementary and secondary programs with the social dancing phase included in the junior high and senior high schools. Those who are opposed to social dancing should have a sound basis for their objections and have a solution in mind particularly if he or she is not in a position to dictate the program content.

A problem closely related to athletics is the attitude toward competition. For some time coaches have jokingly said that when losing, they have been building character. Today, it is not uncommon to find athletic directors and coaches who openly admit that their primary goal is to win, not to build character. Although athletic competition may have many values, these values can be lost in the pressure to win. To a lesser degree this can occur on the informal recreational competitive level. The desire to win at all costs can distort the values of the participant, resulting in dirty, illegal play. The Christian coach or athlete, therefore, must not allow his values to become distorted when under such pressure.

Moreover, the alert Christian athlete will seek opportunities for encouraging students of various racial and ethnic groups to participate in both intramural as well as intercollegiate athletics. The athletic world has made significant progress in the last decade in racial integration, and the Christian should continue to work for a color-blind program. He will do this, not simply because among minority groups are some of the world's greatest athletes, nor because every man stands under the judgment of God for the consideration and respect he shows or should show to others, but simply because it is right.

For the Christian with aspirations in collegiate or professional sports or coaching, the matter of Sunday responsibilities could be a problem. Each individual must arrive at his own solution in line with his interpretation of Scripture regarding the Lord's day.

The Christian athlete is in a unique position to influence other people. Because of the publicity, status, and prestige normally afforded to athletes, he will be known and watched both on and off the field. Therefore, how he conducts himself personally, how he handles praise and glory, and what he says in relation to his faith in Christ is important. The latter is particularly important since an athlete may feel that he is a Christian because he leads a good, moral life, but he may not have made a personal commitment to Christ.

In summary, the Christian should approach courses in health and physical education as an opportunity which will help him glorify God. Physical benefits can help him become a healthy and fit instrument for God's use. A wholesome emotional life aided by the proper handling of stress and tension gives a Christian a clearer view of life, helps him in his social relations, and broadens his interests in ways that will aid in friendship evangelism. Careers in health, physical education, and recreation can provide the Christian with opportunities to grow personally as well as to guide in the development of young lives.

Notes

[1] S. I. McMillen, *None of These Diseases* (Westwood, 1963), p. 7.

[2] Mark 12:30.

[3] Cited in Lester M. Fraley, Warren R. Johnson, and Benjamin H. Massey, *Physical Education and Healthful Living* (Englewood Cliffs, 1954), p. 45.

[4] Arthur M. Kipnis, "Philosophical Aspects of Recreation," *Recreation*, XVLI (Feb. 1953), p. 517.

[5] McMillen, p. 109.

[6] *Time*, 17 Jan. 1955.

[7] Quoted in Fraley, p. 45. The student may also wish to consult Elwood C. Davis, Gene A. Logan, and Wayne C. McKinney, *Biophysical Values of Muscular Activity*, 2nd ed. (Dubuque, 1965); Perry B. Johnson, Wynn F. Updyke, Donald C. Stolberg, and Maryellen Schaefer, *Physical Education—A Probelm-Solving Approach to Health and Fitness* (New York, 1966); and Howard S. Slusher and Aileene S. Lockhart, *Anthology of Contemporary Readings—An Introduction to Physical Education* (Dubuque, 1966).

William H. Young

Education

If you are considering a career in teaching, how do you visualize yourself responding to the following situations? A school superintendent asks about your personal philosophy of classroom control and pupil freedom. A friend wants to know if you expect to go beyond teaching the prescribed curriculum to deal with your pupils' ideals and values. A parent questions whether you see any place for teaching religious knowledge in the public school classroom. How does a Christian understanding apply to these educational issues? Education and Christian thought have frequently interacted around such important concerns in teaching.

Americans have traditionally believed in the power of education to help solve the personal problems of individuals, as well as the social dilemmas of our changing society. In an earlier period of American education, this faith in education was closely linked with faith in God, and religious and moral instruction were a vital feature of education at all levels. Today the program and purposes of American public schools reflect a secular orientation. And in the preparation of teachers, insights from our Christian heritage are frequently neglected. However, despite the secular thrust of our educational system, there are opportunities for Christians to apply their faith constructively to the complex problems of educating contemporary youth.

In order to "turn on" youth, especially in urban schools where social problems are often overwhelming, schools need more teachers with deep personal commitment and a clear sense of direction. For the Christian these qualities are closely linked to a vital relationship to God. But if faith is to have any practical relevance to the teacher, Christian conceptions have to be consciously applied to educational policies. Examples from several major aspects of teaching should illustrate how attitudes and ideas from our Christian faith can relate to educational issues. A Christian preparing to teach can develop a clearer sense of direction by thinking through his own answers to basic questions concerning the nature of human learners and the tasks of teaching knowledge and values.

education and the nature of man

What is the moral nature of those we teach? Teaching methods are based in part on what teachers think are the most fundamental characteristics of human beings and how they will respond in teaching situations. In particular, a teacher's approach to pupil motivation and discipline will typically reflect his views of human nature. The teacher who thinks of people as basically competitive and aggressive will tend to exert a different form of classroom control than one who perceives humans as fundamentally cooperative and agreeable.

Consider also patterns of organizing learning experiences. These range from the highly regimented systems of many traditional schools to the decidedly permissive arrangements characteristic of certain others. On the one hand, many teachers and administrators insist on a carefully-ordered, well-controlled organization of learning, even at the risk of restricting creativity and self-expression. This point of view tends to presume that children require a large measure of external control to regulate their misguided impulses. Such a view of child behavior gives priority to channeling potentially unproductive or disruptive behavior along constructive lines.

Other educators with more faith in the essentially sound impulses of youth and their capacity to direct themselves place considerable emphasis on cultivating their independent thought and action. For such teachers, self-regulation takes precedence over considerations of efficiency and order. Both of these perspectives could find some justification in historic Christian assumptions about man, so that the Christian teacher can work out a synthesis, drawing from elements of both approaches. However, a Christian, conscious of biblical concepts of freedom and the creation of man in God's image, will naturally question the excessive control of human behavior reflected in certain authoritarian forms of teaching. At the same time, a radically permissive approach to education based on the assumption that children's natural impulses are invariably good, as set forth in Alexander S. Neill's account of his famous school, *Summerhill,* will seem excessive to the Christian who believes that youth require more direction than this model provides.

This example indicates the fallacy of an overemphasis on one or another aspect of man's nature and needs which has frequently led to lopsided educational policies. At various times in the history of education an almost exclusive emphasis has been placed on either sharpening man's rational powers, or controling his capacities for selfishness and laziness, or satisfying his need for a free environment to learn and grow, or providing for his happy adjustment to society. While each of these is an appropriate consideration for formulating educational plans, a single, simplified model of human behavior is not likely to do justice to our complex natures. Christians can profit from the varied contributions of secular thought to our understandings of the persons we teach, while at the same time integrating these with such biblical conceptions as the basic human need for love and the pervasive effects of sin in human life.

Furthermore, a Christian teacher in search of an effective approach to human nature can draw insight and inspiration from what the gospels disclose concerning Jesus' understanding of humanity and the ways he led people to the discovery of truth. With respect to forming a balanced approach to human nature in teaching, for instance, Jesus combined incisive understanding of the moral weaknesses of those he taught with conscious effort to draw out potentialities for personal development in the most unlikely people.[1] He maintained high expectations of what frail human nature could achieve under the stimulus of God's redemptive love. Moreover, he was sensitive to the physical and emotional needs of those he taught while seeking to nourish their spiritual lives.[2] Finally, while he understood the basic elements in human nature that men share in common, he took account of the individual differences among them and was sensitive to the particular qualities of individual persons.[3]

value issues in education

Closely related to questions concerning the nature of man in education are the value issues that are an aspect of all educational decisions. How do Christian values relate to secular education? Teaching is permeated throughout with efforts to influence man's choices. Although many people think of schooling primarily in terms of increasing pupils' knowledge, skills, and personal capacities, a considerable part of all educational endeavor aims at cultivating beliefs and commitments and at developing certain attitudes and relationships. Even decisions about what knowledge, skills, and pupil potentialities should be emphasized involve value choices of what is important for pupils to learn.

One definition of education describes it as "the process of deliberately attempting to make of the young something which if left to themselves they would not become."[4] As this definition suggests, education requires deliberate decisions about the worth of various alternative influences on the young, so that value choices are an unavoidable part of teaching. There is considerable controversy over decisions on value issues in education today, and many persons, including youth, are critical of the values of those who control these decisions.

While Christian beliefs are less directly relevant to some value questions in education, such as which plays should be studied in a course in English literature or what should be the school dress code, Christian ideals are pertinent to a wide range of value issues concerning what to teach and the goals of teaching. In some cases, specific Christian beliefs from our cultural heritage have been translated by educators into secular terms.

For example, a current stress on mutual respect and a climate of sympathetic understanding in the classroom is a secular version of what an earlier generation of educators would have called Christian love. In this case there is general agreement on promoting this value, although a Christian's frame of reference for this may differ considerably from that of a non-Christian. In such instances Christian motives and ideals can be expressed in teaching, even when their Christian source is not openly identified.

A Christian music teacher can convey his sense of gratitude for God's gift of music and his wonder at the beauty of musical expression even when he is not free to press the Christian basis for this appreciation on his pupils. A physical educator who has, from a Christian perspective, come to identify moral qualities that he believes are associated with achievement in this field, has ample opportunity to seek to develop these in youth. Moreover, some of the most significant teaching of values takes place not through formal lessons that refer to moral or spiritual concepts as such, but through the communication of attitudes and ideals through teaching and informal interpersonal relationships.

Of course, on occasion, it is appropriate and even desirable for a teacher to acknowledge openly his personal value commitments. In a public school setting he cannot legitimately strive to convince youth to accept personal religious beliefs. Rather, just as a conscientious teacher will alert students to the particular viewpoint of a textbook or other materials they encounter, he may acknowledge openly those presuppositions of his which are incorporated into his teaching, depending on the occasion and the maturity of the group. Certainly the Christian preparing to teach will want to clarify his own values and consider how to express them in his teaching, while he also determines appropriate limits on imposing his values on youth.

While a Christian will often share particular educational ideals in common with educators of other faiths or of no faith, he may also view with jaundiced eye an educational ideology or value system that allows no room for a Christian world view.[5] Some contend that American education has tended to develop a humanistic, naturalistic frame of reference for values that serves as a form of "secular religion." Since modern education has eliminated the religious basis for teaching values in public schools, there is a danger that religion may seem irrelevant to school subjects and students' search for meaning in life. This leads naturally into the consideration of how a Christian may appropriately relate his faith to the curriculum of education, in addition to dealing with value issues in the sphere of human relationships.

the religious dimensions of knowledge
What place is there for studying religious ideas and practices in schools? In an historic decision prohibiting the recitation of prescribed prayers and the devotional use of the Bible in public schools, the Supreme Court acknowledged that the study of the Bible or of religion does have a legitimate place in a secular program of education, provided that such study be conducted in an objective manner.[6] Several states have recently pioneered new educational programs aimed at fulfilling this Supreme Court mandate and reversing the trend toward the neglect of the religious aspects of knowledge in public school curricula. The Court has declared that while teaching religion in the sense of using the public school classroom to propagate particular religious beliefs is unlawful, teaching "about" religions is not.

Therefore, preparation for teaching should allow for developing an awareness of the religious knowledge that has an important place in the school curriculum. Our literature, history, and arts are so interwoven with Christian elements that a Christian preparing to teach these subjects may profitably develop a special understanding of these elements as a background for his teaching. Christian music education students may explore the influence of biblical themes in the development of music, while those in English education may devote particular attention to biblical allusions that fill so much of English literature, or even to the study of the Bible as literature.[7]

Religious aspects of American history have often been slighted in school textbooks and courses of study, so that prospective history teachers may help fill this gap by investigating the role of Christian movements in the settlement of this country and the westward expansion. Prospective science teachers should seek to understand the issues in the long-standing dialogue between science and religion in the Western world. This sort of preparatory study will provide invaluable source material for those who desire to teach those religious aspects of subject areas which form an integral part of the curricula of schools.

Moreover, religion in the broad sense of a comprehensive world view or ultimate commitment is a dimension of most fields of knowledge, as this volume of essays seeks to show. The serious Christian student should seek to understand the relations between biblical truths and the conceptions of truth and methods of discovering it in the disciplines he may have to teach.[8]

Absolute objectivity is clearly unattainable in any field of study, although this does not lesson the teacher's obligation to pursue it. Moreover, the student should realize that the ideal of objectivity is not the opposite of subjective experience, nor does it necessarily conflict with personal commitment. A Christian's subjective appreciation of religious experience should contribute to his ability to teach with sensitivity the religious aspects of any branch of knowledge. Materials are beginning to appear for the guidance and use of teachers who desire to deal responsibly with religion as a human phenomena in public school classrooms.[9]

Some differences of opinion remain concerning the requirements of such objectivity,[10] but one can forcefully argue that neutrality in treating religious subject-matter requires the exercise of personal insight into religious ideas and sentiments, combined with an impartial approach toward variant opinions in classroom discussion. Christians may strive toward this ideal as

they prepare for the challenging task of exploring with youth
realms of truth which the Christian knows have their source
ultimately in God.

Notes

[1] Note expecially the stories of Zacchaeus (Lk. 19:1-10) and the Samaritan woman (Jn. 4).

[2] See, e.g., the feeding of the five thousand (Mk. 6:30-44).

[3] Cf. Jesus' words to Simon the Pharisee with his behavior toward the woman who entered Simon's house. (Lk. 7:36-50).

[4] Van Cleve Morris, *Philosophy and the American School* (New York, 1961), p. 18.

[5] For a book which places greater emphasis than this article can on the differences between a Christian approach to education and the secular view, see Rousas J. Rushdoony, *Intellectual Schizophrenia: Culture, Crisis and Education* (Philadelphia, 1961).

[6] *School District of Abington Township v Schempp,* 374 U. S. 203 (1963).

[7] A recently published resource for teaching the Bible as literature is James S. Ackerman, *On Teaching the Bible as Literature* (Bloomington, 1967).

[8] See Frank E. Gaebelein, *Pattern of God's Truth: Problems of Integration in Christian Education* (New York, 1954), for one evangelical's analysis of some of the relations between Christian truth and the truth in various disciplines. The same subject is treated from a different theological perspective in Philip H. Phenix, *Education and the Worship of God* (Philadelphia, 1966).

[9] Religion-Social Studies Curriculum Project, Florida State University, *Religious Issues in Social Studies I. American Culture* (Tallahassee, 1969), and Indiana Biblical Literature Commission, *Biblical Literature: A Course of Study for Secondary Schools* (Ft. Wayne, 1967).

[10] For various viewpoints on teaching religion objectively see Theodore R. Sizer, ed., *Religion and Public Education* (Boston, 1967).

Robert G. Clouse

History

Those who do not understand the past are doomed to repeat it.
Many of our current tragedies, such as the war in Vietnam,
might have been avoided if our society placed a greater emphasis upon the study of history. The purpose of this discipline is,
therefore, not only to learn details about the past but to use
events that have transpired to help us understand the present
and perhaps even to influence the future course of man. In
order to accomplish this purpose, historians try to ascertain
cause-and-effect relationships; they insist on time perspectives,
emphasize objectivity and tolerance, and occasionally formulate
philosophies of history.

Christianity and history are closely bound together. The reasons for this are apparent when one considers the firm historical
basis for Christian teaching concerning both the nation Israel
and the story of Christ's redemption. Believers also feel that
there is a purpose for and an end to history.

basic presuppositions

The Christian view of history has often been associated with
some particular philosophy or explanation of the movement of

human events.[1] But, beyond the articulation of certain general principles and the affirmation of a few basic values, most Christian historians consider the attempt to construct a philosophy of history invalid.

One can say, however, that the Christian outlook on history contains at least three ingredients—the doctrine of original sin, the idea of a future life, and the relevance of the Christian drama of personal salvation. These views make the believer in Christ especially capable of viewing history in a realistic manner. A realization of the basic sinfulness of all men will keep one from supposing that one class or a single nation represents the prime cause of trouble in the world. For example, some believed that if the liberal democracies could win World War II against the Nazis and Fascists a better world would come. Dictatorship and racism would be defeated and the four freedoms would triumph. Obviously no such result came from that war. Even today in the struggle between the "free world" and the communists, the Christian who is trained in history will realize that the red revolutionaries have no monopoly on sin.

A commitment to the Christian teaching of salvation and to a future life of rewards and punishments will keep a historian from cynicism. As one views the past, it is easy to fall into the habit of believing that the only values are power and strength. History can seem like an endless cycle of man's inhumanity to man. However, the believer has a message of hope for every human situation. The cross of Christ led to the resurrection and to victory over evil. Consequently, all of the gloomy and discouraging details of life are preludes to a glorious tomorrow. Although often the righteous suffer and the wicked prosper, the Christian can assure the historian that "truth will not remain forever on the scaffold."

Christianity will also resist the current trend of thinking of people as groups. Christ died for each man and this emphasis on personal salvation will keep the believer from being unconcerned about the individual. Also, a Christian will extend this view to all people because he realizes the equality of men in the sight of the one who is no respecter of persons. Today, it is often easier to think of men in the image of Nature than in the image of God. One totalitarian dictator who launched a great war and brought misery to many said that in reality he was no more cruel than Nature. But a Christian will look at man in a higher way, for he sees him as God's special creation for whom Christ died.

After noting these basic Christian ideas, a word of caution is in order. It is a mistake to feel that history demonstrates the sinfulness of man or that the Christian message of redemption and its value is obvious to the historian. Actually, these attitudes must be brought to the study of history by the Christian. The cry for an interpretation of the human story is not a desire for history but for "prophecy." Those who wish their history written with a rich interweaving of value judgments and moral statements should turn to an application of the insights of holy Scripture to life. As Professor Herbert Butterfield has put it, "On the decisive question of the . . . interpretation one would give to the whole human story, it would be unwise to surrender one's judgment to a scholar, any more than one would expect a scholar by reason of his technical accomplishments to be more skilled than other people in choosing a wife. . . . Our final interpretation of history is the most sovereign decision we can take . . . and it is inseparable from our decision about the role we are going to play ourselves in that very drama of history."[2]

causal relations

A more crucial task than the search for a philosophy of history for the historian in our day is the attempt to understand through cause-and-effect relationships why events occur. If one is interested, for example, in why the Reformation occurred, the historian will point to the decline of the medieval church, the vibrant faith of Luther, the political, economic and social conditions of the German states in the late fifteenth and early sixteenth centuries and in this way build up a chain of events leading to the new development in western European religion. The search for causal relationships is complex, for behind every human event is a multitude of forces, some known and others unknown, and often these are difficult to relate.

The discipline of history is also uniquely concerned with the significance of time. An understanding of time sequence, for instance, is necessary for a knowledge of cause-and-effect relationships. So, dates become important tools of the trade. Generally, an historian places greater importance on the chronological ordering of events than on the exact dates of the events. Problems of cause and effect and time perspective are important to the believer, but as a historian he would probably treat them as other scholars would.

world civilizations

Two recent developments in the study of the past which have to do with objectivity and tolerance should be of special concern to the Christian. One of these is the emphasis upon world civilization rather than a study of only Western civilization. The second is the concerted effort by many younger historians to make their studies more relevant to the times, a phenomenon especially evident in the addition of black history courses to the curricula of many universities in America.

The rise in the teaching of world civilization since World War II has been very impressive. Prior to this, much emphasis had been laid upon national histories and other Western European traits. If the Afro-Asian areas were considered at all, they were viewed through the eyes of the imperialist West. Several factors have contributed to this change of emphasis—the global position of the United States, improved communications which compel the general recognition of "one world," and the vast increase of accurate historical knowledge about the non-Western world. Symptomatic of this new trend are *The Rise of the West: A History of the Human Community* by William H. McNeill (1963), *The World Since 1500: A Global History* by Leften S. Stavrianos (1966), and the UNESCO publications *Journal of World History* and *History of Mankind.*[3]

Professor McNeill's book has been very well received although there is still considerable misgiving among some scholars about the feasibility of teaching all of world civilization. This can be attempted, according to McNeill, by a rather rigid schematization of history and by an emphasis on the shared relationships between various world civilizations. Fundamental to this approach is the significance of cultural diffusion in history. Thus, he gives special attention to the spread of food crops, political systems, military technologies, and diseases which spanned great distances and affected several cultures.

There are many benefits for the Christian who studies history with this emphasis on world civilization—among these, the larger perspective the concept of world civilization encourages. Often Christians have identified their faith with the social values worked out in the Western world, many of these values going back to the emphasis built into Christianity by the late medieval church. A global approach can liberate the student from this dangerous situation. He will come to identify the essential core of his faith and be able to keep or reject the parts which have only the basis of Western values rather than the more solid foundation of the revealed will of God.[4] By studying other cultures through the avenue of history, one can experience the same reorientation which living in another society brings. Elisabeth Elliot, the well-known former missionary to the Aucas, describes this experience and its life-changing quality in the following words:

> So here are "heathen" people, I told myself. And here is the Word of Truth. There must be evidenced among them a recognition of the difference, for example, between good and evil. Would it be the same for them as it was for me? What did God say about it? What would "Christian" conduct mean to the Aucas? I came to see that my own understanding of these subjects was not nearly as clear as I had supposed. I kept balancing the Auca way of life against the American, or against what I had always taken to be the Christian. . . . A comparison did not convince me of the superiority of any other group. I had come from a society where polygamy was illegal to one where it was permissible. . . . I observed faithfulness and a strong sense of responsibility on the part of Auca husbands. . . . The Aucas were unhampered by clothing

and the caprices of fashion, but stuck firmly to a code of modesty which did not change with the seasons. In their nakedness they accepted themselves and one another for what they were, always abiding by the rules. . . . I saw the Indians live in a harmony which far surpassed anything I had seen among those who call themselves Christians. I found that even their killing had at least as valid reasons as the wars in which my people engaged.[5]

In this same way the confrontation of the Christian with the non-Western world will force him into separating the essential from the non-essential in the Christian outlook.

Another result of studying world civilization will be to show the believer the vastness of the scope of Christian missions. Jesus commanded, "Go therefore and make disciples of all nations, baptizing them in the name of the Father and of the Son and of the Holy Spirit" (Mt. 28:19). As one reads of the non-Western cultures he can see how little has been accomplished to fulfill this commission. Perhaps this will cause a change in the nineteenth-century missionary movement which still dominates evangelical Christianity. New modes of transportation, the example of the Peace Corps, and the need for more advanced technology in the developing nations should suggest a few of the lines along which effort ought to change. It no longer seems to be necessary for those who commit themselves to missionary service to stay in a foreign country for a lifetime. Provision should be made for them to return home more frequently and perhaps to serve for varying lengths of time. Also, it seems evident that the missionary must be a "worker priest" in the sense that he or she contribute some advanced skill in the emerging world along with the preaching of the gospel.

the relevance of history
Besides the challenge of a global study, the new emphasis upon relevance in history deserves the attention of the Christian.[6] The attempt to make history meaningful results in its use as an agent of social change.[7] The recent introduction of black his-

tory into many universities is an example of this effort. As Carter G. Woodson put it several years ago, "Let truth destroy the dividing prejudices of nationality and teach universal love without distinction of race, merit or rank. With the sublime enthusiasm and heavenly vision of the Great Teacher let us help men to rise above the race hate of this age unto the altruism of a rejuvenated universe."[8] To the exponent of Negro history, education is given an important role both as a precipitating factor of racial prejudice and as a corrective of this process. Implicit in much teaching of this subject is the idea that a glorious past is necessary for racial self-respect. Many students of black history believe that the doctrine of white supremacy draws its main inspiration from the overemphasis on the achievements of European peoples as compared with the other civilizations of the world.

However, black history threatens to inject bias into this teaching of the past, a bias which will twist history just as effectively as nationalism has done.[9] The Christian should not object to the Negro's being encouraged by the teaching of Afro-American history. (Too often evangelicals have not been aware of the social sin of the suppression of the blacks.) The Christian and the social theorist ought to welcome moves to make history relevant.

However, the traditional discipline of history has espoused principles of objectivity and tolerance which may not be in harmony with these psychological overtones.[10] Objectivity means the study of historical data in a detached manner attempting to avoid as much as possible the slanting of facts due to personal prejudice. Tolerance means to give a full and impartial hearing to opposing views. Objectivity and tolerance are necessary to history because it can never be classified as an exact science. Thus, a historian must admit that there could be various logical, valid interpretations given for the same historical evidences. This leads him to respect the ideas of his peers even though he might vigorously disagree with these opinions from a personal point of view. A person properly trained in the historical method is capable of doing much to lessen the amount of bigotry in the world, a truly Christlike work.

Unfortunately, the historical technique can be employed as a two-edged sword. In one sense it cuts away prejudice, but the other blade is quite capable of increasing it. The kinds of questions that men ask of the past are conditioned by the society in which they live. If honestly-attempted history suffers from such a serious handicap, one can readily imagine the degree of difficulty associated with the use of history for non-objective purposes. For, if slanted, history can be used to cultivate bigotry because historical accounts can be written in a biased fashion. Beside the zealous black power spokesmen who wish to use history in this way, modern Communist historians are also caught in this approach. Such deliberately distorted history is really not history at all.

Nevertheless, the student faces a very serious problem compounded by the fact that a fine line divides an erroneous interpretation or an unintentional error in methodology on the one hand and a deliberate attempt to propagandize under the guise of historical objectivity on the other. The effect of both would be equally damaging. So, the Christian historian must cultivate a critical approach which keeps a ready guard against the danger of anti-Christian presuppositions and of unreliable materials, interpretations, and conclusions.

Because of the opportunities involved in the global approach to history and in the pressures to make the discipline relevant, these are exciting days for a Christian interested in history. History is not a social science, not a behavioral science, not a humanity, and not an exact science. It is partially all of these contained in one integrated package. It brings together the fragmented educational experiences of our time and produces a broadly-educated, unique scholar, one who has much to offer in an understanding of mankind and in service to his Lord.

Notes

[1] Many volumes could be cited which deal with the relation of the Christian faith and history. Among the more helpful: Hendrikus Berkhof, *Christ, the Meaning of History* (Richmond, 1966); Herbert Butterfield, *Christianity and History* (London, 1949); Alan Richardson, *History, Sacred and Profane* (London, 1964).

Other works which may be consulted on the general theme of philosophy of history include Edward Hallet Carr, *What Is History?* (New York, 1963); Robin G. Collingwood, *The Idea of History* (Oxford, 1946); John Higham, Leonard Krieger, and Felix Gilbert, *History* (Englewood Cliffs, 1965); Erich Kahler, *The Meaning of History* (New York, 1964); Hans Meyerhoff, *The Philosophy of History in Our Time* (New York, 1959); Warren H. Walsh, *An Introduction to the Philosophy of History* (London, 1951).

[2] Butterfield, p. 39.

[3] William H. McNeill's work was originally published by the University of Chicago Press and is available from them in both cloth and paperback. A less expensive edition is available in a Mentor book. Leften S. Stavrianos' book is published by Prentice-Hall and is widely used in the introductory world history course.

[4] For a sample of some historians who have been influenced by their studies to question many evangelical social views, see Robert G. Clouse, Robert D. Linder, and Richard V. Pierard, eds., *Protest and Politics: Christianity and Contemporary Affairs* (Greenwood, 1968).

[5] Elisabeth Elliot, *The Liberty of Obedience* (Waco, 1968). pp. 15-17.

[6] For a consideration of the term *relevance* in the context of the Christian life, see the thoughtful book by Richard C. Halverson, *Relevance, The Role of Christianity in the Twentieth Century* (Waco, 1968).

[7] Examples of this approach can be found in Barton J. Bernstein, ed., *Towards a New Past, Dissenting Essays in American History* (New York, 1969) and Staughton Lynd, "Historical Past and Existential Present," *The Dissenting Academy*, ed. Theodore Roszak (New York, 1968).

[8] Carter G. Woodson, as quoted in Earle Thorpe, *The Mind of the Negro* (Baton Rouge, 1961), p. 442. Dr. Woodson was the founder of the *Journal of Negro History* and a leader of the movement to study black history. Despite some of the warnings in my article, I feel that there is a proper justification for Negro historical studies. "The proper justification for Negro history, as with any other work of scholarly endeavor, is that *it constitutes a contribution to the knowledge and understanding of mankind.* The only inspiration really necessary for the scholar is that he, through his researches and writings, is giving to his generation and

to posterity knowledge and understanding. Any other outlook may be detrimental to scholarship. What more extreme forms of 'filio-pietism' can produce is evident in German historiography of the late nineteenth century Nationalist School and in National Socialist and Fascist and Bolshevik propaganda." Earle E. Thorpe, *Negro Historians in the United States* (Baton Rouge, 1958), p. 9.

For a start on the serious study of black history, one could cite the two publications by the American Historical Association's Service Center for Teachers of History: Philip D. Curtin, *African History* (Washington, 1964) and Louis R. Harlan, *The Negro in American History* (Washington, 1965).

[9] Some historians who celebrate the passing of the nationalist influence on history seem to be unaware of the new dangers to objectivity from the pressures of social relevance. Notice the following statement: "Finally, historians have been able to renounce, if they chose (perhaps have had to renounce, even if they did not choose), the over-demanding conception of their function that required them to demonstrate that all their work was immediately germane to and provided clear directives for dealing with the current problems, dilemmas, and crises of the contemporary world." J. H. Hexter, "Some American Observations," *The New History*, eds. Walter Laquer and George L. Mosse (New York, 1967), p. 10.

[10] The historian ought to be well aware of the difficulty of anyone ever being completely objective. No matter how honest a person tries to be, whatever he writes is the product of his own environment, education and value structure. Notice the discussion of this problem in the following: J. Huizinga, "A Definition of the Concept of History," *Philosophy and History: Essays Presented to Ernst Cassirer*, eds. Raymond Klibansky and Herbert J. Paton (New York, 1963); Patrick Gardiner, *Theories of History* (Glencoe, 1959); and Herbert Muller, *Uses of the Past: Profiles of Former Societies* (New York, 1957).

Gordon R. Lewthwaite

Geography

So it's geography you're taking? What on earth has Christianity to do with that? Surely the world is the world and a map is a map, and neither paganism nor piety should be permitted to bend a single line! After all, didn't Christians get themselves into a lot of trouble by trying to square the circle of the earth and fit their science with Scripture? Surely small thanks are due to those medieval minds who cited Isaiah 11:12 and Revelation 7:1 to clinch the case for "the four corners of the earth," who quoted Joshua 10 and Psalm 19 to prove the sun went round the world, and who insisted that further exploration would certainly discover that angel-guarded Paradise whence the four rivers ran. And didn't some insist that since the gospel had sounded "to the ends of the world" by Paul's day (Rom. 10:18) there could be no inhabitants in any supposed Antipodes? Not to mention the further absurdities of Cosmas Indicopleustes, a monk who pleaded for "Christian topography" and sought (with the aid of some wild exegesis of Hebrews 8 and 9) to reduce the globe to Tabernacle form. Small wonder that four centuries ago Peter Heylen was contemptuously brushed aside with the sneer that "geography is better than divinity,"[1] and that now contemporary professors insist that piety be expunged from the exam papers. Surely the escape of geography from its religious straitjacket has been wholly to the good.

uncovered biblical truths

But—is that the whole story? Like it or not, the Scriptures are rooted and grounded in a geographical setting, and this means that theology and geography cannot help but converge. From Genesis to Revelation, the text is shot through with color. As George Adam Smith[2] and more recently Denis Baly[3] and others have reminded us, the Bible tells the story of a Chosen People in a Chosen Land, and anyone who seeks biblical understanding apart from its geographical setting is bound to miss a good deal of the story. For virtually every jot and tittle of the land—every river, hill and plain—were fraught with meaning for ancient Israel, the people of the Old Covenant. There were the long leagues of steppeland that Abraham traversed from Ur to Canaan, the pastoral uplands that were left to him when Lot made his choice of the rich but perilously-fractured trench of the Dead Sea, the long route of the Exodus that threaded the deserts and oases of the Sinai and the Negev, the productive delta of the Nile where the bondsmen labored, and the rainier uplands of their chosen land.

Nor does the relevance of geography end there. How much we gain in understanding as we pause to localize the struggle against the Canaanites of Palestine, the Philistines of the coastal plain, the Edomites, Moabites, and Ammonites that held the uplands east of the Jordan. And how could Israel forget the seductive wealth of Tyre and Sidon with their Phoenician traders and the cedar trees of Lebanon, and the great empires of the Nile and the Euphrates that ever sought to threaten or cajole? For Israel was located at the crossroads, a modest, corrugated and subdivided land so precariously—and yet so providentially—placed between the steppe and the sown. And though Christ dissolved the place-bonds of worship (Jn. 4:20-24), and Jew and Gentile were alike swept into the worldwide fellowship of the New Covenant, the peculiarities of place and people were still imprinted on the Christian communities that arose in the province of Asia[4] and elsewhere along the beaten routeway of the Roman Empire.

hidden biases

But this very fact that Christianity has been localized in its geographical origin and distribution has become (to some) a barrier to faith. The ancient "stumbling block of particularity"—the fact that the Christian revelation has come to some regions of the earth but not to others—has been reinforced by the prevailing moods of "naturalism" and "religious relativism." Geographers dealing with religion are sometimes liable to insinuate that Christian faith is of purely natural or "cultural" origin, that the faith of one part of the world is no more valid than the faith of any other region, and that the Judeo-Christian claim to revelation is a myth. Further, some argue that the triumphant monotheism of Israel came not from a self-revealing God but from Egyptian or other contacts, that monotheism is a creed for the lonely monotony of the desert but not for the teeming jungle with its polytheistic tendencies, and that the simple message of Jesus was twisted by Paul or a pagan environment into an essentially different form.

But we do well to remember also that such assertions are not derived from any geographical facts but from religious presuppositions, assumptions that underlie a fundamentally anti-Christian faith. They are not neutral data: They are creedal affirmations that must face the trenchant challenge of sober Christian scholarship and the unavoidable either/or of the fact of Christ. There is no room for any ultimate relativism here. As if it were logically possible for the crucifixion to be objective truth in Jerusalem and falsehood in Mecca, and the resurrection fact in London and fiction in Moscow! As if Christian morality were nothing more than the morally-neutral byproduct of geographical and historical accident, and the morality of Nazism on a level with the Sermon on the Mount![5]

For all that Christianity may vary in its form and distribution through time and place, it is our conviction—as the Dutch geographer Gerhard de Jong has phrased it—that the true gospel of Christ "remains unaffected by the diversities . . . of nature," a universal faith for the peoples of plain and mountain, rainforest and desert.[6] This is not, of course, to deny the sympathetic study of other faiths or the validity of the "secular" study of religious geography, for geography, by sheer methodological necessity, must objectively analyze the areal significance of religious phenomena rather than propagate a creed. But it does repudiate any form of relativism which would deny the uniqueness of Jesus Christ and reduce the eternal Kingdom of God to a purely cultural level, a creature of time and place.

And Christian faith affects other aspects of our geography, too: Indeed, it should saturate it with meaning. For our whole approach to the phenomena of earth and man will inevitably be Christian or non-Christian, meaningful or meaningless. Some geographers today, impregnated with the "naturalism" of a supposedly post-Christian era, assume that man and his earth are nothing but the accidental byproducts of a sheerly meaningless process. While a few may grope for faint hope in the dubious hypothesis that matter is continuously coming into being, others are driven by the sheer logic of their dismal faith to share what Bertrand Russell called his "firm foundation of unyielding despair": The whole cosmos, with all its freight of human hopes and achievements, is but the fortuitous byproduct of "accidental collocations of atoms" and is doomed to inevitable "extinction in the vast death of the solar system."[7]

But what nonsense Christian faith makes of this cheerless creed! The geographer is not wasting his time with a meaningless earth, for "the earth is the Lord's and the fulness thereof," and "he formed it to be inhabited." Of course we don't believe that the earth was made in six days in 4004 B.C. or somewhere thereabouts, and of course we needn't seek to define the mode and time of creation or read the precise concepts of modern science into the "phenomenal" language of ancient Scripture.[8] But by faith we believe that the progression from chaos to ordered cosmos was guided by a sure and certain purpose, and by faith we are aware of the illuminating motifs of divine design and human dominion over the earth and its resources. Whatever we may think of some aspects of the search for terrestrial plan and environmental design which Clarence Glacken has traced through early Western thought,[9] whatever we might repudiate in the teleology of such nineteenth-century geographers as Carl Ritter and Arnold Guyot, we cannot deny the sense of divine purpose that pervades the Christian faith—and undergirds the whole of the Judeo-Christian tradition for that matter.

There is no intrinsic conflict with science here. As Richard Hartshorne points out in his *Nature of Geography*, there are "three fundamental facts of geography for which science [has] no explanation—namely the uniqueness of the earth in the universe, . . . the earth as the home of that unique creature, man; and finally—the fundamental explanation of a host of geographic facts—the differentiation in character among the major land units of the world."[10] And it is precisely on such ultimate issues that the Christian revelation sheds its shafts of light.

darwin's view

In point of fact, the Christian mind is thoroughly within its rights in refusing to strain at the gnat of purpose and swallow the camel of happenstance. There are plenty of geographers who may tell you that Charles Darwin gave a death-blow to the Christian idea of a designed earth and any hint of purposefulness in the adaptation of organisms to their geographical environment, but that is nonsense. As if the ideas of time and process were incompatible with plan and purpose! As if the superb and intricate co-ordination of eye and brain and flash of thought—and (with fatal irony) the very fact of reason itself—could be dismissed as sheerly accidental! After all, it was Darwin himself, for all his agnostic waverings, who confessed that "the extreme difficulty or rather impossibility of conceiving this immense and wonderful universe including man . . . as the result of blind chance or necessity . . . compelled [him] to look to a 'First Cause,' " and that the evidence for design often came over him "with overwhelming force."[11] And, as the biochemist Laurence Henderson pointed out, even if Darwin had damaged

the biological arguments for teleology, he had left the staggering
mass of inorganic data quite untouched. Doggedly defending his
agnostic creed by arguing that "science must put aside the
philosophical problems which arise . . . and philosophy must
deny to all men the right to found a system of natural theology
upon the fact," Henderson yet went on to argue "that in
abstract physical and chemical characteristics the actual environment is the fittest possible abode of [any conceivable]
life." Moreover, he affirmed that the solar system, the meteor-
ological cycle, and the organic cycle give an inevitable impression of harmony which undeniably "corresponds to an order in
the universe"[12] —a strange agnosticism indeed!

But we might prefer to agree with the chemist Robert E. D.
Clark[13] that the environmental conditions of this planet are far
too precisely balanced to warrant recourse to the hypothesis of
chance. The distance of the earth from the sun, the particular
size of the globe, the speed of rotation, the tilt of the axis, the
length of day and night, the succession of the seasons, the
global heat balance, the ratio of land to sea—all these and many
another factor are interwoven into a life-sustaining system of
almost incredible complexity. Arthur Smethurst, geochemist
and theologian, was on firm ground when he asserted that

> Nothing but the belief that the universe is the intelligible
> work of a rational designing Mind; nothing but the belief that
> God is a God of Truth who has created the human reason;
> nothing but the belief in one single creative Mind and Will,
> infinite in wisdom and power yet showing diversity in unity;
> nothing but the belief that the world is His creation, can
> justify the assumptions underlying modern science.[14]

the unfinished task

But that is not to say that we believe this is the best of all
possible worlds, that the earth as we know it is perfectly designed for human habitation and man perfectly adjusted to this
earth—though some have curiously charged this belief to Christianity. Far from it! If there is anything made clear in the vivid

imagery of Scripture it is the fact that, though man was stamped with the image of God and given dominion over the earth and its resources, the alienating impact of spiritual revolt has spread its maladjustments through the whole realm of the old creation. There are two sides to the geographical coin.

Actually, there are more sides than two, and we can barely touch upon a few right now. As such Christian philosophers as R. Hooykaas[15] and Hermann Dooyeweerd[16] of the Netherlands have pointed out, the biblical approach banished the ancient deification of the earth and the nature-gods of pagan worship and thus laid bare the earth as a created realm for scientific exploration and human enjoyment: The "cultural mandate" of Genesis calls man to fruitful dominion. But science itself can be robbed of its deepest meaning by the distorting impact of apostasy, and as the geographer de Jong points out, the fulfilment of the mandate to populate and replenish the earth was bound to bring a curse as well as blessing in its train.[17] George Perkins Marsh, the great nineteenth-century geographer and conservationist, in full accord with this thought, urged that thorns and thistles had sprouted in the wake of environmental abuse, that toil and sweat of brow were increasingly exacted by a niggardly earth, and that technological progress had its accompaniment of destructive as well as developmental power. For man had failed to remember that he was but a steward whose "efforts to replenish this earth and subdue it" had been filled with "the ravages committed by man [which] subvert the relations and destroy the balance which nature had established."[18]

The same duality of good and evil also breaks surface in the twin themes of contemporary geography, "areal differentiation" and "spatial interaction." For the areal or "chorological" variations that are woven into the tapestry of the earth can be developed by man for his material and cultural enrichment, and, as de Jong puts it, "the chorological diversity of the earth is one of the treasures of the creation." Location and landforms, vegetation and climate, soils and minerals—all are interwoven to form an areal pattern which man can bring to geographical fruition. This is not to say (as some have) that it is only man who gives an otherwise meaningless earth its meaning—an irony indeed if man himself is meaningless! But it is to say that each region best serves the purpose of replenishing the earth when man develops its particular cultural and economic potential and exchanges its riches for the complementary resources of other lands. The process can of course be perverted, for (given the ambivalence of man) the healthy growth of areal differentiation can be stunted by the imposition of monotony or exaggerated into an unhealthy self-sufficiency, while the beneficial process of spatial interaction can also spread corruption and impoverishment. But the realization of a broader unity with the harmonious exchange of "the blessings of diversity" is surely, as de Jong states, the norm of human geography.[19]

It is impossible, then, for Christian thought to detach the study of geography, however earthy, from its Christian frame. This is not to plead, as Cosmas did, for a specifically "Christian topography"—as ludicrous a concept as "Presbyterian chemistry" or "Roman Catholic botany." The secularization of science and its separation from religious control was both necessary and salutary. But a healthy *methodological* separation is not an *ontological* cleavage: We are human beings with all that that implies. The logical thought that insists on purging the map of all extraneous data leaves the map-maker as human as ever, and if the data are not placed within a Christian framework of thought, they will be placed within a non-Christian framework. We may share the wish of the late Sidney W. Wooldridge, a leader among British geographers, that "the Christian view of man and his world" should form "the philosophical background of education."[20] And we may share the concern of some British graduates that the whole nature of man may be ignored in the reduction of geographical "systems" to a matter of physics or chemistry.[21] For if divine origin and meaning are denied to the earth and man, the geographer is left to find what "values" he can in the passing phenomena of a meaningless "Nature." In the healthy zest of Christian thought, by contrast, man has been molded from the dust of the earth but inbreathed with the breath of life, and the world which has been given into his dominion is not only a realm of rewarding study but in travail with a New Creation, the redeemed cosmos destined to be made manifest in a New Heaven and a New Earth.

Notes

[1] Dr. Peter Heylen, *Cosmographia* (1649), Preface, cited in Sidney W. Wooldridge and W. G. East, *Spirit and Purpose of Geography* (London, 1956), p. 5.

[2] George A. Smith, *Historical Geography of the Holy Land* (London, 1896).

[3] Denis Baly, *Geography of the Bible: A Study in Historical Geography* (London, 1964), p. 4.

[4] For a summary view, see Edward M. Blaiklock, *The Seven Churches of Asia* (Auckland, New Zealand, n.d.).

[5] Though this is a matter of comparative religion rather than geography, it is often relevant to geographers. So you might find useful reading in C. S. Lewis' *Mere Christianity* (New York, 1956), pp. 3-25; *Abolition of Man* (New York, 1947); and *Christian Reflections* (Grand Rapids, 1967), esp. pp. 44-56, 72-81. See also Hendrik Kraemer, *Why Christianity of All Religions?* (Philadelphia, 1962); Stephen Neill, *Christian Faith and Other Faiths* (London, 1961); and J. N. D. Anderson, *World's Religions* (Chicago, 1950).

[6] Gerhard de Jong, *Chorological Differentiation as the Fundamental Principle of Geography* (Groningen, 1962), p. 134.

[7] Bertrand Russell, "Free Man's Worship," *Mysticism and Logic* (London, 1919), pp. 47 ff.

[8] One can find many views on this topic, with particularly lively discussion of the form revelation assumes in Genesis 1—11. For a defense of a literal approach to early Genesis and the rejection of uniformitarianism in favor of catastrophic geographical changes, see John C. Whitcomb and Henry M. Morris, *Genesis Flood* (Nutley, 1960) and Donald W. Patten, *Biblical Flood and the Ice Age* (Seattle, 1966). The present writer's viewpoint more closely approximates that found in Bernard Ramm, *The Christian View of Science and Scripture* (London, 1955).

[9] Clarence J. Glacken, *Traces on the Rhodian Shore: Nature and Culture in Western Thought from Ancient Times to the End of the Eighteenth Century* (Berkeley, 1967).

[10] Richard Hartshorne, *The Nature of Geography* (Lancaster, 1961), p. 60.

[11] Charles Darwin and Sir Francis Darwin, *Autobiography of Charles Darwin* (London, 1949), pp. 149, 153.

[12] Lawrence J. Henderson, *The Order of Nature* (Cambridge, Mass., 1917), pp. iii, 118. See also Lawrence J. Henderson, *Fitness of the Environment* (Boston, 1958).

[13] Robert E. D. Clark, *The Universe: Plan or Accident?* (London, 1949), esp. pp. 59-64.

[14] Arthur F. Smethurst, *Modern Science and Christian Beliefs* (Nashville, 1955), pp. 19 ff.

[15] Reijer Hooykaas, *Christian Approach to the Teaching of Science* (London, 1960), pp. 12-15.

[16] Herman Dooyeweerd, *In the Twilight of Western Thought: Studies in the Pretended Autonomy of Philosophical Thought* (Philadelphia, 1960), pp. 39-42, 171-196 and *New Critique of Theoretical Thought* (Amsterdam, 1953), 4 vols., trans. David H. Freeman, et al.

[17] Gerhard de Jong, "Nature of Human Geography in the Light of the Ordinances of Creation," *Free University Quarterly*, V (1957-58), 97-119 and *Chorological Differentiation*, pp. 137-39.

[18] George P. Marsh, *Man and Nature: Or Physical Geography as Modified by Human Action* (New York, 1869), pp. 56, 43.

[19] de Jong, *Chorological Differentiation*, p. 137.

[20] Sidney W. Wooldridge, *The Geographer as Scientist* (London, 1956), p. 30.

[21] "Human Knowledge: Models and Reality," Report of Research Students' Christian Fellowship, *Christian Graduate* (Mar. 1967), pp. 27-28.

E. Mansell Pattison

Psychology

There is a sense of paradox in a discussion of the relationship of Christian presuppositions (or philosophy, if you will) to the field of psychology. On the one hand, psychology as a science has tried to disavow its philosophical heritage; on the other hand, the questions which psychology faces arise out of and ultimately revert back to philosophical issues.[1]

the pursuits of psychology
So far as psychology is concerned, the student should recall that traditional philosophy dealt with two major questions: (1) What is the nature of man? and (2) What is good, healthy, moral behavior?

The demise of traditional philosophy in the late ninteenth century followed upon the conclusion that philosophy could only speculate about these questions and was unable to provide substantive answers. In turn, twentieth-century philosophy became a scientific discipline concerned with the logic and syntax of language. In a sense, philosophy ruled itself out of the game of discussing questions about man and his behavior.[2]

This shift in the field of philosophy carried with it a similar relegation of religious philosophy to speculation or merely irrelevance. Until then, the twentieth-century philosophical inquiry had been closely tied to religious inquiry. But the movement of philosophical inquiry into the domain of science left religious inquiry with seemingly no relevant base for the study and understanding of man.

The traditional concerns of philosophy were then inherited by psychology, which attempted to answer the questions via the experimental method, without philosophical concern or perhaps even theory.[3] For example, in a popular text on psychological theory, Melvin Marx says, "Recent trends have been clearly away from an emphasis on formal theory and towards a non-theoretical—even anti-theoretical orientation."[4] Critics of the experimental approach waggishly said that psychology had first lost its soul, then its consciousness, and it was about to lose its mind!

This is perhaps too harsh a view of the experimental revolution which swept the American psychological scene during the first half of the twentieth century. For this was the time in which psychology was establishing its domain as a science and was developing experimental methods of inquiry germane to the study of human personality and behavior. Thus the historical development of psychology as the study of man has had a marked pragmatic flavor. It was not the philosophical issues that were examined and found wanting, but rather the experimental method was producing new, exciting, and provocative information about the nature of man. Philosophical issues in a sense were left behind in the dust of the rush down a new road of discovery.

Although there were and continue to be some ardent experimentalists who would frame the field of psychology solely in terms of the laboratory method, most contemporary psychologists would hold to more limited concerns and goals. Thus, most would acknowledge that animal behavior experiments cannot be held to represent exact analogues of human behavior. Nor would the results of laboratory experimentation with human subjects be considered sufficient data for adequately understanding the total nature of man. Rather, the experimentalist would hold that by close adherence to externally observable, replicable, experimental data great gains can be made in the study of man.

That such data may be incomplete, inadequate, or even distorted would not necessarily be of concern, since the experimentalist is not aiming for a totally comprehensive understanding of man. Nor perhaps should we expect the experimentalist to look toward such goals, but leave that task to the theoreticians and clinicians. In this view, laboratory experimental data and the psychological scientists involved in that enterprise become one part of a larger psychological enterprise, rather than representing the totality.[5]

It is, then, not to the experimental side of psychology, but to the theoretical and applied aspects that Christian philosophy bears most relevance.

Although the subjective, philosophical, and comprehensive aspects of psychology have not been totally submerged, perhaps living most viably in the clinical aspects of psychology, it was not until about 1950 that significant movements developed in psychology to restore the concepts of mind, consciousness, and soul into psychological conceptualizations of man.[6]

philosophy in psychology

Do philosophical issues clearly relate to a psychological view of man? The phenomenal success of the experimental method for a long time allowed psychologists to ignore the logical processes and philosophical assumptions of their period. Yet early in this century, E. A. Burtt in his *Metaphysical Foundations of Modern Science* called attention to the importance of assumptions regarding (1) reality, (2) causality, and (3) the human mind. Psychology in large part ignored these assumptions as it attempted to break away from speculative philosophy and attempted to ape the methodology of the physical sciences. More recently, philosophers of science have suggested that the social sciences, including psychology, are only in part sciences built on the model of the physical sciences, and that philosophical issues are part of the indispensable fabric that makes social science the study of man.[8]

In addressing the American Psychological Association in 1959, Herbert Feigl, the eminent philosopher of science, spoke on the "Philosophical Embarrassments of Psychology."[9] He argued that no one wished to return to speculative thinking which posed unanswerable questions. But then he criticized a contemporary psychology that operates on unexamined assumptions. The importance of metaphysical bias is underscored by Hall and Lindzey in their standard text *Theories of Personality,* where they observe that a given theorist will define personality completely in accord with his particular preference.[10]

In another recent text *Personality and the Good,* Bertocci and Millard conclude that any view of the nature of man reflects some presuppositions about illness and health.[11] They assert that any personality theory is grounded in philosophy, whether the theorist is aware of it or not. The problem, says Bunge, is that psychologists assume whatever metaphysical philosophy was popular in their graduate school experience and unwittingly incorporate it into their psychology.[12]

There is probably little substantive relevance of Christian philosophy to the framing and interpretation of circumscribed psychological theory. But at the broader level of general personality theory, and the application of experimental data to the interpretation of human behavior, the opportunity for cross-communication and cross-fertilization does exist.[13]

Further, there are several levels of theory building, ranging from simple theories closely tied to experimental data to complex embracing theories of the whole totality of human existence that may bear loose connection to any experimental or clinical data. Unfortunately this has been often overlooked. For example, Freud's theories were flatly rejected by many Christians because they misunderstood his emphasis on the biological drives of human nature, while other psychoanalytic theorists were accepted because they appeared more sympathetic to religion and Christian concepts. No discrimination was made between Freud's personal religious views (agnostic but not amoral), his significant clinical discoveries (the importance of biology and interdependence of mind and body), and his metaphysical speculations on man and society (interesting but myopic). Freud's early associate Carl Jung was seen as much more acceptable, especially among Roman Catholics, because he suggested that man had religious needs. Yet Jung was just as agnostic and caustic about Christian doctrines as Freud.

Other psychoanalytic pioneers, Rank, Adler, Horney, and Fromm, in turn won religious favor because they emphasized the social utility of religion; Carl Rogers because he championed positive ideals; Gordon Allport and Abraham Maslow because they stressed the altruistic potential of man; and O. Hobart Mowrer because he talked about the reality of sin (although not the historic Christian concept of sin). This changing historical list reflects some piece of Christian doctrine. Yet in each instance this was a "pseudorapprochement," for the basic assumptions of these men were ignored or superficially grasped, when in fact their theories were not necessarily related at all closely to historic Christian views of man.[14]

The lesson suggested here is that the Christian community is seriously misled in seeking to espouse some "one" personality theory. All personality theories have scientific assets and liabilities with no necessary Christian or anti-Christian bias. The student should never assume that we will emerge with some definitive "spiritual psychology," for psychological theory must remain at the level of scientific hypotheses. As such, every psychological view of man is temporary, expedient, and subject to new experimental and clinical data. Thus we should be alert to any theology that attempts to take over and "Christianize" a particular personality theory.

Likewise, there is a tendency to christen theological doctrines of man with unjustified permanency and authority. Theological concepts of man in part reflect the psychological concepts which theologians hold. Theologians often have not realized the implications of their psychological assumptions. Yet as Tillich observed, no doctrine of man is possible without an understanding of the processes of man.[15] If we take the Bible to be primarily a revelation of the nature of God, then its portrayal of man is a correlate of its description of God. That is, it is a portrayal of man in relationship to God, not an intimate description of the processes of man. The portrayal of man can be held to be an accurate presentation of the basic aspects of what it means to be human, but still, any spiritual concept of man is a theological extrapolation—in theological terms, biblical anthropology. As such, a theological doctrine of man is tenuous and subject to critical re-evaluation just as is a psychological concept of man. It is just this critical re-evaluation task that is the task of philosophical theology.

To summarize, there should be a continuing dialogue of re-evaluation of the ultimate nature of man from the viewpoint of theology and the proximate processes of the nature of man from the viewpoint of psychology. No perfect "fit" should be expected. Rather, the points of disparity and ambiguity should help to define further areas of inquiry from both fields and hopefully enable each to contribute to the other.

nature of man

Now let us turn to several of the most significant assumptions about the nature of man.

What is the nature of good and evil in man? Both Allport and Maslow see man as a creature with potentiality for self-actualization. They believe humanity is capable of some ultimate good state toward which it can move. A somewhat less idealistic view is taken by Carl Rogers who, nevertheless, espouses the essential goodness of man. To Rogers, man behaves in evil fashion only because of neurotic conflict; once freed of neurosis, man will act in good and noble fashion.

These optimistic views are more beneficent than most American psychologists would maintain. More typically, they follow a naturalistic assumption that man is neither good nor evil, but merely an organism to be described by his behavior without evaluation. The naturalistic premise eliminates any principles, goals, or components higher than those that can be determined by the study of organismic behavior. This position is rationalistic; that is, personality can be fully comprehended by rational, scientific processes; and it is a materialistic reductionism; that is, man is solely a complex assemblage of biologic mechanisms.

In American psychology there are no real exponents of the view that man is intrinsically evil. Freud's dual instinct theory which posits a metaphysical death wish—Thanatos—comes closest to such a view. Thanatos ultimately leads to each man's destruction in death. Yet even the most prominent advocate of a death drive, Karl Menninger, could not be said to see man as evil, for to Menninger, man lives out a struggle between both good and evil forces within himself.

Theological views vary as much as do the psychological. On the one hand, we have dour "Calvinists" who see all human behavior as intransigently evil, while on the other hand, the pietist "holiness" groups have held that man can achieve a state of perfect, holy, sinless behavior.

In contrast to the naturalistic premise that man is neither good nor evil, our current insights from both theology and psychology suggest that man is *both* good and evil—not in some discrete proportions, but admixed inseparably throughout the fabric of personality and behavior. We observe good and bad motives and behavior in everyone in everyday life irrespective of the theology or psychology they claim. The apostle Paul describes man as existing in a state of tension between conflicting motives and impulses; "I do not do the good thing that I want to do, but I do practice the evil things that I do not want to do" (Rom. 7:19—Williams). The human condition is precisely the ongoing enterprise to forge from the noble and ignoble, creative and destructive, parts of ourselves a self-respecting yet realistic view of ourselves.

A second major assuption concerns the degree to which human behavior is freely chosen or ineluctably determined by physical, psychological, and social forces. Classic psychoanalytic theory emphasized the unconscious, determined, irrational components of behavior; while in the laboratory a deterministic position was held to be the only feasible operational stand to take. In contrast, contemporary existential theory and the whole movement of humanistic psychology has emphasized the role of personal freedom, responsibility, and conscious decision; while again current revisions of the philosophy of science suggest that a strict determinism is not a necessary precondition for successful experimentation.

Perhaps the more abstract elements of this debate diminish in the light of the everyday human aspects of this problem. Long ago Freud pointed out that our behavior was more determined by our unconscious aspects of personality than we were willing to admit, and that we were more responsible and able to change our behavior than we were willing to accept. Again, in the affairs of living, this debate may be seen as a matter of perspective. For example, Gatch and Temerlin compared psychotherapy reports from classic psychoanalysts and from existential psychoanalysts.[16] Interestingly, there were no actual differences in their clinical behavior despite their theoretical opposition: Both treated events in the patient's past as if they had been totally determined and not the patient's responsibility, while both treated decisions for the future as totally a matter of free choice of the patient who had the total responsibility for making those decisions.

The counterpart of this issue can be observed in theology where determinism versus free will has been a central issue in major theological and denominational systems, such as the extreme determinism of some branches of Calvinism and the ardent exposition of free will by groups in the Arminian tradition.

This debate over determinism and free will perhaps provides an excellent example where fruitful dialogue may occur between psychological and theological approaches to human existence. Experimental and clinical data may indicate the degrees to which human behavior reflects chosen and determined elements, and theology may help to focus on the consequences for human existence of extending either extreme as a general assumption.[17]

A third major assumption concerns the conceptualization of man as a psychological being (mind) versus a biological being (body). The attempt to synthesize mind and body has perplexed philosophers and psychologists since the time of Plato. He placed mind over against body with the rational faculties of mind-self (the good part of man) striving for control over the irrational passions of the body (the bad part of man). Philosophers posed various dualistic and monistic models, none satisfactory, until psychology declared the controversy at an end by resolving to study only brain. But that, too, has brought a reaction from those psychologists who note that even brain does not exist in isolation.

Thoughts and emotions affect our bodies, and illness certainly affects our personalities. We can readily see the relations between brain states and psychological states in sleep, arousal, anxiety, fear, appetite, and sexual arousal. There is no dichotomy in life. Although psychology categorically ruled out the mind-body problem 50 years ago, the discussion has been reopened. A recent book, *Theories of the Mind,* provides a broad range of suggestions, yet it contains this conclusion by Jordan Scher: "When all this has been said, mind remains largely an enigmatic elephant of unknown dimensions and uncoordinated aspects."[18] We can no longer accept the notion of mind and body as antithetical elements of good and bad; nor can a psychology that poses man as uniquely mind or uniquely body claim a hearing.

The same may be said for theology, for much of Christian theology has been heavily influenced by the Platonic dichotomy. The long history of Christian asceticism which viewed body with suspicion was founded upon Greek and Gnostic dualism, not biblical Hebraicism. Much of Christian theology has not taken the body aspect of personality seriously. Reducing personality to biology is one-sided, but so also is the elimination of biology. The biblical concept of man is that of a unitary being, of which body, mind, and spirit are not separate entities, but reflections of an integral self. Physical is part of spiritual and spiritual is part of physical. Asceticism denigrates the body; hedonism exalts the body; Christianity affirms that man is an indivisible being.

troublesome areas

Now we shall turn to a brief examination of some specific aspects of human behavior around which there has been considerable tension in theological-psychological discussions. In each instance I want to illustrate how specific words can lead to confusion because theological discourse and psychological discourse may use the same word or topic to refer to different dimensions of human experience.

The first is *anxiety*. In theology this has become a particularly popular theme, especially in existential circles following Kierkegaard's emphasis on the existential anxiety of life. A variety of biblical passages immediately come to mind regarding anxiety, such as "be anxious for nothing."

However, both the existential-philosophical concept of anxiety and the more everyday idea of "peace of mind" popular in religious circles (such as Norman Vincent Peale's religious tranquility themes) are rather wide of the definition of anxiety in a psychological frame of reference. In psychological terms, we refer to anxiety as the combination of physical and psychological reactions that accompany fright. Anxiety is the built-in response of the psycho-physiological organism to apprehended danger, mobilizing the organism to either fight or flight. In this context anxiety is a necessary component for normal functioning of the human organism. Too little anxiety response indicates inadequate organism response to environment, perhaps resulting in insensitive foolhardiness. Too much anxiety response leads to immobilization or neurotic defenses against unneeded or inappropriate arousal of the organism.

Maturity does not imply the absence of anxiety, stress, or conflict. This is illustrated by a recent study of "normal" YMCA college students who exhibited no overt conflicts or anxieties in life but in personality were dull, drab, and uncreative.[19] Creativity and leadership involve a certain amount of ferment in ones's life and personality. Hence the notion that the religiously devout should not experience anxiety, stress, and conflict, in the psychological sense we are describing, is absurd. Rather, Christian commitments bring tensions to one's life because one is thereby committed to oneself, one's friends and family, one's society, and one's God. Bertocci has suggested that the Christian life is not the search for some banal peace and tranquility, but the search for an implementation of creative anxiety.[20]

A quite different concept is involved when we turn to Kierkegaard's existential anxiety (some would prefer the term ontological anxiety). This is a kind of ultimate concern for life and its meaning—what might be termed spiritual anxiety. Here we are not concerned with current stress and conflict except as they reflect underlying lack of ultimate security and peace.

A good example might be the marriage relationship. If a couple has not achieved a sense of basic trust and commitment to each other, then each small conflict in the marriage will tend to arouse anxiety about the whole basis for the marriage relationship. On the other hand, if there is a sense of relationship, security, and commitment, then living together is not threatened by everyday stress and conflicts. These can be realistically faced and worked out in a mutually satisfying fashion. Even so, Christian commitment may be seen as providing a basis for ultimate security, a resolution of ultimate anxiety, so that one can courageously deal with the ongoing psychological anxieties of everyday life.

A second topic is *aggression*. Both psychology and theology have had difficulty in separating the various aspects of rage, anger, hostility, and basic aggressive instinctual drives. Aggression in a psychological sense may best be seen as the basic biologically-related driving energy for life. People vary in the amount of "aggressive drive" intrinsic to their personalities. The critical factor involved is the appropriate channeling of this basic aggressive drive, for basic aggressiveness can be either constructive or destructive. An analogy is the automobile that requires a driver to steer its power along a purposeful course.

Anger, like anxiety, is part of the psycho-physiological make-up of man, a defensive mobilization of the organism in reaction to fear or frustration. Rage would be the situation where anger overwhelms the personality and little purposeful reaction is possible. Anger, however, is a very necessary and useful reaction. It is a signal to the person that he is being threatened or frustrated and must take appropriate action. Anger is appropriate as a communication of feeling in reaction to another's behavior. Anger is inappropriate when there is no real danger or when the anger leads to hostility, which may be defined as the purposeful desire to destroy another. Anger followed by hostility is dysfunctional. Everyone experiences hostility to some degree, but we should seek to understand what has made us angry and use this knowledge to resolve angry conflicts instead of indulging in hostile retaliation. This is the best sense of the biblical injunction to "be angry and sin not."

A third topic is *guilt.* I have found it useful to distinguish between four types of guilt: objective, subjective, existential, and ontological. Each refers to quite different issues.[21]

Objective guilt is a violation of given arbitrary social laws. Objective guilt is arbitrary and not necessarily moral. For example, during World War II, the Jews were found objectively guilty of violating Nazi law. Another example: A man drives through a red light to take an expectant mother to the hospital to deliver her baby. The driver is guilty of violating an objective law, but is not behaving in an immoral fashion. The history of the Christian church is replete with examples of people adjudged guilty in terms of objective guilt according to the arbitrary mores of the social climate of that church society, mores bearing no relation to ultimate moral mandates.

Subjective guilt is the common combination of physical and mental phenomena that we all experience when we say we "feel guilty." This is usually what we mean by conscience. However, this subjective guilt is likewise not necessarily a reliable guide to moral action because we feel guilty only about the things we have been taught to feel guilty about. People often feel guilty over trivia, but have no qualms of conscience over vital issues. For example, a minister I knew would feel guilty if he did not put his weekly tithe in the offering plate, but after each service he would unconscionably grab a fistful of bills from the offering as his weekly "spending money."

Alternatively, feelings of guilt may produce overwhelming condemnations rather than a signal of concern. As a consequence, a person may bribe his conscience rather than seek to evaluate the source and reality of his guilt feelings—this is a common source of neurosis. We cannot and should not seek to eradicate guilt feelings, but part of moral maturity involves remodeling our childhood guilt feelings so that we only feel guilty about things that are part of our mature adult moral code, so that our guilt feelings are not sources of condemnation, but spurs to moral action.

Existential guilt is not a feeling, but a situation: It is the condition of estrangement between two persons. It is the violation of one's commitments to another, the repudiation of a relationship of love, concern, and involvement. The resolution of existential guilt—the estrangement in a loving relationship—cannot be accomplished by a mechanical repayment, a prostration of self, or the sacrifice of myself or another. Rather, existential forgiveness of existential guilt can only come through reconciliation and restoration of a loving relationship.

For example, if a husband is angry at his wife, he may have guilt feelings. He may come home with chocolates and flowers and then not feel guilty. But although he no longer feels guilty, the violations of the loving relationship may be still unresolved and hidden. On the other hand, the existential estrangement between husband and wife can only be resolved by mutual resolution of the conflict, which makes flowers and candy irrelevant—or merely symbols of the reconcilation that has already occurred.

Ontological guilt may be defined as the problem of man justifying his existence and his decisions in life. Jean Paul Sartre observes that if God does not exist to affirm the freedom of man to act, then how can man justify himself? Sartre, as an atheist, concludes that life is meaningless and therefore unjustifiable, absurd, forlorn. Or as Dostoievski puts it in *Brothers Karamazov*: If man is responsible for everything, then man is guilty of everything. In this sense ontological guilt is a description of the fact that man as an isolated being cannot justify his existence.

Perhaps guilt is not the right word here, except that theological use of the word guilt has essentially revolved around this issue. This is the sin to which redemption is addressed, not specific everyday problems, although they obviously bear a relation to each other. Ontological guilt as a concept may be seen as closely related to the concept of ontological anxiety. Neither is a strictly psychological concept, nor is psychotherapy directed in the usual sense toward these aspects of anxiety and guilt.

The Christian message of salvation—to be free in Christ—suggests that when man is moored in God, he then has the freedom to live his life. As Saint Augustine said, "Believe in God and go out and do what you want." It is a strange paradox that the Christian religion which has ostensibly proffered freedom to man has often produced anxious, tense, worried, guilt-ridden believers who experience anything but the freedom to live![22]

A fourth topic is the concept of *pride*. Pride as the downfall of man is a literary theme as old as the Hebrew prophets and the "hubris" of the Greek tragedians. Pride that is disastrous is that which is presumptuous. Over-weaning pride is the overestimation of self, the thrusting of self forward at the expense of others. It reflects the omnipotent phantasies of power and importance that children universally display. That type of pride in the adult may be considered neurotic in psychological terms, or sinful in biblical terms.

However, presumptuous pride should not be confused with realistic and proper self-regard and self-respect. The latter is the acknowledgement of one's true worth, the satisfaction of effective performance, and the gratification of necessary achievement and competence. St. Paul's declaration that "I count myself as nothing" has often been torn out of theological context and "psychologized" into a neurotic attitude of worthlessness, hopelessness, and a view of utter depravity of human endeavor. Were this true, no one could function. All of us need to respect ourselves and be respected by others. If we cannot accept ourselves, we will not accept others. It is no accident that Christ stated that the second great commandment was to "love others as we love ourselves."

The difference between a humanistic and a Christian concept of pride is that the humanist views man as self-justifying, whereas the Christian sees man as justified and accepted of God *as man is*. Paul Tillich grasps this in his sermon *You are Accepted*: "Do not seek for anything; do not perform anything; do not intend anything. Simply accept the fact that you are accepted."[23] The Christian concept of pride suggests that when accepted in Christ, we can accept ourselves with wholesome recognition of what we are in relation to ourselves, others, and God.

A final major topic of confluence between psychology and theology has to do with *morality*. At the outset of this essay, I noted that the task of defining moral behavior had passed from philosophy to psychology. Now most academic psychologists as well as most practicing psychotherapists would quickly wish to disavow that the mantle of responsibility had been thrust upon them. Morality has been traditionally said to be the province of the church. However in the twentieth century, the role of the church as moral arbiter has been seriously challenged and undermined, for both justifiable and questionable reasons. Regardless of cause, our society developed a significant moral vacuum into which the psychological professions have been pulled or pushed.

To a large degree psychology has replaced theology as the moral arbiter of our society, for who but experts in psychology tell us how to live healthily, maturely, sanely, etc. To be sure, the words have a "scientific" flavor, but the function is moral.[24] In a comprehensive study of the philosophy of psychotherapy, Joseph Margolis concludes, "Psychotherapy, then, is primarily concerned with a technical goal, the preservation and restoration of mental health; nevertheless its own development leads it, inevitably, to take up the role of moral legislator."[25] Other social scientists and psychologists have recently pointed to the same conclusion, as illustrated by over 160 references I have recently collated on current concerns in morality in the psychological literature.[26]

Now this state of affairs is not necessarily an undesirable

development, for the moral stances of the church have often ignored human need and formulated moral dicta that were psychologically naive and humanly unrealistic. The recent discussions of situation ethics have proved a healthy corrective to some of the stifling immorality of traditional morality. For example, divorce was long held to be immoral, which ignored the destructive effects on the children and the lives of both partners merely to keep intact a social contract.

Yet the situational ethicists, be they philosophers, theologians, or psychologists, have ignored the necessary reality of a moral structure in society. Clyde Kluckhohn, the late Harvard anthropologist summed it up well:

> There is a need for a moral order. Human life is necessarily a moral life precisely because it is a social life, and in the case of the human animal the minimum requirements for predictability of social behavior that will insure some stability and continuity are not taken care of automatically by biologically inherited instincts, as is the case with the bees and the ants. Hence there must be generally accepted standards of conduct, and these values are invested with divine authority and continually symbolized in rites that appeal to the senses.[27]

This issue of morality may prove to be the most vital of all in the dialogue between psychology and theology. Theology cannot produce a morality without a knowledge of human process and affairs. Psychology can tell us what effect moral values have on behavior, how moral values are made in the person and society, and how moral values operate within the structure of personality. Yet on the other hand, psychology cannot produce a moral ethic solely as matter of science. Heinz Hartmann, the eminent psychoanalyst, highlighted the inadequacy of psychology alone when he observed that psychoanalysis can make for unity but not goodness; psychoanalysis can enable us to understand how we create our values and enable us to act with integrity, but it cannot tell us how to choose our values or establish the criteria that we shall use.[28]   Here is the task of theology and the church in dialogue with our society. Thus the contemporary concern over morality in both psychology and theology may open the doors to collaboration in the most vital enterprise of our society.

summary

In this essay I have indicated that theology and philosophy, closely intertwined, were the historic disciplines concerned with the study of the nature of man and the analysis of human behavior. The development of an experimental scientific psychology in the twentieth century coincided with the abnegation of philosophy and the disenfranchisement of theology. Consequently there was little effective dialogue between philosophy, psychology, and theology during the first half of the twentieth century. The scene has been changing rapidly in the second half of this century.

Numerous areas of confluence exist between psychological and theological concerns. However effective, dialogue and mutual contributions cannot develop by merely seeking to find areas of superficial agreement. In fact the most productive collaboration may come from exploration of areas of divergent points of view.

Notes

[1]For convenience I shall use the term *psychology* and *psychologist* in this chapter as generic terms, since teaching, research, and therapeutic practice cross lines of professional identity as psychologist or psychiatrist. The issues with which we are concerned are germane to the field in general, not merely to a particular professional group or one segment of a profession. The discussion in this chapter inevitably reflects my personal views which are based on the conviction that we can neither artificially separate religious and philosophical thinking from psychology as some Christian professionals advocate, nor can we glibly accept easy answers that do not do justice to an open and rigorous attitude of thinking in both theology and psychology. See E. Mansell Pattison, "Psychiatry," *Christianity and the World of Thought,* ed. Hudson T. Armerding (Chicago, 1968); and Lars Granberg, " 'Christian' Psychologist?" *Journal of the American Scientific Affiliation,* XIX (1967), 88-89.

[2]See William Barrett and Howard Aiken, *Philosophy in the Twentieth Century,* 4 vols. (New York, 1962).

[3]For a critical analysis of the assumptions of this philosophy see Irving L. Horowitz, *Philosophy, Science, and the Sociology of Knowledge* (Springfield, Ill., 1961). Nor is the theological problem limited to psychology. See John Dillenberger, *Protestant Thought and Natural Science* (Garden City, N. Y., 1960).

[4]Melvin H. Marx, "General Nature of Theory Construction," *Theories in Contemporary Psychology* (New York, 1963).

[5]Some Christian psychologists feel that the empirical approach, although limited, is the most feasible base for psychology. Therefore, it is perhaps unnecessary or impossible to adequately deal with "Christian" issues. See Robert F. Ettinger and C. Eugene Walker, "Behaviorism and Existentialism: Views of Skinner and Tillich," *Journal of Religion and Health,* V (1966), 151-157.

[6]For example, see *Humanistic Viewpoints in Psychology,* ed. Frank T. Severin (New York, 1965).

[7]Edwin A. Burtt, *Metaphysical Foundations of Modern Science,* rev. ed. (Garden City, N. Y., 1932).

[8]See Talcott Parsons, "Unity and Diversity in the Modern Intellectual Disciplines: The Role of the Social Sciences," *Daedalus,* CVI (1965), 39-65.

[9]Herbert Feigl, "Philosophical Embarrassments of Psychology," *American Psychologist,* XIV (1959), 115-128.

[10]Calvin S. Hall and Gardner Lindzey, *Theories of Personality* (New York, 1957).

[11] Peter A. Bertocci and Robert Millard, *Personality and the Good* (New York, 1963).

[12] Mario Bunge, *Metascientific Queries* (Springfield, Ill., 1959).

[13] This brief summary skirts an immense area of epistomological inquiry. To what degree do scientific discourse and religious-philosophical discourse overlap in language and knowledge? Is the knowledge provided by both types of inquiry of the same category; that is, complementary views of the same object, or are the two types of inquiry discrete investigations of basically dissimilar objects of existence? For introductions to these issues see James E. Royce, *Man and Meaning* (New York, 1969).

[14] Examples of some currently popular adaptations of a particular theory to a Christian theology include Jung's collective unconscious by Victor White and James Knight; Combs and Snygg's perceptual psychology by Orlo Strunk, Jr.; Frankl's logotherapy by Donald Tweedie; Mowrer's reality therapy by John Drakeford.

[15] Paul Tillich, "Impact of Pastoral Psychology on Theological Thought," *Ministry and Mental Health*, ed. Hans Hoffman (New York, 1960).

[16] Vern M. Gatch and Mark K. Temerlin, "Belief in Psychic Determinism and the Behavior of the Psychotherapist," *Review of Existential Psychology and Psychiatry*, V (1965), 16-33.

[17] See John N. Lapsley, *Concept of Willing* (New York, 1968).

[18] Jordan Scher, ed., *Theories of the Mind* (New York, 1962).

[19] Roy Grinker, "Mentally Healthy Young Males (Homoclites)," *Archives of General Psychiatry*, VI (1962), 405-453.

[20] Peter A. Bertocci, *Religion as Creative Insecurity* (New York, 1958).

[21] E. Mansell Pattison, "On the Failure to Forgive or to be Forgiven," *American Journal of Psychotherapy*, XIX (1965), 106-115.

[22] See James A. Knight, *Conscience and Guilt* (New York, 1969).

[23] Paul Tillich, "You Are Accepted," *Shaking of the Foundations* (Boston, 1948).

[24] This thesis is not mine alone, but is expressed by leading students of the social function of the mental health disciplines. See Paul Halmos, *Faith of the Counsellors* (New York, 1966); and Philip Rieff, *Triumph of the Therapeutic: Uses of Faith After Freud* (New York, 1966).

[25] Joseph Margolis, *Psychotherapy and Morality* (New York, 1966).

[26] E. Mansell Pattison, "Ego Morality: An Emerging Psychotherapeutic Concept," *Psychoanalytic Review*, LII (1968), 187-222.

[27] Clyde Kluckhohn, "Introduction," *Reader in Comparative Religion: An Anthropological Approach*, 2nd ed., eds. William A. Lessa and Ezra Z. Vogt (New York, 1966).

[28] Heinz Hartmann, *Psychoanalysis and Moral Values* (New York, 1960).

Walfred H. Peterson

Political Science

Like it or not, modern man is a child of government. Not only is he affected by government in innumerable ways that might at first glance seem trivial—he rises on government-standardized time, washes in government-purified water, and eats government-inspected bacon fried on government-priced gas—but his basic attitudes are also affected by government.

Man learns what is right and wrong in considerable measure from government. Laws of the society are passed and enforced not merely to control behavior but also to shape beliefs. While it is true that law in part rests on a general public morality, that morality in part rests on law. To illustrate: one reason men know what stealing is and that it is bad is that the law identifies it and calls it illegal. Modern government also shapes beliefs in its educational programs. From the ABCs to advanced physics and metaphysics, government is society's chief formal educator. True, men learn from other agencies, but government directly and indirectly influences these agencies in many ways.

As a dutiful child of government, modern man gives government his loyalty and devotion. For all the common grumbling about government officials and policy, most men are still rather patriotic. Christian citizens of the United States will kill Christian citizens of Germany with some enthusiasm when asked or ordered by government to do so. So, too, Marxists of, let us say, Russia and China. For what other agency than government will so many so willingly kill and die?

All this means that the state, governmental structures, the processes of governing, and relations between the governors and the governed need study, for they affect our lives deeply. This study is the job of political science. As political scientists do their job well, they merit the attention of all college students. While many political scientists would say that their discipline is still in its infancy, they have accumulated enough data and developed enough theories to occupy most students to advantage for a very long time.

The study of political science ought to have a special interest to the Christian student or to any other student who tries to find his ultimate values and loyalties outside government and law. For if values and loyalties are not merely products of government action, then all government action must be measured against them. That is, if an ultimate justice exists beyond the justice of our law, then our law should be squared with that ultimate justice as far as possible. So, the man of ideals needs to know something about what government does and something about how it does it. If he objects to what it does or does not do, he will need to know how to manipulate it to produce the remedy for his objection. He will need political science.

Another point merits passing attention from the Christian student of political science. Some of the most richly descriptive terms in the Christian vocabulary stem from politics. *Kingdom, law, liberty, rebellion,* and *slavery,* while now often used in some churches in a purely spiritual context, found their meaning initially in a political context. Paul used *redemption* in his day because his readers knew that military captives or legal slaves found a new life when their freedom was purchased. The reason for this transfer of vocabulary is obvious. Christianity is from one view a series of relationships between God, man, and other people. Political life is also a series of relationships between the ruler, the ruled, and other people. These sets of relationships are so similar that the words developed for one can become apt words for the other. This means that the imaginative student in political science may very well learn some secular things that open his eyes more fully to some religious things.

the nature of political knowledge

Political scientists do not agree on the scope, objectives, or methods of political science. Indeed, they are divided into loose alliances of warring camps that rage at each other in the supposedly dispassionate pages of learned journals and studious sessions of professional conferences. Classification of these warring camps and generalization about them are impossible in the space available here. But two tendencies in the methodology of political science merit brief attention.

Some political scientists stress that it is political *science* which they pursue. Many of these call their approach "behavioral" because they focus attention on the political behavior of persons. They aim at a more objective, quantifiable, and theoretical structure for the study. They argue that political science sorely needs a greater body of verifiable data, and that political theory must build its abstract models proportionate to the sharply limited body of such knowledge now available. They say that issues of morality or justice are not the concern of political *science* except as data indicate that people act on beliefs about what is thought to be moral or just. They feel akin to psychologists, sociologists, and economists. Their approach to the study of politics is more dominant every year in American classrooms.[1]

Other political scientists are more likely to discount the possibility of achieving a science of politics. Of these, many would perhaps most aptly be called political philosophers. They regard political knowledge as more fruitfully developed by logical manipulation of certain basic propositions, data, and insights. They argue for the ready availability of foundational political knowledge useful for extensive theorizing. This group includes admirers of the political thought of Plato and Aristotle, because that thought turns the focus of political theory toward the definition and achievement of the just society. They feel akin to the more traditional social thinkers, philosophers, and, in some cases, to theologians. The reader must be warned that most of what follows would best be classified as political philosophy.[2]

The student beginning the study of political science will scarcely feel qualified to take a position on the methodology of the study for a long time. For certain kinds of knowledge, however, one with a Christian world-view can accept the utility of both approaches just described. There are Christian political scientists of a variety of methodological persuasions, though few of them would fit into the "scientific" or "behavioral" approach by the definitions proposed by its most outspoken advocates.

If a conflict over methodology develops between the Christian and political scientists from either tendency, it will most likely appear when one or the other insists that his route to knowledge is the only route—a not uncommon experience. In the climate of our age it is made most aggressively by those who conceive of the discipline as a science. This fact tends to put the Christian student on the defensive in the field when questions of basic method arise. Indeed, it forces some to compartmentalize their thought: Part of life becomes the arena of science where all things are questioned and measurable tests are required and another part of life becomes the arena of faith where nothing is questioned and no tests are allowed.

the place of revelation

For the Christian one route to knowledge is revelation. However valid and useful other routes may be, they do not obviate the need for revelation. It can be both a starting point for important knowledge, and it can serve as a standard against which other knowledge is checked.

But caution is needed. The Christian should realize the limits of revelation for purposes of social study: Revelation does not specify data or theories about many important aspects of society's life. It reveals that man is self-seeking, but it does not reveal how he will act in a certain situation—a thing empirical research may do. It reveals that man should seek justice, but it does not necessarily reveal that a specific relationship is unjust —a thing moral theory may do. It speaks for the dignity of man, but it does not tell how laws should be written to promote it—a thing that may require both empirical research and profound legal theorizing. Revelation, for all its grandeur and spiritual adequacy, would not alone be sufficient for the drafting of a good constitution for a given state. It needs the aid of as much sound political science and moral philosophy as men can give. It too is only one route to knowledge.

Two present-day American political thinkers who bring the knowledge of revelation to play on some of the basic problems of political science are René de Visme Williamson of Louisiana State University and John H. Hallowell of Duke University. From different theological perspectives, both criticize some recent emphases in the discipline, and both try to develop a political theory compatible with a Christian world-view.[3]

the nature of man

The caution that revelation does not give all the knowledge that the social sciences need does not in any way minimize its importance for them. Revelation gives some of the most basic knowledge of all. For example, it outlines the nature of man.

Man is several things in Christian thought. He is spiritual. This implies that any purely materialistic or mechanistic theories about society will be inadequate. He is social. This implies that any theory that treats the existence of social institutions like the family or the state as a mere matter of convenience will be inadequate. He is a moral agent. This implies that he must both identify and promote the good as distinguished from the bad. He is at once a creature of great dignity and creativity and of depravity and destructiveness.

The natural mixture in man of creativity and destructiveness, of potentials for good and evil, has more than spiritual dimensions. It is at the center of any Christian understanding of the political order. On the one hand, it calls for some measure of freedom so that man's creative powers can be unleashed. On the other hand, it calls for some measure of control so that man's destructive powers can be limited. The problem of the prudent balance between these opposite and complementary measures has been a major theme in Western political thought in part because that thought reflected this dual Christian premise. Reinhold Niebuhr's *The Children of Light and the Children of Darkness* provocatively defends the wisdom of democracy based on the implications of this natural dualism.[4] This little book should not be missed.

the nature of political authority

"Every person must submit to the supreme authorities. There is no authority but by act of God, and the existing authorities are instituted by him; consequently anyone who rebels against authority is resisting a divine institution . . . [The authorities] . . . are God's agents working for your good."

From these words, the remainder of Romans 13, and related passages, it is clear that the New Testament is concerned with the nature of political authority. But what are its implications? Does any authority, regardless of origin, deserve obedience? What of a situation where two competing authorities demand obedience? In relating the authority to that which is good, does the apostle imply that obedience is required only for authority directed to the good? Who decides the good?

Perhaps we can agree on this: The New Testament implies that the relationship of ruler to ruled is necessary for man's welfare in society. That is, the function of government is necessary. Pure anarchy is not an acceptable option. Even dictatorship is preferable to it. But this does not imply that any government activity is, therefore, justifiable. After all, the apostles disobeyed constituted authority, and in the book of Revelation government actions are denounced. Support of government as a necessary institution does not imply support of a given government policy. The Christian can stand in opposition.

What is proper opposition? Revolution? It is hard to square revolution with New Testament political suggestions, though many people have tried. Riots? The task of justifying these may be even more difficult than that of justifying revolution. Presumably the revolutionary is trying to create a more just society, but the rioter typically has no better alternative to offer. He is merely venting his anger (righteous or not) against some alleged evil. Civil disobedience? This—the deliberate disobedience of law without revolutionary intent—is the approach that Peter and John took when the authorities told them not to preach. Martin Luther King's writings have explicated it for our day. Legal opposition within the framework of government? Many Christians say this is the proper route of opposition, but at times it may seem completely ineffective. Do not suppose that the choice here is easy. Some religious men—for example, Dietrich Bonhoeffer in Nazi Germany—have even accepted opposition by assassination!

In a brief and provocative book emphasizing the political interests of the New Testament, Oscar Cullman takes up the matter of the Christian's relation to government. He argues that the state within its limited temporal sphere is an institution created by God for man's good. Beyond this temporal sphere, however, is the eternal realm. There the state has no competence at all. Since the eternal is with us in part now, this means that state functions are limited now.[5] This view makes both the anarchists' attack upon the existence of the state and the totalitarians' complete surrender to the state unacceptable within Christian thought.

other authorities

The phrase quoted above from Romans probably relates solely to government as we think of it. Yet, Paul would certainly say that in its sphere of action, the church is as much instituted of God as the state. Could we not add the family? That is, man has binding relationships in several directions.

In recognition of the plurality of binding relationships, a political system acceptable to the Christian must make some sort of allowance for this plurality of authorities. But however skill-fully lawmakers separate out the spheres of these authorities, their activities must overlap. This fact can create conflict be-tween agencies that the individual is obligated to serve. The individual is then caught in the dilemma of trying to serve two or more masters.

The dilemma is especially difficult when the two masters are state and church. The former has awesome weapons at its com-mand to coerce obedience, including the hangman's noose. It also has in our age the loyalty of nationalism. The church, however, should not coerce obedience in any way. Yet it, too, has loyalty, a loyalty that should be deeper than that given to the state. The student can find moving illustrations of the di-lemma's impact on individuals all through Christian history from the early martyrs to, for example, present-day religious pacifists.

some concluding observations

The Christian view of the nature of man, of the authority of the state, and of the authority of other institutions, when put to-gether, makes for a complex view of political life. Some mem-bers of the New Left have oversimplified things by abandoning some claims to authority which God, the state, or family have placed upon them. Many of them look to the state as the one final authority. Others point to some political party or to some sort of communal group as finally superior to all else. But the Christian view calls for a nice balancing of several authorities. When Christ said, "Render therefore to Caesar the things that are Caesar's and to God the things that are God's," he only gave us our duty and two categories of things. We must put the experiences of life into such categories. Political science can help us to that.

Of course, the ordinary political science course does not often have occasion to wrestle with these fundamental issues. Courses must and do go on for months exploring much less fundamental issues than these. The student must not forget, however, that these and similarly important matters are always in the background of any study. He would do well to try to trace out the connections between this background and the day-to-day materials on which he works.

One caution may be especially important for the social science student today. In courses emphasizing one approach to knowledge, he should consciously try to keep from being dominated by the habits appropriate to that approach where those habits are inappropriate. He should recognize that any academic methodology for finding truth is only a means and not the end. In most political science departments today this recognition should not be too difficult. Both individual professors and departments are, in fact, wonderfully eclectic about basic things.

Notes

[1] See Heinz Eulau, *The Behavioral Persuasion in Politics* (New York, 1964).

[2] See James C. Charlesworth, ed., *The Limits of Behavioralism in Political Science* (Philadelphia, 1962) and *A Design for Political Science: Scope, Objective, and Methods* (Philadelphia, 1966).

[3] René de Visme Williamson, *Independence and Involvement, A Christian Reorientation in Political Science* (Baton Rouge, 1964); John H. Hallowell, *Main Currents in Modern Political Thought* (New York, 1950). See Hallowell's discussion on Reinhold Niebuhr.

[4] Reinhold Niebuhr, *The Children of Light and the Children of Darkness* (New York, 1944).

[5] Oscar Cullman, *The State in the New Testament* (New York, 1956).

Thomas E. Van Dahm

Economics

" 'Christian economist'—isn't that a contradiction in terms?"
This question was once put to me, partly in jest, but the fact
that it was asked at all probably indicates an unconscious feeling that economics, concerned as it inevitably is with the
"things of this world," is something that Christians should not
approach too closely. Since the aim of this essay is to suggest
the relevance of the Christian faith to the study of economics,
we had better clear the air at the outset by attempting to establish the legitimacy of economics as a field for the Christian
student. May I suggest that misconceptions concerning the nature of economics or Christianity, or both, are the basis for any
uneasiness regarding the propriety of mentioning Christianity
and economics in the same breath.

First, there is often, on the part of those without formal
training in economics, the belief that economics is the study of
how to "make more money," that is, how to acquire more
income and wealth. Admittedly, a knowledge of economics may
serve this purpose; but so may a knowledge of chemistry, or
French, or even theology! While not without its "practical"
aspects (in the sense of personal monetary gain), economics has

quite a different focus.

In the words of a classic definition of the field: "Economics is the science which studies human behavior as a relationship between ends and scarce means which have alternative uses."[1] So economics *can* be used to "make more money," if that is one's goal; but it can also be used by criminal syndicates to further their evil ends, by school boards in allocating available tax revenues so as to achieve their educational goals as effectively as possible, by the Department of Defense, the PTA, and so on.

If we were to "Christianize" this definition of economics, by specifying that the ultimate *ends* are to glorify God and carry out his will, and that the appropriate uses of *means* are those which are compatible with the Christian view of man and the material world, we would have a concise statement of the doctrine of stewardship. Thus, for example, if Christian families and individuals are responsibly systematic and careful in allocating their contributions to those uses in which they are expected to be the most helpful in advancing Christ's kingdom, they are using economics, whether they realize it or not. Economics, in brief, being a science, is ethically neutral, its principles suitable for use for the loftiest as well as the most depraved ends.

Misconceptions concerning the nature of Christianity also are responsible for doubts as to the suitability of economics for study by Christians. There are those who, impressed by biblical admonitions against becoming too closely attached to this world, see Christianity as almost purely "other-worldly" in its essential nature. Surely this is a distorted view of Christianity. At the same time we are painfully aware of the pathological attachment of most Americans to material things, we must bear in mind that God created the world and has made man responsible to him for the use of its resources. Even though the Christian's ultimate citizenship is in heaven, there is work to be done here. Man must use all the resources at his disposal in order that God may be glorified and his will be done on earth. This is clearly, forcefully, and repeatedly taught in both Old and New Testaments.

Thus, if both economics and Christianity are correctly under-stood, it is apparent that, far from being antithetical, they actually complement each other.

a christian approach to the study of economics

Will the fact that the student approaches economics from the standpoint of a Christian world-and-life view cause any problems for him in cases where the professor or the authors of the course materials hold other views? No, provided that neither the student nor the professor and authors allow their views on religious questions to interfere with their use of logic in reasoning or to affect their perception of data, and provided that they can keep separate any cases of disagreement arising solely from differences in underlying premises concerning the nature of God, man, and the physical world and their interrelationships. Such disagreements simply are not economic, but philosophical; therefore they have no bearing on one's understanding of economics per se. Student and professor may, of course, disagree over other matters, not because the student is a Christian but because of differences in interpretation of data, errors in logic, or differing social philosophies.

Still there are certain respects in which being a Christian makes a difference in one's approach to economics. We turn now to an explication of this point, using a familiar threefold classification of the subject matter of economics: facts, theory, and policy.

facts, theory, and policy

One would not expect any problems in the area of facts. After all, if the unemployment rate is 4% of the labor force, or the Consumer Price Index has risen 2.5% over the past year, what is there to argue about? Unfortunately, it is not quite that simple. In the first place, two sets of data may appear to contradict each other. Which should we accept? Second, the available data may not be exactly what we need or would like, in the way of coverage or reliability. How much confidence should we place in the data? It is in selecting and evaluating data that man—

fallen as he is—often shows his true nature. Consciously or unconsciously, he tends to select those facts which support his preconceived views, ignoring or explaining away the bits of evidence which seem to contradict them. Thus, two people—two Christians, in fact—faced with identical assortments of information concerning a particular matter, could come away with completely different conclusions about what the "facts" really are.

The Christian, then, having a particular view of the nature of man, should be on guard against the tendency in himself, as well as others, to view the "facts" from a perspective distorted by pride and self-seeking. The intellectual sin of rationalization is subtle and dangerous because it is so difficult for the guilty one to recognize.

Economic facts consist of information concerning what *was* and what *is,* with respect to economic conditions, developments, and events. Economic theory embodies attempts to arrive at valid explanations of (1) how what was became what is and (2) how a particular economic system functioned or functions, that is, how the parts fit together to constitute an integrated whole. Theory and facts reinforce each other in that the facts suggest generalizations and, in turn, generalizations are checked against facts and suggest the kinds of data needed for verification. There are numerous pitfalls of logic that can trap the wariest theorist, so the beginner obviously needs to be constantly on the alert.

There are two basic criteria used in evaluating an economic theory or principle: *formal* validity (conclusions relate logically to premises) and *empirical* validity (theory corresponds, in some sense, with the "real world"). Notice that no mention has been made of any specific "Christian" criterion. To accept a theory as "Christian" despite its failure to pass one or both of the "validity" tests, or to reject as "unChristian" a theory which is valid in both respects would be an insult to the creator of human reason.

Yet disagreements over theoretical questions can and do arise, even among Christians. Although the question of formal validity can be settled ultimately by appeal to principles of logic, two stubborn causes of dispute remain: (1) the imperfect state of economic theory, due especially to the difficulties of verification and (2) the tendency for pride and self-interest to predispose one to accept or reject a particular "brand" of theory insofar as it does or does not suit one's advantage or even one's preconceptions.

The first of these reasons needs little comment. Economic literature contains the remains of numerous theories which *seemed* to explain the operation of the economic system, or some subsystem, but which later events demonstrated to have succeeded only because of the existence of certain special circumstances whose importance was not grasped.

The second reason for theoretical disputes can profit from an illustration or two. Consider, for example, Marxist economics. Millions of people embrace certain conclusions of Marx's reasoning because these conclusions are emotionally appealing to them, even though the theoretical foundations are demonstrably based on errors of logic and observation. And, closer home, numerous influential Christians reject much of the work in economic analysis of the past three decades, comprising what is called "macroeconomics" or "aggregate economics" in most texts, not because the analysis is formally or empirically invalid but because they dislike one of the implications, namely, that the federal government is able, through the exercise of its tax and expenditure powers, to influence the level of economic activity, hastening recovery from recession and reducing the pace of inflation.

Moving now to a more personal level, should the Christian student approach economic theory with the expectation that it will yield answers to the everyday problems faced by the housewife, employee, consumer, etc.? For the most part, the answer must be, No, not directly. In this respect, economics is much like history, physics, or literature. These and other disciplines throw light on various aspects of human behavior or of the created order, but they do not furnish explicit guidance for coping with the problems of which refrigerator to buy, how to fill out an income-tax form, or what career to prepare for.

Economic theory can make an important *indirect* contribution to personal decisions, however. The emphasis of economics on the choice-making process should heighten the student's awareness of the fact that he is constantly faced with situations involving choice. Hopefully, the Christian student of economics, now more alert to such situations, will therefore be more likely to choose an alternative that is consistent with his commitment. Of course, there are occupations in industry and government which depend heavily on a knowledge of economic theory; but these will involve relatively few college graduates early in their careers.

The really significant possibilities for the application of economic theory for most readers of these pages will be in various "second occupations": as citizen, as member of a church and of other organizations, and perhaps as a direct participant in important decisions of these organizations. Armed with a working knowledge of economic theory, one should be in a position to exert his influence toward more rational decision-making in private organizations with which he associates and to evaluate more intelligently the economic aspects of government policy proposals and programs.

The third and final aspect of economics is policy: the area concerned with the use of government to influence the behavior of the economic order. It is in the area of policy that most economic controversy occurs—and no wonder! Not only are facts and theory involved, but social philosophy as well. In other words, we can expect some disagreement even among Christians over policy matters, not only because they may differ in their views of the facts or of the significance of these facts for the functioning of the economy, but also because of differences over the importance of various alternative national economic goals or the propriety of using particular methods to accomplish them. Quite possibly, therefore, Christians can be found on all sides of any policy issue.

goals and means
Among commonly-accepted economic goals are (1) high-level

employment, (2) stable price level, (3) substantial rate of economic growth, (4) equitable distribution of income, (5) freedom in decision-making, and (6) economic security. The methods of achieving them include (1) changing taxes and tax rates, (2) changing the level and direction of government spending, and (3) various prohibitions, limits, and requirements affecting economic activity.

All of these goals and means are subjects of controversy, as we know. It would be convenient if we could push all such matters aside and leave them to professionals; but followers of Christ are not permitted to do so, because policy decisions involve judgments as to the nature of man and of the good society. Thus, questions of justice, of the manner in which people live—their health, self-respect, chances to better themselves—and hence their attitudes toward God and their fellowmen are all involved in policy decisions. We have the duty to inform ourselves, so far as we have the opportunity, of the economic facts, their meaning, and whether a particular economic goal or program directed toward a certain goal or goals appears to be compatible with the perceived will of God.

As a matter of fact, for the Christian, one of the most valuable outcomes of the systematic study of economics is an enhanced awareness of the complexity of the economic system and of the consequent necessity of careful, logical thinking in evaluating economic policies and proposals. No matter how completely dedicated one is to God, or how sound his theology, there is no substitute for technical competence and rigorous thinking in making valid economic judgments and decisions.

To illustrate this point, when a group decides to construct a church building, it does not simply hold a prayer meeting, disperse to collect any and all kinds of building materials, and then knock it all together, trusting in God and their feelings as to what is "right." Rather, they generally rely on someone who knows both architecture and the purposes and functions of a church building, telling him what they have in mind and expecting him to come up with plans that will be feasible.

By exact analogy, it is foolish to rely on simple faith, good will, and "feeling"—one's own or others'—in formulating opinions concerning complex economic policy issues, such as the question of foreign economic aid, labor-management relations, tax reform, and others. Unfortunately, numerous well-meaning Christians, ministers and laymen, theologically liberal and conservative and in-between, who would never think of venturing an opinion on bridge construction or the treatment of mononucleosis, do not hesitate to make high-sounding pronouncements outlining "the" Christian approach to any problem involving economic policy, in terms often far stronger in emotive content than in economic quality.

The Christian must pay close attention not merely to the person's apparent sincerity and dedication to Christ but also to his economic competence. It is simply irresponsible to decide in favor of one view or another primarily on the basis of the number of fervent references to our God-given heritage, or to the communistic or fascistic leanings of the opposition, or even the number of biblical "proof-texts" (sometimes wrenched out of context) tossed into the discussion.

Hopefully, too, the Christian will develop habits of reasoning that will carry over into church "economic policy." The church, after all, has acute problems of allocating scarce resources to accomplish its ends; yet rigorous analysis is often sadly lacking in approaching this task. For example, a missionary gives a rather discouraging report, citing the small number of converts over the past few years in his field. "But," he asks rhetorically, "is all the money in the world too much to pay for a single soul won for Christ?" Of course not. But the economics-oriented person would object to the way the question was put; he would look at the situation in terms of alternatives. If one field is comparatively infertile and has a poor outlook, while some other field shows signs of real harvest potential, then Christian stewardship demands that we allocate more of our resources—manpower, literature, supplies, and equipment—to the more productive field, perhaps phasing out or curtailing activities in the less-productive one.[2]

In conclusion, this brief essay has not attempted to deal with the many substantive issues of economic policy and personal economic problems. Its intent rather has been to develop the elements of a Christian approach to the study of economics, an approach which can almost be summarized in the form of three requirements:

(1) To use our time and intelligence as best we can to understand the issues involved, the alternatives available, and their probable consequences,

(2) To seek divine guidance in evaluating these alternatives, with the ultimate goal of doing God's will, and

(3) To approach these issues with humility in the realization that all of us are tainted with a self-seeking nature and are limited in our knowledge.[3]

Notes

[1] Lionel Robbins, *Essay on the Nature and Significance of Economic Science* (New York, 1935), p. 16.

[2] This idea is developed forcefully in Donald A. McGavran's article, "Have We Lost Our Way in Missions?" *Christian Herald,* reprinted in *Church Herald,* 11 Apr. 1958, pp. 12-15.

[3] The student can find helpful discussions in John C. Bennett, et al., *Christian Values and Economic Life* (New York, 1954); D. L. Munby, *Christianity and Economic Problems* (New York, 1956); John F. Sleeman, *Basic Economic Problems: A Christian Approach* (London, 1953); and Josiah Stamp, *Christianity and Economics* (New York, 1939).

III. The Natural Sciences

Charles E. Hummel

The Natural Sciences

The twentieth century has witnessed unprecedented prosperity for much of the Western world. The magnificent achievements of the natural sciences have released us from the ravages of many diseases and much drudgery in our daily work. They promise indefinite progress in unlocking nature's secrets, from subatomic entities to the vast reaches of interstellar space. Yet these achievements have brought us to a technological crisis of terrifying proportions which threatens mankind's very existence.

Never before has our capacity for destruction been so great. The same genius which sends astronauts to the moon also deploys nuclear missiles poised to obliterate a hundred million people in one strike. Our vast industrial machine works its destructive effects less obviously on our environment through increasing air and water pollution. Even more subtle and dangerous in the long run is the technological environment we are producing to subordinate human values to efficiency, to make man the servant of his machines, even in our educational institutions.

Scientific research and technological innovation have also

contributed immensely to both the effectiveness and cost of modern weapons. As a result, the arms race against the Russians has produced our huge military-industrial complex, against which the late President Eisenhower warned. Firmly entrenched in our burgeoning economy, this complex threatens both escalation of militaristic diplomacy and squandering of natural resources so urgently needed to renovate our society.

We boast of our scientific progress, yet for most people life today appears more perplexing and beset with problems than ever before. Modern literature and art forms reflect this sense of frustration; our writers and artists continue to be the most perceptive observers of the human situation. Ironically, anxiety matches affluence as our technological skills have reached peak efficiency in a climate of apparent meaninglessness, moral irresponsibility, and impersonal manipulation.

Protest against this plight has become commonplace, but where do we turn for a sense of direction and the moral dynamic to pursue the right path? How can we enjoy the achievements of science and technology without their destroying our natural environment and ourselves through depersonalization, even if we escape nuclear annihilation? Surely the first step is to assess the nature of the scientific enterprise, to understand its objectives, limitations, and means of control. We shall do this with an historical approach which examines the work of several eminent scientists who led the scientific revolution of the sixteenth and seventeenth centuries. George Santayana once asserted that he who does not learn from history is doomed to repeat its errors. This chapter, therefore, briefly reviews the scientific revolution of the sixteenth and seventeenth centuries which produced the modern scientific method as a discipline distinct from philosophy and theology.

In this historical context, we shall endeavor to understand the nature of the scientific approach to the natural world and its relationship to other equally valid perspectives. We shall also perceive the dilemma of our own century. While Christianity contributed to the climate in which modern science matured, during the nineteenth century Western culture discarded traditional Christian morality as a value base and turned to science for its guidance. Ironically, having freed itself from philosophy and religion, science was then made to cope with philosophical and religious problems of meaning, value, and purpose—questions alien to its nature. This misuse of science by our culture, actually the promulgation of certain philosophies in the name of science, has contributed to the technological crisis which Wilbur Ferry describes so perceptively. "Here is where all the trouble begins—in the American confidence that technology is ultimately the medicine for all ills. Technology is the American theology, promising salvation by material works."[1]

The following historical sketch will provide the background for this problem. As we understand the purpose of the modern scientific approach to nature, we shall appreciate both its value and its inherent limitations. Then we shall perceive the role of science in contemporary society and the need for moral guidelines beyond science to enable it to perform as a helpful servant rather than a tyrannical master.

the scientific revolution

Usually revolutions, whether political or intellectual, have both an extended period of unrest preceding the opening salvos and subsequent skirmishes after the decisive battle has been fought. The Renaissance and Reformation prepared the climate for the scientific revolution of the sixteenth and seventeenth centuries, while another two hundred years extended the new regime's influence. In this section, we shall focus on the 150-year period beginning with Copernicus and ending with Newton. From the many men of scientific genius who led this great complex movement, we select four whose crucial discoveries in the realm of astronomy and physics laid the foundations for modern science.

Copernicus, Kepler, Galileo, and Newton revolutionized the nature of scientific explanation. They also illustrate, as men of faith and reason, the relationship of the emerging new science to Christianity. While today many of our most critical concerns center in the life sciences, especially the possibilities of controlling future human development, their rapid advance came two centuries later and represent an extension of the scientific method into new realms of natural science. For this reason we concentrate on the arenas of astronomy and physics in which the modern scientific method largely forged its identity.

Before we examine the work of these four scientists, however, we shall take a brief flashback to the origin of science in Greek thought and its marriage to theology under Aquinas which set the stage for the scientific revolution. Then we shall have an historical basis for understanding the critical issues confronting science, theology, and philosophy today.

From the dawn of civilization men have tried to understand the natural world of their physical and biological environment. While the Egyptians formulated mathematical rules for land measurements, and the Babylonians developed an interest in observing the movements of the heavenly bodies, the Greeks hold undisputed title as the original thinkers and scientists of ancient Europe. From the outset, Greek philosophy was bound up with mathematics and pursued knowledge for its own sake in the spirit of free inquiry. The earliest Ionian philosopher, Thales of Miletus (640-550 B.C.), was a mixture of practical scientist and philosopher.[2] The Milesian school of philosophy was the first to assume that the whole universe is natural and can potentially be explained by ordinary knowledge and rational thought. This assumption also undergirds the modern scientific enterprise.

The most influential Greek philosopher, however, for understanding the scientific revolution was Aristotle (384-322 B.C.), the greatest collector and organizer of knowledge in the ancient world.[3] He produced an encyclopedia of information within a system of thought that molded the mind of the Western world for almost 2,000 years. This system combined both science and philosophy since it sought to explain natural phenomena ultimately in terms of meaning and purpose.

Aristotle's system of thought stimulated scientific investigation during the following centuries which witnessed the disintegration of the Greek Empire and the rise of Rome. Hipparchus and Ptolemy developed their astronomy within Aristotle's framework which placed the earth as the center of the universe around which the sun, moon, and planets revolve. During the Dark Ages, the flame of secular learning flickered near extinction, but in the treatises of Boethius—a Roman noble and Christian martyr—the light of Aristotle illuminated the medieval mind of western Europe.

Between A.D. 1200 and 1225 the complete works of Aristotle were recovered and translated into Latin, opening up a new world to the medieval mind. During this century Thomas Aquinas (A.D. 1225-1274) synthesized Aristotelian natural philosophy with Christian theology.[4] In his great works, *Summa Philosophica contra Gentiles* and *Summa Theologica,* Aquinas showed that philosophy and theology, human reason and divine revelation, must be compatible. While he thought the existence of God can be demonstrated by reason, biblical doctrines such as the Trinity and Incarnation, for example, are to be received by faith. Aquinas developed his system within Aristotle's philosophical framework in which logic professes to give rigorous proof from accepted premises. This method supported the idea of knowledge derived by reason from intuitive axioms and ecclesiastical authority. Such a method is hardly conducive to the free investigation of nature![5]

Scholastic philosophy reached its greatest strength under Aquinas, although its influence waned in the fourteenth century with the rise of nominalism. During the Renaissance, however, the alliance between Aristotelianism and theology gained strength. With science, philosophy, and theology welded into one system, any questioning of Aristotle could be construed as an attack upon the church. This marriage of Aristotelian natural philosophy and Christian theology, harmonious as it was at the start, set the stage for the domestic quarrels of the seventeenth century and produced problem children who reacted strongly against their home environment. It also demonstrated that a theology which marries the philosophy of one era is likely to become a widow in the next.

The Middle Ages, having provided the seed-bed for the growth of modern thought, gave way to the Renaissance and

Reformation. During the early fifteenth century, many competent teachers from the Mideast brought their manuscripts with them to the West; thus humanism, the study of these "humane letters," spread throughout Europe. The sixteenth century also witnessed political and religious revolution. The Reformation, started in 1517 when Martin Luther nailed his 95 theses to the church door in Wittenburg, soon spread through northern Europe. Old centers of authority were breaking up as a new world was opening. In this context of the Renaissance and the disruption of Western Christianity, the scientific revolution took place.

copernicus and kepler

Throughout the 150-year period from Copernicus to Newton, major controversy concerned the nature of motion, a problem that had baffled many of the finest minds for two millenia.[6] According to Aristotle, all bodies tend naturally to travel toward the center of the universe, which he understood to be the earth. Other motion, considered "unnatural," is caused by a continuing force necessary to sustain it; hence the concept of an original Prime Mover. Astronomers Copernicus and Kepler investigated the motion of the heavenly bodies, Galileo studied the movement of smaller objects on the earth, and Newton synthesized the phenomena of celestial and terrestrial motion in one mathematical explanation. The work of these men not only radically altered our concept of motion and the structure of the universe, but it also played a major role in developing the modern scientific approach to nature.

Nicolaus Koppernigk[7] (1473-1543) was born of a Polish father and German mother who Latinized his name as Copernicus. In 1496 he went to Italy as a student of mathematics and astronomy. At that time the accepted Ptolemaic theory considered the sun and planets to revolve around the earth. This system required 80 wheels (cycles and epicycles) to describe the planetary motions since their orbits were assumed to be circular.[8] As a keen mathematician, Copernicus had difficulty accepting such a complicated arrangement.[9] Using Ptolemy's own principle of the simplest geometrical scheme, he tried to simplify the diagram. In his study of ancient Greek writings he came upon the heliocentric idea. By placing the sun in the center, with the planets including the earth revolving around it, Copernicus reduced the number of wheels to 34. When Pope Clement VII heard about this work, he requested the astronomer, an active member of the Catholic Church, to publish it in full. In 1543 Copernicus finally completed his book, *Concerning the Revolutions of the Celestial Spheres,* which he dedicated to Pope Paul III. This new theory, contravening 2,000 years of astronomical tradition, made a major break with the entire system of Aristotle, for whom the earth was the center of the scientific, philosophical, and religious universe.

Copernicus was not a great observer of nature, nor did he work with data unknown to his predecessors. His great achievement was to arrange the pieces of the puzzle already at hand into a different picture, one with greater mathematical economy and symmetry.[10] As a geometer, he was convinced that the key to the universe is number, so that what is mathematically true is really true in astronomy. He held to his theory even though he could not adequately answer the objections it raised; significantly most of the scholars who supported it during the rest of the sixteenth century were mathematicians. Copernicus both closes an old epoch and opens a new one. The importance of his influence lies not so much in the actual system he produced as the stimulus he gave to other men. Furthermore, his interpretation of the data marked a significant step away from a common sense understanding of nature toward the abstract description of reality so characteristic of modern science. Thus while our eyes tell us that the sun moves, mathematics assures us that it is really the earth which moves around the sun.

Johannes Kepler (1571-1630) also formed a link between the old and new eras. A Protestant, he studied at Tübingen where he became convinced that the Copernican hypothesis was correct. His contribution to mathematics, which prepared the way for the calculus of Newton and Leibnitz, alone would have insured his fame. In 1600 Kepler became the assistant to Tycho Brahe of Copenhagen, the greatest observational astronomer since Hipparchus. A year later Brahe's sudden death left his "chaos of data" to which Kepler added mathematical genius. Convinced that God had created the world in accordance with the principle of perfect numbers, he passionately sought to discover the mathematical harmonies of nature. Kepler combined this approach with the insistence that every hypothesis be exactly verified through observation, since he was also greatly concerned with physical (efficient) causality.

Kepler approached the immense collection of observations with the Aristotelian conviction which had gripped the astronomical mind for almost 2,000 years: Planets must move in perfect circles. But this theory would not fit the data. After laboriously trying other hypotheses, Kepler finally demonstrated Mars' orbit to be an ellipse.[11] This discovery led to the first of his three planetary laws which summarized a vast amount of data and to this day remain an elegant statement of mathematical truth. It also made another radical break in Aristotle's system of natural philosophy. Kepler interpreted causality in terms of mathematical simplicity and harmony. This harmony discoverable from the observed facts is sufficient scientific explanation, and the idea of a final cause involving the purpose of the phenomenon is superfluous. Kepler characterized his research as "thinking God's thoughts after him;" a mystical urge impelled this great scientist to reduce the universe to mechanical law in order to show God's consistency.

galileo and newton

Galileo Galilei (1564-1642), born at Pisa, entered the university and became professor of mathematics at the age of twenty-five. While his astronomical observation with the newly-invented telescope confirmed the Copernican hypothesis, Galileo turned his attention to the motions of smaller bodies in daily experience. His mathematical genius gave birth to the new science of terrestrial dynamics.

Galileo set out to solve the problem of acceleration by exact mathematical description. Abandoning the idea of final causality, the *ultimate why*, he concentrated on the *immediate how* as the principle of scientific explanation. Galileo had no confidence in observation he could not explain theoretically; for him the book of nature was written in the language of mathematics. Galileo is often considered the father of modern scientific method because of his combined use of mathematical analysis and experimental data. Experimenting with bodies rolling down an inclined plane, Galileo finally reversed Aristotle's teaching that heavier objects fall faster and formuated his law that the distance any body falls increases as the square of the time. He also overturned Aristotle by discovering that not motion itself, but a change in motion, requires a force.

For a while Galileo had the support of high church leaders in Rome. But eventually the implications of his research ran completely counter to his scientific Aristotelian colleagues at the University of Padua, who had a vested interest in the status quo. Galileo published his ideas in the Italian vernacular in *Dialogue Concerning the Two Chief World Systems,* a writing remarkable for its polemical scorn and literary skill. These controversial dialogues were used by his scientific opponents to bring Galileo before the Inquisition which condemned him to prison, although Pope Urban remitted the sentence.

Galileo's clash with the church still ranks for many as the epitome of science's fight for freedom from the toils of religion. He is pictured as a brave martyr suffering the persecution of religious dogmatism. But this version, still enjoying widespread popularity, is actually a rationalist myth spawned in the last century. Historical research has shown that Galileo's conflict was not with the biblical revelation but with Aristotelian natural philosophy defended by scholasticism. Both he and his adversaries were in the Roman Catholic church, which had experienced much greater controversy in the Reformation. Further, Galileo and his opponents were scientists in the universities of their day, and every generation has witnessed conflict among scientists tinged with elements of pride, ambition, and prejudice common to man.

Far from being a simple struggle of science against Christianity, it was a revolt of the new scientists against the old Aristotelian system synthesized with scholastic theology. Proponents of the latter used the authority of the church in an attempt to maintain the status quo and their own positions of
power. While the Inquisition's action was deplorable, Whitehead
reminds us, "In a generation which saw the Thirty Years' War
and remembered Alva in the Netherlands, the worst that happened to men of science was that Galileo suffered an honour-
able detention and a mild reproof before dying peacefully in his
bed."[12] We should also note that Galileo's conflict with religious authority was not typical of Europe. In England, for
example, there was no such struggle. Francis Bacon was Lord
Keeper of the Great Seal to Queen Elizabeth when he published
his *Novum Organum* in 1620, while at the end of that century
Queen Anne knighted Isaac Newton and appointed him Master
of the Mint.

Following Galileo, other important discoveries prepared the
way for the final solution of the problem of motion. By the
1660s the harvest was ripe, but it required an outstanding
genius to reap it. Isaac Newton (1642-1727) proved to be that
genius. He studied at Cambridge University, where he became a
Fellow in 1665. A superb mathematician, Newton assigned
mathematics the central place in natural science but with a deep
appreciation of the empirical and experimental. In 1665-66 he
began to think about the earth's gravity extending as far as the
moon and providing the force necessary to keep the moon from
moving away in a straight line. He discovered that the planets
observe Kepler's three laws if they are drawn toward the sun by
a force inversely proportional to the square of their distance
from the sun. Comparing a stone whirling in a sling and the
moon revolving around the earth, Newton found the two motions explainable by the same formula.

His law of gravitation which reduced the major phenomena
of the universe to a single mathematical statement ranks as one
of the greatest achievements of the human mind. The whole

intricate motion of the solar system could now be worked out from the one assumption that the attraction between any two bodies is proportional to the product of their masses and inversely proportional to the square of the distance between them. Dissatisfied with certain points, Newton put away his work for two decades. In 1687 he published refined calculations in his epochal *Principia Mathematica,* which presented in his three laws of motion the solution to a problem that had challenged the best minds for 2,000 years.[13]

Newton never considered his scientific research and discoveries to be at odds with biblical revelation and his Christian faith. He wrote almost as many theological treatises as scientific classics, never doubting God's existence and control over nature. Although the scientific and religious are fundamentally different interpretations of the universe, Newton held that in the last analysis the scientist and his work are dependent upon God.

Newton's research culminated the scientific revolution of the sixteenth and seventeenth centuries which provided the alternative scientific system to Aristotle and laid the foundation for modern science. From it emerged the concept of scientific explanation of natural phenomena free from philosophical and religious considerations. While the struggle often pitted new ideas against philosophical and religious dogmatism, it was not the simple battle between Christianity and science so often pictured; rather the new men of science were rebelling against the authority of Aristotelian natural philosophy wedded to scholastic theology.

Although medieval thought often obstructed the new science, it also provided the context in which modern science developed. The transition was marked by a complex mixture of both continuity and discontinuity with ancient Greek thought. Furthermore, the scientific revolution of the sixteenth and seventeenth centuries fails to demonstrate inherent conflict between a Christian world view and scientific progress. The modern scientific movement developed in a culture stamped by the biblical revelation of a God who is personal, rational, and unchanging. Not only Copernicus, Kepler, Galileo, and Newton, but also other great scientists of this era, worked within the thought structure of an orderly world produced by this God. Only later, under the influence of rationalistic and materialistic philosophy in the eighteenth and nineteenth centuries, was modern science largely cut off from its Christian heritage and made to appear antagonistic to Christianity.

from newton to einstein

The preceding discussion of the scientific revolution concentrated on the problem of motion in astronomy and physics in order to demonstrate the emergence of the modern scientific method. But this "century of genius" (as Whitehead describes it) witnessed marked progress in other realms of natural science as well as in mathematics and philosophy. Francis Bacon, Harvey, Boyle, Pascal, Huyghens, Descartes, Leibnitz, Locke, and Spinoza are but a few of the great thinkers who shaped the new scientific era.

The contributions of Robert Boyle (1627-1691)to the structure of matter, especially his discussion of what constituted a chemical element, laid the foundations of modern chemistry, although it required another century to erect the full structure of the science of chemistry. William Harvey (1578-1637), stimulated by the physiologists at the University of Padua, advanced the cause of biology not merely by dissection and discussion, but also by clinical observation and actual experiment which produced his revolutionary discovery of the circulation of the blood within the body. John Ray (1627-1705) published a series of works on systematic botany and also made a significant contribution to comparative anatomy. Meanwhile, other scholars were rapidly pushing back the frontiers of knowledge at a variety of points.

While this essay cannot possibly describe the scientific progress of the following two centuries, several major developments should be noted briefly before concluding with a summary of modern scientific method with its strengths and limitations. Toward the end of the seventeenth century, an equally important literary movement molded a new view of life and the universe. The French writer Fontenelle made the discoveries of science intelligible and amusing to the general reading public. These discoveries were translated into a new world view, not by scientists themselves, but by the followers of Fontenelle. While eighteenth-century science made progress on many fronts, especially in chemistry, the intellectual leadership of Europe was grasped by this influential group of French writers. Newton's French disciples taught that the Newtonian system demonstrated reality as a great machine so that man, body and soul, became part of a mechanical necessity. Science was thus made to substantiate deterministic and materialistic philosophies. This movement also transposed the scientific methodical doubt of Descartes into an ordinary unbelieving attitude, the very kind of skepticism which he had tried to guard against but which remains so popular today.[14]

The eighteenth century also brought the revolutionary concept of progress and evolution. The immutability of nature gave place to a view of the universe itself possessing a history existing in time as well as space. Thus science and history combined to present the idea that all nature is advancing slowly but persistently from some origin. This concept set the stage for the development of geology and paleontology during the first half of the nineteenth century.[15] Then in 1859, Darwin's *Origin of Species* launched not only the theory of organic evolution but also a new conflict between certain scientists and theologians reminiscent of Galileo's struggle three centuries earlier. This conflict, which cannot be dealt with here, repeated the pattern of seventeenth-century resistance to scientific advance on philosophical and religious grounds and eighteenth-century misuse of science to attack Christianity.[16]

The twentieth century has witnessed an equally profound revolution, not in scientific method, but in our understanding of the nature of scientific laws or theories. This revolution, initially effected by theoretical and experimental physics at the subatomic level, has been augmented by linguistic analysis in philosophy and a radical reappraisal of the nature of mathematics. While Newtonian physics reigned supreme for two and a half centuries, its ultimate inability to explain the experimental data led to the invention of quantum physics and relativity pioneered by Albert Einstein in the early decades of our own century.[17] Quantum theory especially refused to fit in with the old concept of scientific laws and stimulated a redefinition of their relationship to the natural world. The modern concept of the nature of scientific theories has made most of the nineteenth-century objections to theism inapplicable.[18]

modern scientific method

This brief study of the work of four great thinkers in the sixteenth and seventeenth centuries has identified the essential characteristics of the method now utilized by the natural sciences. Based on conceptual logic and the fit between theory and data, this method employs mathematics as its prime tool. The scientist measures and quantifies in his search for a mathematical explanation of phenomena which correlates them and makes prediction possible.

Copernicus used the principle of economy to produce a simpler explanation of the celestial data. In doing so, he moved from the realm of common sense observation (I see the sun setting) to abstract explanation (the earth rotates so that the sun only appears to set). Kepler insisted that a scientific theory be tested by the data. He interpreted causality in terms of mathematical harmony, discoverable from the observed facts and sufficient as scientific explanation. Galileo also abandoned the idea of a final cause, the ultimate why of the phenomena, and concentrated on the immediate how as the the principle of scientific explanation. As a corollary to Kepler, he had no confidence in observed data he could not explain theoretically. Newton also assigned mathematics the central place in natural science, but with a corresponding deep appreciation of experimental data and the empirical approach to phenomena.

Combining methods of mathematical analysis and experiment, the scientific method as developed by Galileo isolates the phenomena to be studied, produces a mathematical analysis or demonstration, and verifies it by experiment. Newton followed essentially the same procedure, beginning and ending with experimentation. His scientific method oscillates between mathematical theory and empirical data.

How, then, are scientific principles discovered? To this question involving the genius of insight and invention there is no simple answer. Butterfield highlights the ability to perceive the same data in a new pattern. Hanson argues that scientific discovery comes neither from pure deduction nor induction, but through the process of retroduction which suggests that something *may be.*[19] Historically new theories have come in a variety of ways. Archimedes suddenly discovered his principle of liquid displacement during a bath. Kepler labored over his data like a man possessed until he saw the planetary orbit as an ellipse. In his interaction with the data a scientist gains an insight or grasps a pattern which may provide these data new structure and intelligibility. Yet by whatever means he may make such a discovery, the scientist gives his hypothesis mathematical formulation and tests it by experiment. Verification of such a hypothesis, however conceived, yields a scientific theory or law which serves as an explanation of the natural phenomena until a more adequate or even revolutionary theory replaces it.

The modern scientific approach to nature has four significant characteristics frequently unrecognized. First, its main tool, mathematics, produces an abstract explanation of reality often at odds with a common sense view. Second, it has divorced itself from philosophy and theology as disciplines. Third, as a consequence, it represents only a partial view of reality, effective as this view may be for its own purposes. Finally, the scientific method yields not final truth but provisional insights or understanding of the natural world always subject to change.

While the scientific method endeavors to explain the experience of our senses in the world, it does so in abstract terms which move away from common sense explanation. Thus the Copernican hypothesis asserts that the earth (which appears stationary) moves around the sun (which we see moving). While the nineteenth century emphasized mechanical models as literal representations of reality, modern scientific theory discourages visualization of phenomena, such as electrons, even though mechanical models are still used as preliminary and oversimplified depictions of natural forces. Seeing is no longer believing. Viewing a blazing sunset, we see a red ball slowly disappearing below the horizon. But on three counts modern science tells us we are wrong. Not the sun but the earth is moving; the sun's light is not really red but white; furthermore, the sun is not actually at the horizon but is already below it since the light we see left the sun about eight minutes ago. And we are quite happy to believe this explanation which contradicts our senses!

Also we must recognize that science, where it is true to its historical genius, no longer concerns itself directly with questions of philosophy and theology. Not for a moment, however, does this mean that science has no philosophical or religious presuppositions. Like all disciplines, the scientific method must start with assumptions. Several basic presuppositions are the reality of the natural world, its rationality or consistency, and its understandability—at least in part. The validity of sense perception (in reading a gauge, for example) and the basic rules of logic are also assumed. Furthermore, one ethical or moral presupposition is also held to be essential: honesty in reporting the experimental data. The "fudge factor" sometimes used by students in elementary laboratory courses is not acceptable. Nevertheless, the scientific method doesn't deal with or produce answers to questions of purpose, value, and meaning. To illustrate this point Henry Margenau observes: "Science will tell us what things are real but will refuse to say what is *reality*. . . . One can practice science without ever using the word *real;* indeed, as a rule, the less said about reality, the better the quality of the science." [20] Margenau affirms the presence of metaphysical elements and assumptions in any science; yet competent physicists can hold widely differing philosophical and religious positions.

As a consequence, the scientific approach to nature provides only a partial view of reality, contrary to the popular idea propounded by many scientists that it is the best or only valid explanation of the natural world. Science looks at nature's forces and phenomena through a mathematical lens and so sees them in terms of formulas. But we have other equally valid perspectives on reality. Consider four men standing on a hilltop surveying the countryside bathed in late afternoon sunlight. All are *looking at* the same scene, but each *sees* something different and represents it in his own medium. Physicist Einstein describes the relative motion of sun and earth scientifically in mathematical formulas. Beethoven, the musican, writes his *Pastoral Symphony*. Artist Gauguin paints the glories of the sunset in richly varied hues, while the psalmist David writes, "The heavens declare the glory of God, and the firmament shows his handiwork." Here are four ways of describing the same scene, each magnificent and meaningful in its own terms from its particular perspective, all enriching our understanding of the natural world. While Einstein's formulas are required to land a man on the moon, would we not prefer a Gauguin over the mantlepiece in our living room?

Finally, the scientific method yields provisional, not final, understanding of the natural world. Through measurement and mathematical analysis, science develops theories or laws to explain the forces of nature. These formulations, representing our best understanding at present, are always subject to revision or rejection. Scientific theories are effective tools, subject to sharpening or replacement, which may be used for good or evil. The glory of science lies in its constant pilgrimage, always traveling but never arriving at final or absolute truth. Karl Popper writes, "Science never pursues the illusory aim of making its answers final, or even probable. Its advance is, rather, towards the infinite yet attainable aim of ever discovering new, deeper, and more general problems, and of subjecting its ever tentative answers to ever renewed and ever more rigorous tests."[21]

nature of scientific theories

During the nineteenth century, the scientific method became absolutized in the minds of many scholars. Having freed itself from philosophy and theology, science tended to usurp the prerogatives of these disciplines. In the twentieth century, how-

ever, developments in science, philosophy, and the political up-
heavals of our age have forced a re-evaluation of the role of
science in modern life. During the last hundred years, three
major views of the nature of scientific theories or laws have
been prominent: literal, instrumental, and a mediating position
viewing them as models.

Nineteenth-century science absolutized Newton's laws to
make the universe a giant machine running smoothly and pre-
dictably according to built-in mechanical laws. Newtonian
mechanics became the ultimate system giving *the* true picture of
the world as it really is. On this view a scientific law corresponds to physical reality much the way a blueprint describes a
machine, or the way a science laboratory atomic model of
tennis balls and marbles pictures neutrons and electrons. In
other words, a scientific law literally describes things as they
actually exist. This literalistic view, still widely held by the
popular mind, was questioned as early as 1889 by Ernst Mach.
But his voice crying in the wilderness was echoed only after the
turn of the century in the instrumental view.

This view holds that a scientific theory is not a genuine assertion about the nature of the world; rather it is an instrument or
convention or definition which simply correlates the data and
predicts phenomena. Thus Watson states, "What we have called
the laws of nature are the laws of our methods of representing
it."[22] What, then, is an electron? Certainly not the infinitesimal
marble depicted by the literal view. The electron is simply a
name, a useful term for something whose effects we measure. If
we suppose "electrons" to be active in a black box impenetrable
to our view, we can measure the energy input and the effects of
the resulting activity, but our theories tell us nothing about
what is actually happening in this box, nor do they need to. So
it is meaningless to talk about an electron itself apart from our
mathematical equations. In recent decades this instrumental
view has become less widely held.

A mediating position between the literal and instrumental
views regards scientific theory as a model or a map which does
tell us something about the nature of reality, even though it is

not a literal description. A model gives a partial view which highlights certain features of interest so they can be studied more easily. The model (usually mathematical or logical and not mechanical) is determined by the forces it explains and so tells something about them. According to Margenau, science tells us that an electron is real (contrary to instrumentalism), but it does not tell us what an electron really is (contrary to literalism).

Toulmin prefers the metaphor of a map.[23] Different kinds of maps describe the same territory: highway, topographical, economic, sociological, etc. Each map tells us something about the terrain without being a literal description. For example, the road map locates a highway with a red line. This line indicates the direction and curves of the highway, but not its color—the highway itself isn't red. The map depicts the towns as circles; but while the towns are at those places, their shape is not circular. The map is not the terrain, but is so related to it that we can find our way around.

Whether model or map, this concept of scientific theories is both satisfying and useful. As a partial view of reality a scientific law explains the phenomena, satisfying our desire to understand more about the natural world, and proves useful in stimulating further research. So different is this modern concept of scientific laws from the prevailing nineteenth-century view that Mascall writes, "Far more important than any revolution in scientific theories themselves is the revolution in what a scientific theory is."[24]

summary

This brief historical survey has sketched the interrelationship of science with philosophy and theology during the scientific revolution of the sixteenth and seventeenth centuries. In the struggles of this era, the new science was frequently opposed by contemporary scholars on theological as well as philosophical grounds, although pioneers such as Copernicus, Kepler, Galileo, and Newton worked within the structure of a Christian world-and-life view. But the very success of modern science in explaining natural phenomena led to its deification in the nineteenth century. Scientism has now become a modern religion whose devotees claim the potential, given enough time, to solve all human problems. Yet insofar as science attempts to answer ultimate questions of meaning, value, and purpose, it proves untrue to its genius and heritage.

As we face the pressing problems of our age, let us fully value the scientific method for what it can produce. But let us also recognize that as a partial view of reality, science by its very nature cannot solve our deepest human problems. Its results must be guided by an ethic and morality whose source is elsewhere. Since the popular mind is slow to relinquish myths, we must constantly reaffirm that science itself can never guide the use of its achievements. For example, science gives us atomic power; but do we use it to generate electricity or to annihilate our fellow men? Modern technology can land men on the moon; but should the billions of dollars be spent instead to relieve human misery in our large cities? We can produce the supersonic transport; but is the noise cost to millions of people worth the price of faster air travel?

Clearly science and technology must by guided and controlled by human values. Thus Ferry argues: "There is a growing list of things we *can* do [but] that we *must not* do. My view is that toxic and tonic potentialities are mingled in technology and that our most challenging task is to sort them out. . . . What is needed is a firm grasp on the technology itself, and an equally clear conviction of the primacy of men, women and children in all our calculations."[25] Man must look beyond modern scientific method for the ethical and moral guidelines to exercise this control.

But where do we turn for this guidance? We discover it in history, in the self-revelation of God as Creator and Redeemer, the Lord of both nature and human history. "In many and various ways God spoke of old to our fathers by the prophets; but in these last days he has spoken to us by a Son, whom he appointed the heir of all things, through whom also he created the world" (Heb. 1:1-2). This statement summarizes the Old and New Testament revelation of God whose acts of judgment and mercy culminated in the coming of Jesus Christ. Here we find our answers to the deepest human questions of meaning, value, and purpose in life. While chemistry depicts man as a complex of compounds and biology describes him as an animal organism in a population, the Bible represents man uniquely created in the image of God, that image defaced through sin but restorable in Jesus Christ. In Christ, man experiences full reality and from him gains both the perspective and motivation to use the results of science for the glory of God and the good of his fellow men. Christian men of science and technology thus have the insight and moral responsibility, both professionally and as citizens, to work for the primacy of human values so that science can indeed be a good servant rather than the power that will eventually destroy us.

Notes

[1] Wilbur H. Ferry, "Must We Rewrite the Constitution?" *Saturday Review*, 2 Mar. 1968, p. 50. Ferry's analysis is perceptive and his title dramatizes the magnitude of the crisis, although his solution might well create more problems than it solves.

[2] William C. Dampier, *History of Science*, 4th ed. (Cambridge, England, 1961), pp. 14 ff. This history of science related to philosophy and religion is comprehensive and readable. Recent research, however, renders this volume no longer authoritative in many areas.

[3] Frederick Copleston, *History of Philosophy*, I (London, 1961), pp. 266 ff. This comprehensive survey is both lucid and thorough.

[4] Copleston, *History*, II (London, 1964), pp. 302 ff.

[5] Alan Richardson, *Bible in the Age of Science* (London, 1961), pp. 11 ff. This first chapter presents a brief and readable account of the scientific revolution.

[6] Herbert Butterfield, *Origins of Modern Science, 1300-1800* (London, 1962). Chapter 1 describes the problem of motion at the outset of the scientific revolution and its place in this great period of discovery.

[7] Copleston, *History*, III (London, 1963), pp. 282 ff.

[8] While the planetary orbits are ellipses, they can be represented as circular by this much more complicated arrangement.

[9] Butterfield, chap. 2. The author treats fascinatingly the way in which Copernicus came to see the same data in a radically new pattern or model.

[10] Edwin A. Burtt, *Metaphysical Foundations of Modern Physical Science* (London, 1932), p. 35. Chapter II, "Copernicus and Kepler," demonstrates the role of mathematics and the emergence of the new metaphysics and scientific method.

[11] Norwood R. Hanson, *Patterns of Discovery* (Cambridge, England, 1961), pp. 72 ff. This detailed description of Kepler's calculations illustrates scientific discovery by "retroduction" rather than by simple deduction or induction.

[12] Alfred N. Whitehead, *Science and the Modern World* (New York, 1925), p. 2.

[13] A. Rupert Hall, *From Galileo to Newton 1630-1720* (New York, 1963) provides an excellent survey of seventeenth-century science. Thomas S. Kuhn, *Structure of Scientific Revolutions* (Chicago, 1962) is essential to understanding properly the scientific revolution.

[14] Butterfield describes this movement in chapter 9 and the emerging ideas of progress in chapter 12.

[15] Charles C. Gillispie, *Genesis and Geology* (New York, 1959) traces the development of geology and paleontology during the first half of the eighteenth century.

[16] John C. Greene, *Darwin and the Modern World View* (New York, 1963) explores the impact of Darwin's evolutionary biology on the religious and intellectual thought of the last century. Jan Lever, *Creation and Evolution* (Grand Rapids, 1958) perceptively describes the modern scientific and biblical descriptions of the origin and types of life. A recent volume by Ian G. Barbour, *Issues in Science and Religion* (Englewood Cliffs, 1966), sets forth the history and methods of science and religion, then deals with four basic issues. See chapters 4 and 12 on creation and evolution.

[17] Lincoln Barnett, *Universe and Dr. Einstein* (New York, 1957) lucidly describes for the layman Einstein's work in quantum physics and relativity.

[18] Eric L. Mascall, *Christian Theology and Natural Science* (London, 1956). Chapter 2, "Nature of Scientific Theories," provides an excellent study of this subject which is reviewed briefly at the end of the next section.

[19] Hanson, p. 85. Hanson traces this concept of "abduction" or "retroduction" to Aristotle and quotes Charles Peirce: "Deduction proves that something *must be;* induction shows that something *actually is* operative; abduction merely suggests that something may be." See also pp. 216 ff.

[20] Henry Margenau, *Nature of Physical Reality* (New York, 1950), p. 12. A lucid though somewhat mathematically technical philosophy of modern physics.

[21] Karl R. Popper, *Logic of Scientific Discovery* (New York, 1961), p. 281. David Dye ably describes the scientific method and assumptions in *Faith and the Physical World* (Grand Rapids, 1966), pp. 19 ff.

[22] William H. Watson, *Understanding Physics Today* (Cambridge, England, 1963), p. 52. Likewise Bridgman asserts, "From the point of view of operations, light means nothing more than *things* lighted" [*Logic of Modern Physics* (New York, 1960), p. 151]. Operationalism holds that a scientific concept is simply synonymous with the operations by which its measurement is defined.

[23] Stephen Toulmin, "Theories and Maps," *Philosophy of Science* (New York, 1960), pp. 105 ff.

[24] Mascall, p. 76. Hanson, pp. 99 ff. discusses five uses of scientific theories. See also his Chapter 4, "Theories," pp. 70 ff.

[25] Ferry, pp. 50, 52.

J. Frank Cassel

Biology

For me, the last lecture of a course is always a race with the
final bell. I finished discussing the evidences of evolution and
began to summarize—
  "In living organisms similarity of phenotype reflects similarity of genotype—a similar DNA code. We have found that
each individual is the readout of a code normally formed by the
combination of half of the genetic material from each parent.
This material is passed continuously from parent to offspring
(continuity of germ plasm).
  "In our study of population genetics, we found how differences in the code may arise in population. But what of basic
similarities? Is it simply that no changes have taken place in
ancestral generations? Some basically quite different animals
have striking similarities. The body form of *Ichthysauris* (the
swimming reptile of the Cretaceous), sharks, and porpoises is a
good example. Animals of three different classes are adapted to
a common habitat—the ocean.
  "Every day we draw still other conclusions from certain similarities. When my wife and I go into a china shop, I can see a
difference between saucers, salad plates, luncheon plates, dinner

plates, and platters, and I can usually tell which go together by the similarity of their decorations and by the way the shopkeeper has arranged the display. My wife, better versed than I, gets even more pleasure from our visit as she recognizes Wedgewood and Franciscan and Spode.

"Similarities in organisms may, then, be interpreted in at least three ways:

They may indicate a certain genetic code passed on by
the organism's ancestors.

They may indicate adaptation to similar environment.

They may indicate a basic design.

These interpretations, representing different levels of reasoning, may all be true for any particular species. They are not mutually exclusive.

"At yet another level, you may wish to assume that a design demands a designer. To say that such an assumption is not biological (that is, scientific) does not make it invalid.

"What you personally do with these ideas depends upon many facets of your background—upon your whole frame of reference. Consideration of a designer is beyond the scope of this course, but the existence of a designer—of God—is not negated by the data."

The bell rang! With their usual sigh of relief, the students shuffled out of their last class in Zool 111: Principles of Zoology.

A girl paused in the press.

"Thank you, Doctor Cassel," she said. "Some of the kids have been worrying about taking zoology. I'll tell them they don't need to worry." And she was gone.

Puzzling over her remark, I have often wondered what she was trying to tell me. Can there be university students who won't take a course—a science course—because they fear its content? What reason might they have for such concern?

Implicit in education is an exchange of ideas. Ideas change people. Most of us look forward to such change. But some of our ideas are precious to us. We think of them as part of our authentic selves. We resist being changed and so hold bearers of new ideas as suspect—suspect not so much for their ideas as for the threat their ideas are to our security.

On the other hand, sound scholarship demands that we test all ideas. The idea of the university is, I think, to expose us to the universe of ideas so that we may have adequate data for our testing. Testing does not necessarily mean changing or discarding positions. It means asking many questions. It means assessing ideas carefully in relation to other ideas. It means discovering some questions may have no answers. It means finding answers to some questions not asked.

A student matures to the extent that he gains security in dealing with ideas. Security with ideas, I believe, leads to acceptance of persons presenting ideas. This should lead to self-acceptance and personal adjustment.

Yet most of us live in constant tension. Consistency and stability are not characteristics of our everyday experience. It seems that the more ideas we get, the fewer "resolutions" or satisfying answers we find.

Here, the Christian affirms, is where the gospel comes in. Jesus Christ brings "resolution" to our lives—makes us real persons. Our security rests in him rather than in ideas, in others, or in ourselves.

But those of us who have accepted the gospel—who call ourselves Christian because of our relationship to Christ—find that we are still living in tension. While some areas of our life seem more secure, others seem more fouled up than ever. Particularly in the realm of our intellectual life—of our scholarship, in the realm of ideas—the problems seem to be intensified. Christ's role in our lives, it seems, is not so much to resolve the tensions as to help us live with them.

The purpose of this essay is twofold. I wish to suggest some "resolutions" which have helped me, and to point out some areas of biology which seem to raise significant moral issues for man today.

the bible and science

In the face of modern science, it is difficult to remain forthrightly and satisfyingly biblical. Is any synthesis possible? On the one hand one hears:

The Bible is the inspired, inerrant, authoritative word of God.
The earth is six thousand years old.
On the fifth day, God made fish that swim in the water and birds that fly in the air. On the sixth day he made cattle, and creeping things . . . and man.
Creation . . . after its kind.
The Bible is not a textbook of science.
There are no conflicts between science and the Bible.
In points of conflict, the Christian must choose the Bible.

On the other:

The Cambrian began five hundred million years ago.
Fish are first found in the Devonian, reptiles in the Permian, mammals in the Triassic, birds in the Jurassic.
Omnia viva ex vivo.
DNA
Mutation
Natural selection
Descent with modification
Synthesis of protoplasm

Evolution seems to present an area of great tension in any discussion of a biblical approach to biology.[1] Some who are of conservative biblical tradition hold evolution to be in direct conflict with the Bible. In fact, the national office of one Christian student organization once received a letter requesting that they state their position on evolution so that the writer would know if he could recommend them for support as a Christian organization.

The question as to the relationship between God and the universe is not new. Discussing it with the Colossians, the apostle Paul suggested, "Christ is both the first principle and the upholding principle of the whole scheme of creation." God is the focal point of any facet of knowledge—philosophy, sociology, mathematics, or biology.

What threat is posed when each new fact tells more of God? The universe is what it is because of God. Since God is the source of both the Bible and the world, there can be no real conflict when both the universe and the Bible are properly interpreted. But much is unknown. "How unsearchable are thy precepts, O Lord, and thy ways past finding out!"

Current understanding (interpretation) of the geological record does *not* seem to correspond directly to a "literal" interpretation of the first chapters of Genesis. But to modify any interpretation simply to match another would be either bad science or bad theology. On the other hand, unwillingness to modify the interpretations in the light of the results of continued scientific and biblical research is both bad science and bad theology. Hence, the thoughtful person respects present knowledge in both areas and keeps searching for new information and insight. In the meantime, he must reserve judgment, saying simply, "I don't know where the proper synthesis lies." The tension remains as the search continues.

biology as revelation

The most complex of created structures, the most intricate of machines, the most involved of systems are biological. Yet life eludes satisfactory description or definition. From the intricacy of DNA and the genetic system in the cell to the complexity of the interrelationships in the ecosystem as it harnesses the sun's energy, the grandeur of life staggers the mind of man. Man himself (and particularly his mind) is equally magnificent. The poet, I think, comes closer to understanding life and its implications than does the biologist. Gerard Manley Hopkins tried to express it in "The Windhover."[2]

> I caught this morning morning's minion, king-
>   dom of daylight's dauphin, dapple-dawn-drawn Falcon, in
>   his riding
> Of the rolling level underneath him steady air,

   and striding
High there, how he rung upon the rein of the wimpling wing
In his ecstasy! then off, off forth on swing,
   As a skate's heel sweeps smooth on a bow-bend: the hurl
      and gliding
   Rebuffed the big wind. My heart in hiding
Stirred for a bird,—the achieve of, the mastery of the thing!

Brute beauty and valour and act, oh, air, pride, plume, here
   Buckle! AND the fire that breaks from thee then, a billion
Times told lovelier, more dangerous, O my chevalier!
   No wonder of it: shéer plód makes plough down sillion
Shine, and blue-bleak embers, ah my dear,
   Fall, gall themselves, and gash gold-vermillion.

That he dedicated this poem "To Christ our Lord" seems particularly significant. Modern man has, I think, lost his awe of Nature. With it, he has lost something of his ability to worship. Can we postulate a lesser cause than God? Bowing before him in awe may not be "scientific," but it is certainly not irrational.

But the skeptic pities me in my ecstacy and worship. "What," he asks, "about cancer? Is your God a God of suffering? And what of war? Is God a God of evil, too? The God of the Establishment seems no God at all!" Can man blame God for his current plight? What is of God—and what of man? I cannot here deal with the philosophical and theological ramifications of such serious questions. On the other hand, several pressing problems of our existence and society have both biological and Christian bases and must be considered by concerned students.

life in the laboratory

Most beginning biology texts discuss the experiment by Miller (1953) which resulted in the production of amino acids when an electric spark was passed through a mixture of hydrogen, water, ammonia, and methane. Such experiments indicate that it may be possible, as we gain more knowledge of self-regulating, self-perpetuating systems, to synthesize living protoplasm.

Many students feel quite insecure about this possibility. They seem to feel that God will certainly stop us short of this achievement, with the tacit assumption that should we accomplish this feat we would be creators—gods with no further need of God. Actually, as we learn more of the nature of and the possibilities within the biological world, we are but probing more deeply into creation. When we synthesize a living system from non-living substances, we will only have discovered one way in which God may have achieved this step originally. (We shall never know through science how he actually did achieve it, for we cannot observe past historical events as they took place.)

We have perfected the technique of growing tissue under controlled conditions outside the organism. Recently, even mammalian embryos have been grown in much the same way. They can be maintained to quite an advanced stage.

Little is known of early human development. Much can be learned by raising a human embryo under controlled, observable conditions. What should be a Christian's attitude toward such experimentation? How is the fetus to be disposed of after the experimental work has been completed? Or if advanced technique allows full development, whose is this laboratory child? God is allowing us to discover a great deal about his universe. Is there a limit? If so, how may it be recognized?

The means and morality of restricting child bearing is an old issue. Do the same questions apply to increasing the possibilities? Modern techniques of artificial insemination are being applied to humans. Sperm can be stored for long periods of time. Should we establish sperm banks of sperm from men of high ability—labelled as to possible characteristics? Who may draw from such a bank?

Embryos can also be transplanted from one individual to another. Hence a woman in ill health could have her baby borne by a foster mother. Or a woman unable to conceive could receive an embryo transplant. What guidelines are available for assessing the morality of such practices?

Under public pressure, many legislative bodies have been considering "modernizing" their abortion laws. Abortion is closely related to birth control. In considering abortion, the same questions arise as those raised by experimenting with human embryos. At what point in his development does an individual become "man" in the biblical sense?

These are questions upon which we will all be asked to make decisions, upon which we will have to vote in the process of establishing some legal parameters. I, personally, see no clear biblical resolution to most of these questions. We need, I think, the considered and objective appraisal of each by biblical scholars as well as by biologists, psychologists, sociologists, and legislators.

disease and death

Physiological systems, elegant as they are, do not always work precisely. Sometimes organs fail to develop properly in the growing fetus. Often non-human organisms overpower the human. As Weisz (1966) says, "We can define disease as any structural or functional breakdown of steady-state controls, one form of a temporary unsteady state. Other still intact controls may then initiate self repair." Physiological response to disease, in fact, impresses us with the underlying provision of Nature.

Disease can also be diagnosed and treated. Drugs kill or control pathogenic organisms. Corrective surgery restores normal function. Electric shock and psychological therapy bring deviant minds into line. Natural systems may malfunction, but natural or man-initiated countermeasures also function as part of the sustaining principles of the universe.

Organ transplants are among the more recent therapeutic practices to raise moral issues. If the transplanted organ is rejected by the recipient and death ensues, who is responsible? If a possible "cure" in the form of a transplant, transfusion, or medicine is refused by the patient or his relatives, who is responsible? When is man playing God? When is God acting—or when are his acts being thwarted?

Recent research (Sonneborn, 1966) shows that corrective therapy is within our grasp at the chromosomal level. Continuing experiments hint that *directive* control is possible as well. Not only can the DNA molecule be manipulated to prevent "bad" effects, but also it can, perhaps, be manipulated to bring about "improvements"—more productive crops, tastier meat. Some have suggested the possibility of "better men." Will *you* serve on the committee to decide what is "better"? Or which individuals shall benefit? I am continually sobered by the potential of man's knowledge.

Suffering and death also are recognized in biological terms. The biological cannot be separated from the psychological. To the biologist, death (and any accompanying suffering) is part of the scheme of things—necessary to the intricate ecosystem through which the energy of the sun flows to all living things. Only plants can harness and convert this energy into food. The food produced is used not only by the plants but also by animals. Many of these in turn are food for other animals. Man is part of this food chain. Only seldom does he fall prey to predators. More often his body contributes energy to disease organisms. Upon his death, decomposers complete the cycle.

The whole of Nature is finely woven into the web of life made of many food chains. Each population continues as part of its community. Individuals from each population are utilized that the system may be perpetuated.

Suffering is a result of sensitivity to environmental pressures. Sensitivity is mandatory for the adjustment of individuals to stresses in their environment. Sometimes they achieve only partial adjustment. Then the stress continues and suffering ensues. Lack of sensitivity and the resultant lack of response might bring about the death of the individual because it cannot adjust.

the world we live in

Man is probably the most adjustable of organisms. Not only does he make personal adjustments, but he is also continually controlling his environment for his own benefit. He tills the land and plants seed genetically controlled so that he may harvest more seed with which to feed himself. He carefully husbands certain animals for the same purpose. He manages wild plants and animals for materials, food, and sport. From time to time he disturbs the dynamic balance of the system so much that he destroys it.

Many current problems, such as some of our devastating floods, indicate that man misuses his bounty. Some even question his right to use it at all. Certainly with our ever-increasing knowledge of our universe and our continually-improving technology comes greater and greater responsibility. Who can measure the value of our resources? At what cost can we use them? For what purposes?

Our most pressing challenge, many feel, is to meet the explosive increase in our human population. Space is limited. The productive potential of food organisms is limited. Does the answer lie in limiting the population before we out-produce our environment? Several biological means are available for limiting human productivity. Men differ on how these means should be applied within God's law. Certainly you must decide for yourself how you will face this crisis.

On the other hand, before his planned limitations take effect, man may find himself self-limiting. Not only does he have problems with wise use of resources, but he is finding more and more trouble disposing of his waste products. Some studies have indicated that more carbon dioxide is being introduced into our atmosphere than is being used in the process of photosynthesis. An increase in this imbalance might change the climate of the earth.

Other extraneous matter in the air threatens our health. So does foreign matter in our water. Industrial wastes have ruined many streams. Organic wastes from people and animals are altering many others. Besides making it difficult to get pure water for our uses, such wastes destroy or completely change the aquatic ecosystems. Even marine fish populations, a principle food source for many people, are in great danger of being reduced or destroyed.

To compound the problem, each growing season we employ many substances to kill weeds and insects. Few of these affect only those organisms toward which they are specifically directed. The residue further contaminates our world.

black and white
The turmoil in the United States over race issues is appalling. Distinction and therefore social discrimination between blacks and whites is based on color. Color depends upon the amount of pigment in the skin. Pigment in the skin is controlled by two sets of genes (four genes). Each gene which is "for pigment" adds a little more pigment. Four genes "for pigment" result in "black," no genes "for pigment" result in "white" with shades of brown (mulatto) in between. What a slim basis for hate!

Human populations show many similar variations: hair color, eye color, height, blood type—perhaps even intelligence. Neither the intelligent man nor the conscientious Christian finds a retreat in biology as a basis for racism. Biology will not excuse atrocity of man to man.

responsible citizenship and responsible christianity
Biology impinges on or raises many moral issues. Few clear-cut solutions are apparent. In ecological terms, man can control the world environment. In biblical terms, he is husbandman of the world. Through study of God's sustaining biological principles, man knows how his body and mind function. He knows how the ecosystem operates. He produces food, clothing, and shelter. He enjoys the pleasures of being part of God's universe. The power of his knowledge gives him an awesome responsibility—not only to himself, his brothers, his children, and his children's children—but to God himself.

To act responsibly, you need knowledge. That is why you study biology.[3]

Notes

[1] The following works which critically evaluate these areas are by a scientist (Kerkut), a theologian (Ramm), one who qualifies as both (Barbour), and by specialists in various fields (Bube, Jeeves, Mackay, and Mixter): Ian G. Barbour, *Issues in Science and Religion* (Englewood Cliffs, 1966); Richard Bube, ed., *Encounter between Christianity and Science* (Grand Rapids, 1968); Malcolm Jeeves, *Scientific Enterprise and Christian Faith* (Chicago, 1969); G. A. Kerkut, *Implications of Evolution* (New York, 1960); Donald M. Mackay, ed., *Christianity in a Mechanistic Universe* (London, 1965); S. L. Miller, "Production of Amino Acids under Possible Primitive Earth Conditions," *Science*, CXVII (1953), 528-29; Russell L. Mixter, ed., *Evolution and Christian Thought Today* (Grand Rapids, 1959); Bernard Ramm, *Christian View of Science and Scripture* (Grand Rapids, 1954); T. M. Sonneborn, ed., *Control of Human Heredity and Evolution* (New York, 1965); and Paul T. Weisz, *Science of Zoology* (New York, 1966). Periodical publications of the Creation Research Society, the American Scientific Affiliation, and the journal *Zygon* carry current papers along these lines.

[2] From *The Poems of Gerard Manley Hopkins*, eds., W. H. Gardner and N. H. MacKenzie, 4th ed. (New York, 1967), p. 69.

[3] While numerous individuals have given helpful suggestions in the preparation of this chapter, I wish particularly to acknowledge my debt to my college student sons, Jay and David, who, being exactly one student generation apart (four years), tried to tell it to me like it is.

George W. Andrews

Geology

The more flamboyant aspects of the conflict between geological science and the Christian religion reached the explosive stage in the latter half of the nineteenth century and gradually sputtered out in the first half of the twentieth century. But a fair amount of sniping still remains between some scientists and some Christians; this largely results from intemperate positions held by both parties. Two of the most important points of present-day contention concern the age of the earth and the evolution of life.

nature of geology

The science of geology consists of a body of information on the nature of the earth and some logically inferred premises on its origin and history. Geology had its origin in the speculations of the ancients, but the science as we know it today is largely the result of the sifting and winnowing of facts and theories during the last 175 years. Modern geology represents the consensus of a host of able thinkers. Although its details are constantly being refined in response to new information, the basic system of geologic thought has stood the test of much critical examination, and it is not likely to be overthrown by some completely new system. The relative ages of the rocks have been carefully and thoughtfully determined by the study of superposition of sedimentary rock strata (that is, in rocks deposited as sediments the lowermost is necessarily the oldest), and absolute age values have been determined by the decay of radioactive minerals in rocks. Although scientists are constantly making refinements in geologic dating, it is most improbable that radical changes will be made in the age of the earth or its rocks. The vast majority of geologists honestly seek to present the truth scrupulously as they understand it. The oft-repeated tale that there has been some grand conspiracy by geologists and their cohorts to discredit Christianity is a myth.

A certain amount of inference is healthy, and indeed necessary, for a science such as geology to move forward. The scientist, however, may become so enamored of his scientific method that he may infer more than he ought. *Science,* knowledge obtained and shown to be correct by accurate observation and thinking, is one thing; *scientism,* a belief that only scientific methods can fruitfully be used in the pursuit of knowledge and should be used in areas of investigation, is quite a different thing. Scientism resembles a religion. Its faith is based in the scientific method as the supreme revealer of truth just as in Christianity faith is based in God as the supreme revealer of truth.

evolutionism

Probably the most vocal sect in scientism is that of evolutionism. Here, again, we must distinguish between *evolution,* a series of related changes in a certain direction, particularly in organic development, and *evolutionism,* the adherence to or belief in evolution. Organic evolution is a theory of origin of living organisms which has largely been developed by biologists rather than geologists. However, biologists usually deal only with living things, and the fossil record provides much confirmatory evidence for evolution and gives historical verification to the biological theory. Evolution as a science is based on a body of fact which would be most difficult to refute. Evolutionism, on the other hand, as a faith may be legitimately questioned. Some evolutionists develop a religious fervor for the process of evolution that borders on fanaticism. In some of their writings one might conceivably strike out the word "evolution," substitute the word "God," and with a little imagination produce a tract plausibly defending Christianity. Such extreme positions have, of course, provoked response in kind from some Christians who feel strongly motivated to defend their faith. But the conflict here is not really between science and Christianity, but between two differing religious viewpoints. Perhaps one could say that the conflict lies between faith exclusively in human reason and faith exclusively in divine revelation.

Although science has its religious fantasies, it by no means holds a monopoly in exotic thinking. Defenders of Christianity have too often lapsed into absurdities which grossly violate both science and reason. One common fallacy among religious writers is to blame all the ills of the world—communism, materialism, anarchy, or what have you—on evolution. Organic evolution is a scientific theory of the development of life on earth and nothing more. Popular thinkers, particularly in the late nineteenth century, applied the tenets of organic evolution to the social situation. This probably served as only an excuse to justify unethical and dishonest business practices such as cutthroat competition and economic exploitation of the working classes and was not a valid application. The most casual examination of history does not even suggest that the world suffered a great proliferation of evil because of the discovery of organic evolution. It is reprehensible to blame all of the world's ills on evolution just because one does not agree with the religious viewpoints of some outspoken evolutionists.

deceptive arguments
Flood geology, another popular fallacy, reappears periodically in discussions of Christianity and geology. Flood geology holds that all of the sedimentary strata of the earth's crust were deposited during the Noachian deluge. It implies that the earth

is very young, and some of the theory's proponents would adhere to Archbishop James Ussher's date for the creation of the world in 4004 B.C. Flood geology began as a legitimate geologic theory to account for the origin of rock strata. However, as geology developed as a science, so much irrefutable evidence accumulated against it that the idea was discarded by reputable geologists well over a hundred years ago. This was before Darwin seriously raised the question of evolution in 1859 and long before the discovery of radioactive dating of rocks.

We cannot here pursue a lengthy argument against flood geology, but one example may suffice. There are about 30,000 feet of sedimentary rocks deposited in the Gulf Coast geosyncline in the southern United States. All of these rocks show evidence of deposition in shallow-water continental and marine environments similar to those found in the modern Mississippi River delta area. Yet the flood geologist must deposit these sediments in less than a year's time! Flood geology ignores or explains away the evidence of the radioactive dating of the earth's crust. As a theory, it lacks scientific merit and simply allows some Christian writers to justify their particular bias about the earth's age. Professional geologists hardly consider it worth discussing, feeling that it ought to be shunned by anyone seriously studying the earth's history.[1]

Some creationists use another perennial concept, the creation of the earth with an apparent but false age, to discount the great antiquity of the earth and the evolutionary development of life. This idea assumes the separate, instantaneous, divine creation of all organisms and, if this is so, then claims that they must have been created with an appearance of age. The reasoning continues that the earth also may have been created with the appearance of great age—perhaps in 4004 B.C. or even yesterday if men were created with divinely constituted memories! No one has yet satisfactorily explained what the purpose of Deity was in this enormously complicated deception. Why indeed should an omnipotent God degrade himself to create such a grand and superfluous lie? Apparent-age theories should be recognized for what the are—devices to reconcile scientific facts with a particular religious viewpoint. They represent a variety of specious reasoning and special pleading which serious students should reject.[2]

If we then repudiate the extreme positions of some scientists and some Christians with regard to the inter-relation of geology and Christianity, what basis can we make for peaceful coexistence? The scientific method of investigation, certainly valid and demonstrated in many ways to be a boon to civilization, does not necessarily hold a monopoly on truth. When one moves beyond the realm of scientific facts and begins to probe the purpose and cause of things, he enters into some form of religion even though he may not consider himself to be a religious person. The devoutly mechanistic evolutionist will vehemently deny any cause or purpose for organic life. Yet he must explain the fact that life exists in great complexity, and sometimes he attributes this to evolution with as much faith as a devout Christian attributes it to God. Clearly, science has extended itself beyond its rational limits when it attempts to answer questions of purpose and cause. Conceivably, the universe, the earth, and organic life may have come about only as the result of chance, but I think that this is highly unlikely.

the genesis account

The first chapters of the book of Genesis give an answer to the questions of cause and purpose which seem more satisfactory. In examining the Genesis account of creation, a student needs to look at the record objectively and divest himself of several millenia of ingrained traditional interpretation. It is useless to argue about the meaning and purpose of the six days of creation, for example, while ignoring the important and basic concepts set forth. The most striking and important fact of the creation account is that the universe, the earth, and organic life were created by a single Supreme Being. The cause is clearly defined, while a purpose is hinted at and developed elsewhere in the Bible. We learn that it was done and who did it, but we can infer very little as to how it was done. If we attempt to determine how the universe came about only on the basis of this account, we begin to trespass on ground that rightly belongs to science and we encounter great difficulties.

Perhaps at this point we could legitimately suggest a Christian cosmogony sympathetic with science.[3] A great deal of Christian writing on this subject tends to be anti-science, and most scientific writing ignores the Christian perspective. Reflection can rationally synthesize the two viewpoints. The astronomer, rather than the geologist, can better answer questions of the origin of the universe and the solar system. The Genesis account states only that God brought these systems into existence but does not elaborate on how they were created. One should study the theories of origin proposed by astronomers, but with the realization that they are subject to modification in line with new evidence.

We now understand that the earth is only a small planet in a universe whose limits are so vast that they have yet to be measured. The Genesis account of creation, on the other hand, centers on the earth, but this is indeed appropriate to its revelation to the ancients with their limited concepts of the nature of the universe. Perhaps this account was given as a revelation to an observer standing on earth. If so, it does at some points interestingly correlate with the scientific record.

The first stage that our hypothetical observer sees is that "the earth was without form and void, and darkness was upon the face of the deep" (Gen. 1:2). Geologists readily accede that the earth began its existence as a hot planet, the evidence being the high degree of volcanic and igneous activity shown by the oldest rocks. Temperatures almost certainly exceeded those necessary to boil off liquid water, and this would result in a dense cloud cover allowing no sunlight to penetrate to the earth's surface. Then, very early, the earth began to rotate—why, geology cannot say—and day and night were differentiated (Gen. 1:3-4). Perhaps as the result of some cooling of the earth, the cloud cover was diminished so that day and night could be detected by our observer.

The next event is the cooling of the earth to the point where liquid water could exist on the earth's surface but with the temperature still warm enough to produce an unbroken cloud cover (Gen. 1:6-8). The clouds now have risen from the surface, and ocean is distinctly separated from the cloud blanket. Scripture shows some insight into this stage of earth history with the query, "Who shut in the sea with doors, when it burst forth . . . ; when I made clouds its garment, and thick darkness its swaddling band . . . ?" (Job 38:8-9). Perhaps at this stage of earth history the planet was bathed in a universal ocean—geology has no certain evidence on this point—or perhaps it appeared so to our observer.

However, continents and ocean basins were clearly differentiated in the next act of creation: "And God said, 'Let the waters under the heavens be gathered together into one place, and let the dry land appear.' And it was so" (Gen. 1:9). "Hitherto shalt thou come, but no further: and here shall thy proud waves be stayed" (Job 38:11—KJV). The stage is now set for the origin of life, with land and sea differentiated and temperature extremes buffered by extensive oceans and an atmosphere rich in water vapor.

Genesis deals with organic life mainly in a categorical sense, but yet it does reflect some basic chronological truth. The first life recorded is that of plants—not only primitive plants, but also advanced types as well (Gen. 1:11-12). This may be a purely categorical grouping, or perhaps it hints that primitive plants had the potential for producing advanced types.

The next Genesis event appears at first glance to be out of place—the creation of the sun, moon and stars (Gen 1:14-18). This, however, must mean that these things appeared for the first time to our observer on the earth's surface. Probably at this stage in earth history, the cloud cover became broken to the extent that the heavenly bodies were visible. The creation of marine and flying animals separate from land animals in the account again reflects a more categorical than chronological treatment. Nevertheless, the account does indicate that plants existed before animals, and of course photosynthetic plants capable of food production must have preceded animal life.

Then, perhaps, if our observer were given a brief glimpse of geologic time, he would have been impressed with the predominant marine life of the Paleozoic and Mesozoic eras (570—65 million years ago) and then with the great proliferation of terrestrial mammalian life during the Cenozoic era (65 million years ago to present). We must honestly face the fact that, with all due respect to the Genesis creation account, it is not a textbook of geology. The main message of the record is that of creation by one all-powerful God. We can learn more about the history of creation by the examination of the geologic record.

conclusion

The conflict between divine creation and naturalistic evolution has, since the time of Darwin, generated more heat than light. It cannot be plumbed to any great depth here, but it does seem desirable to raise some questions about this controversy. Could not a Supreme Being, in his infinite wisdom, initiate life, sustain it, and change it through geologic time to produce present-day life? Life in its varied forms exists. Is it any less wonderful because it was produced by a God-directed evolution than by a fiat magical creation? Is it more reasonable to assume that life in its complexity was produced by a purposeless, mindless, directionless process of mechanistic evolution rather than by a divinely-driven progressive evolutionary creation? I shall spare the reader dogmatic answers and suggest that he ponder these things carefully.

Both geology and the Genesis record have their place in a reasoned discussion of earth history. Geology supplies the facts and interpretations as to how the earth originated. One cannot successfully dispute these facts and interpretations by religious arguments. Revealed religion, on the other hand, answers questions of the cause and purpose of things, and it cannot be legitimately disputed by scientific arguments. To reject geologic science on the basis of religious belief is unjustified, and the rejection of Christianity on the basis of geologic science is equally unjustified. Geology, restricted to its scientific aspects, compels no one to become a Christian; nor can it provide one with a valid excuse for not becoming a Christian. The basic question to face is, Did the universe, the earth, organic life, and man come about by mere chance? Science itself does not provide the answer, and consequently some scientists have drifted into atheism or agnosticism. It would seem at least as logical to accept the biblical claim that there is a cause for our existence on this earth, namely, a God. If, for the moment, we accept this working hypothesis, it might be worth our while to examine the nature of God as revealed in the Bible to learn something of the purpose of our existence.

Notes

[1] A modern version of flood geology can be found in John C. Whitcomb and Henry M. Morris, *Genesis Flood* (Philadelphia, 1961).

[2] For a contemporary account of the apparent-age theory see Whitcomb and Morris, pp. 232-39.

[3] The following works provide helpful information on the relationship between science and Christianity: American Scientific Affiliation, *Modern Science and the Christian Faith* (Wheaton, 1950); Richard H. Bube, ed., *Encounter between Christianity and Science* (Grand Rapids, 1968); Derek Kidner, *Genesis, an Introduction and Commentary* (Chicago, 1967); Russell L. Mixter, ed., *Evolution and Christian Thought Today* (Grand Rapids, 1959); and Bernard Ramm, *Christian View of Science and Scripture* (Grand Rapids, 1955).

Walter R. Hearn

Chemistry

Nineteen thousand students are enrolled at my university this year, about 16,000 of them undergraduates. Only 130 of these are chemistry majors, plus 30 more in biochemistry, yet 3,500 are taking introductory chemistry. Why? A few because they liked high school chemistry. Others because a year of physical science is required for general education—and chemistry is rumored to be easier than physics. For many students, no doubt, freshman chemistry is just a hurdle, a prerequisite for other courses.

In twenty years of teaching biochemistry I have known hundreds of students personally. Did any take chemistry primarily to gain more understanding of God's creation? I wonder, since chemistry deals with the "stuff" of God's universe: the structure and properties of substances and the reactions that change them into other substances. Does that leave out *anything*? Energy, perhaps—the realm of physics—but physical chemistry overlaps with physics in studying how the various forms of energy interact with matter. No wonder chemistry is a prerequisite for other sciences that deal with special groups of substances: geology with rocks, astronomy with stars, biology with protoplasm. Chemistry overlaps with these in geochemistry, astrochemistry (or cosmochemistry) and biochemistry.

It is remarkable that chemistry can account for transformations of so many created things—from rocks and stars to human beings—on the basis of a small number of theories and laws. And most of our chemical understanding is relatively recent. The most important of all chemical theories, the atomic theory, dates back less than 200 years to John Dalton (1766-1844). Even the concept of molecules as discrete particles accounting for properties of gases goes back only 300 years to Robert Boyle (1627-1691). Boyle and Dalton, both Englishmen, were also devout Christians, as were many pioneers of modern science. Antoine Lavoisier (1743-1794) is generally considered the founder of modern chemistry for his careful use of the analytical balance. With it he dealt the final blow to "phlogiston" (a "principle of combustion" thought to escape when something burned) and established the law of conservation of mass. He clarified the difference between the important gases carbon dioxide, nitrogen, hydrogen, and oxygen and gave the latter two their present names. Before being guillotined as a member of the French establishment, Lavoisier also worked out a rational scheme for naming chemical compounds, still the basis of chemical nomenclature.[1]

Thus the whole analytical period of chemical history is younger than the United States. Before it began, iatrochemists had searched for chemical cures for disease, and generations of alchemists had tried to transmute ordinary metals into gold and gain other magical powers over nature. Chemical arts like metallurgy, fermentation, and dyeing are mentioned in ancient writings of China, Egypt, and Mesopotamia, The word *chemistry,* derived from Arabic, is said to have come from a Greek word (*chyma*) meaning things melted and poured out. It may also have come from *Khem,* "the land of Egypt," so named from the dark color of its soil. According to this derivation, al-chemy was the "art of the black country," the "black art." When Arabian Mohammedans dominated Egypt, they learned the secrets of ancient temple laboratories, finally passing them on to the Europeans.[2]

chemistry and controversy

Through the long course of its development as occult art and then as modern science, chemistry has been a lively human drama. The nature of combustion, the number of elements, atomic weights, the formula of water—almost every law, theory and "fact" taught in introductory chemistry today—was fought out between protagonists of opposing views. As in other branches of science, arguments were resolved by further experimentation. The "winning" view was the one best able to explain observations and predict the outcome of new experiments. Unfortunately, with so much verified information to get across, most of this exciting "life" of chemistry has been squeezed out of introductory courses along with the false theories and erroneous observations.

Even today the science of chemistry is full of controversy, though about subjects undreamed of in the days of "fixed air" and phlogiston. In my own field, chemists disagree sharply about how to account for the catalytic efficiency of enzymes. They debate whether memory is encoded in polymeric molecules in the brain and differ on the chemical bases of hormone activity. As in the past, experimentation will eventually settle such questions.

But, in addition, "value questions" pervade chemistry today: What are the proper goals for chemical research? How should chemistry be taught? Even the sequence of chemistry courses traditional for majors—inorganic, analytical, physical and organic—has been called obsolete by a number of leading chemists. They think the curriculum should be completely reorganized around "concepts" such as chemical structure (inorganic and organic blended together) and chemical dynamics (energetics, kinetics, reaction mechanisms, etc.).

Introductory chemistry courses are continually being revised. The course for majors now often includes much that was formerly taught in physical chemistry, with a lab that used to be sophomore quantitative analysis. But what should be in a course for non-majors? How much theory and how much "descriptive chemistry"? Should lab work be emphasized or dropped? (Many a chemistry student can now describe the orbital overlap in the HCl molecule but cannot suggest a reaction for its preparation.) Chemistry professors find it hard to keep up with their rapidly changing subject themselves, let alone decide what parts to introduce to students.

The course you take will represent a compromise and may seem poorly suited to your interests. Part of your responsibility as a student might be to help improve it. In these days of openness between students and faculty you are likely to get a hearing if you can make a case for a better way of teaching. Be critical, in the best tradition of science, but be sympathetic also. Teaching chemistry to students of widely varying abilities and interests is at least as difficult as learning it.

But no matter what the format or the quality of the course you take, keep in mind that its content, the subject matter of chemical science, is also the handiwork of God. Why shouldn't we rejoice in the opportunity to see how God has put together the universe, our planet earth, our bodies, our brains? Chemistry has spiritual dimensions. If you are a Christian, whatever you pray about very likely involves matter. Even people are chemical. Maybe not *merely* chemical, but certainly they are *at least* chemical. In order to pray for people (and things) intelligently, in order to bring out the best that is in them, you need to understand them. If you want to be creative and redemptive in this world, a knowledge of chemistry should help.

where chemistry and theology meet
The Bible serves Christians as a source of spiritual wisdom. It introduces us to Jesus Christ, "whom God made our wisdom, our righteousness, and sanctification and redemption." For whatever knowledge of chemistry we need in order to "work out our own salvation," we have to look elsewhere. What slight chemical information is found in the Bible is generally accurate in description and free from superstitious explanation.[3] Influenced by their cultural surroundings, biblical writers knew what

was known or thought to be true about material things. Thus Job 28 accurately refers to the mining and smelting of ore, but the "elements" of 2 Peter 3:10 probably meant nothing more sophisticated than "earth, air, fire, and water," or some other pre-scientific catalog of the building blocks of matter. The religious message is not affected one way or the other: However we classify them, all matter and energy are God's creation.

Chemistry has some direct bearing on biblical interpretation through its contributions to archeology. One of the most dramatic advances in archeology was the discovery and development of radiocarbon dating by the physical chemist and Nobel prize winner, W. F. Libby.[4] Modern chemical techniques establish the history and authenticity of artifacts from Bible lands. The ancient glassmaking industry, for instance, has left a chemical record of its sources of raw materials and pigments, and of particular geographical centers of glass manufacture. Each individual type of glass yields a characteristic chemical analysis and spectrum.[5]

Where chemistry overlaps with physics or biology, it indirectly influences theology. For example, determining the relative abundance of lead isotopes provides one means of dating the earth. Chemical compositions of stars (from spectra), and now actual analyses of moon rocks, set limits on possible theories for formation of heavenly bodies. Some have constructed an "entropological argument" for the existence of God out of current physico-chemical theories of the origin of the universe. But philosopher-theologian E. L. Mascall warns us not to tie up Christianity with arguments based on verbal confusions or on merely temporary scientific views:

> The Christian may well rejoice in the fact that the heavens declare the glory of God and the firmament showeth his handiwork, while adopting an attitude of extreme detachment towards arguments that attempt to prove the existence of God from the Second Law of Thermodynamics or the recession of the extra-galactic nebulae. So far as they are reliable, the findings of modern science tell us a great deal for

which we should be grateful about the nature of the universe that God has made, but we shall be wise if we build our conviction that God has made it upon other foundations than those of modern science.[6]

The Second Law of Thermodynamics has been misunderstood, in my opinion, by well-meaning writers who argue that because of it, life could not possibly have arisen through a sequence of physico-chemical processes. Scientific investigation is to them intrinsically unable to account for the origin of life from inanimate matter. In their interpretation, God must have made living creatures by instantaneous formation or rearrangement of matter. Such a mental picture of the creation of life, and of man, has been held by many Christians, including some with excellent scientific training. It is possible, however, to hold an equally strong view of the Bible as the written word of God without that narrow a definition of creation.[8] Other Christians, also trained in science, regard the early chapters of Genesis as parabolic, inspired by God, and analogous to the New Testament parables of Jesus. The parables of our Lord are "true" whether or not their hearers also regard them as historical accounts or accurate statements of scientific principles—for primarily they are religious instruction.

A Christian who holds this broader view will affirm that the God of the Bible is the Creator of matter and of life and of human beings, whatever the current scientific explanation of their interrelationship. He will not limit creation to miraculous (magical), instantaneous events, but can be awed at the miraculous (deeply mystical) fact of even his own creation, though believing that the Creator used a long history of chemical processes to bring him into existence. He need not regard "creation of life in a test-tube" by biochemists as intrinsically impossible, even if very difficult to achieve. Such a chemical triumph, if scored in his lifetime, will not undermine his faith in God or in Christ or in the Bible. He will realize that any primitive metabolizing system in that test-tube shows the handiwork of God just as all matter does—whatever its complexity or entropic state.[9]

We are obliged to "speak the truth in love," and the truth you learn from chemistry and other courses is part of that truth. At times you may have to explain to a fellow Christian how your theological views are influenced by scientific knowledge. At other times you may have to testify (perhaps to a chemistry professor) that your knowledge of God through Jesus Christ is personal, going beyond what you can know of matter or understand of God through reason. An intelligent Christian doesn't have to choose between faith and reason, or between science and the Bible. Sometimes, though, we do have to choose between speaking in theological categories and speaking in scientific categories. Both theology and science are full of unresolved controversies, each area deserving our best thought. Make connections between them whenever you can, but "with all lowliness and meekness, with patience, forbearing one another in love, eager to maintain the unity of the Spirit in the bond of peace."

Someday, perhaps, chemistry may tell us in detail how our brain functions when we pray.[10] Atheists and agnostics will delight in that knowledge, and Christians may find it hard to take. But if some of us who love God also love chemistry, maybe we can demonstrate that prayer, like "fine gold" or life itself, is no less precious because it can be described in chemical terms.

better things—and bigger problems—through chemistry

As this is being written, the question at hand is not so much whether "prayer is chemical" but whether chemistry has a prayer-of-a-chance to continue developing in the United States. A depressed economic climate has meant loss of employment for thousands of scientists. Chemistry has always had close ties to industry, but now even chemists in academic life are beginning to see hard times. In 1965 a report by the National Academy of Sciences indicated that U.S. chemistry was dropping behind in research support.[11] Now, after more inflation and vast military expenditures, the situation has become far more serious. Industrial firms have cut research budgets drastically, and research funds from federal agencies are rapidly drying up.

Eventually, a decrease in military expenditures and an up-swing in the nation's economy may enable scientific research to recover its vigor, but chemistry faces another problem not so likely to "blow over." The chemical industry is one of the most obvious sources of pollution of our environment, and the mood of the American public toward the environment may have changed permanently from one of exploitation to one of con-servation. Only a few years ago chemistry was proud of having made possible the age of plastics, high-octane gasoline, deter-gents and DDT. Now everyone is aware of adverse effects from each of these discoveries. Chlorinated hydrocarbons like DDT got rid of malaria-bearing mosquitoes in many parts of the world, but pesticide residues kept accumulating until birds be-gan dying and now the health of human beings may be endan-gered. Detergents and fertilizer run-off have filled rivers and lakes with nutrients beyond the capacity of these ecosystems to purify themselves. Leaded gas burned in millions of cars adds to discharges pouring into the atmosphere from industrial smoke-stacks. And plastic has become not only a solid waste disposal problem but a pejorative term: Plastic symbolizes technological pandering to mass tastes manipulated by advertising—without regard for the integrity of personalities or the environment. Chemistry itself may have become something of a dirty word, symbolic no longer of what science can do for us ("Better Things for Better Living through Chemistry") but of what science is doing to us ("The Silent Spring" and Napalm).

Turmoil over what to do about this situation is evident in the 110,000-member American Chemical Society, the largest scien-tific society in the world. Articles and letters in its weekly *Chemical and Engineering News* magazine indicate a variety of response from soul-searching and guilt-feelings to an occasional recalcitrant ecology-be-damned attitude.[12] Among chemists I know in academic life, I see a new willingness to consider both sides of technological innovation. Many feel moral responsibil-ity to turn their research efforts toward solving urgent human problems, including those brought on by technology. Very few scientists today seem to think that ecological problems can be solved through more science and technology alone. Chemists have learned that they have to be "more than chemists," since chemical problems so often involve personal, political, or economic choices—and even philosophical and theological values.[13]

Of course, Christians could have told them that. In fact, that has always been an important role of Christians who are chemists, to demonstrate to our colleagues that life is more than chemistry. That is one good reason for a Christian to take up the study of chemistry, to be able to witness within this branch of human endeavor in the language spoken by its practitioners.[14] But Christians have another good reason to study even a little chemistry: to be able to make informed decisions about technological questions. Thus Christians living in a democracy today have to be "more than Christians," since being a responsible citizen requires some knowledge of science, some understanding of economics, political effectiveness—and many other things.

a personal response to the study of chemistry

To sum up, if you take your study of chemistry seriously you will find it "relevant" in more ways than you might have expected. It should sharpen your theological awareness and help you grapple with the deep questions of God's relationship to the world and the means by which God and man can communicate. In your personal spiritual life it may deepen your sense of awe and humility before both the complexity and simplicity of God's patterns in nature. It may give you opportunity to witness more effectively to non-Christians trained in science or influenced by our science-oriented culture. It may give you knowledge and insight to help people avoid superstitious beliefs or harmful practices. It may equip you better as a voter or perhaps even as a public leader to redirect technology into useful rather than destructive purposes. It may help you in many practical ways to cope with the material world, and beyond that to "feel at home" in the world.

True, we are guests and not permanent residents in this world of chemical substances. But this is the world our Father made for us through his Son, "the first-born of all creation, for in him all things were created, in heaven and on earth, visible and invisible." All this chemistry around us and in us was created through Jesus Christ and for him, the Scripture says. As Christians we are heirs with him of both heavenly and earthly things. And this is the only earth we have.

Notes

[1] For fascinating information about famous chemists and other scientists, see Isaac Asimov, *Asimov's Biographical Encyclopedia of Science and Technology* (New York, 1964). Arthur F. Smethurst, *Modern Science and Christian Beliefs* (London, 1955), discusses the Christian faith of seventeenth-century pioneers of modern science, arguing that their religious outlook was directly responsible for the rise of modern science. Smethurst is a chemist-theologian. For a criticism of Smethurst's view see the work of physicist-theologian Greville D. Yarnold, *Spiritual Crisis of the Scientific Age* (London, 1959).

[2] See René Taton, ed., *Ancient and Medieval Science* (New York, 1963); Charles Singer, *Short History of Scientific Ideas to 1900* (London, 1959); or a more specialized work such as James Campbell Brown, *History of Chemistry from the Earliest Times*, 2nd ed. (Philadelphia, 1920). For a glimpse at sixteenth-century alchemy just before its transition into science, see Henry M. Pachter, *Magic into Science, The Story of Paracelsus* (New York, 1951).

[3] R. Laird Harris, "Bible and Chemical Knowledge," in American Scientific Affiliation, *Modern Science and Christian Faith* (Wheaton, 1948), pp. 250-59.

[4] Willard F. Libby, *Radiocarbon Dating*, 2nd ed. (Chicago, 1955).

[5] Ray Winfield Smith, "History Revealed in Ancient Glass," *National Geographic*, CXXVI (1964), 346.

[6] Eric L. Mascall, *Christian Theology and Natural Science* (London, 1956), p. 166. All of chapter 4, "Creation in Theology and Science," is excellent.

[7] Such writers include Robert E. D. Clark, *Darwin, Before and After* (London, 1958); Henry M. Morris, *Twilight of Evolution* (Philadelphia, 1963); and A. E. Wilder-Smith, *Creation of Life* (Wheaton, 1970). Clark is a chemist, Morris a civil engineer and Wilder-Smith a pharmacologist.

[8] See, for example, Aldert van der Ziel, *Genesis and Scientific Inquiry* (Minneapolis, 1965); Walter R. Hearn and Richard A. Hendry, "Origin of Life," in Russell L. Mixter, ed., *Evolution and Christian Thought Today* (Grand Rapids, 1959); or Walter R. Hearn, "Meaning of Creation," *Journal of the American Scientific Affiliation*, XVIII (1966), 26.

[9] Walter R. Hearn, "Creation of Life," *Gordon Review*, CLVI (1958), 4.

[10] Francis Crick, an Englishman who won the Nobel prize in chemistry along with Watson and Wilkins for establishing the structure of the DNA molecule by X-ray diffraction, has proposed, more or less whimsically, the study of "biochemical theology." Crick writes, "So many people pray that one finds it difficult to believe that they do not get

some satisfaction from it, and a good molecular biologist will naturally believe that this can be expressed, at least in part, in molecular terms. Part of it, of course, would involve the molecular biology of the synapse and the overall organization of the nervous system, but the principal effect is probably hormonal, and one would not be surprised to find hormone levels that were affected by prayer. No doubt before long some 'with-it' church in America will take up the topic." See his "Molecular Biology in the Year 2000," *Nature*, CCXXVIII (14 Nov. 1970), 613-15.

[11] National Academy of Sciences, National Research Council, *Chemistry: Opportunities and Needs* (NAS-NRC 1292), (Washington, D. C., 1965). Known as the "Westheimer Report," this survey of pure and applied chemical research in the United States gives a good picture of what chemists have been accomplishing in recent years.

[12] A subscription to *Chemical and Engineering News* costs, at present, $7.00 per annum and is an excellent way to keep abreast of current developments. In addition to *C&EN* and research journals, the American Chemical Society also publishes two journals primarily for students: *Chemistry* (for high school students) and *Journal of Chemical Education*—both obtainable from the ACS Subscription Service Department, 1155 Sixteenth St., N. W., Washington, D. C. 20036.

[13] Moral and social issues faced by scientists are discussed by Charles A. Coulson, *Science, Technology, and the Christian* (New York, 1960); and Ian G. Barbour, *Christianity and the Scientist* (New York, 1960).

[14] Valuable examples of witness by practicing scientists include Charles A. Coulson, *Science and Christian Belief* (London, 1955); Robert E. D. Clark, *Christian Belief and Science* (London, 1960); Aldert van der Ziel, *Natural Sciences and the Christian Message* (Minneapolis, 1960); Donald M. Mackay, ed., *Christianity in a Mechanistic Universe* (Chicago, 1965); David L. Dye, *Faith and the Physical World: A Comprehensive View* (Grand Rapids, 1966); Richard H. Bube, ed., *Encounter Between Christianity and Science* (Grand Rapids, 1968); and Malcolm A. Jeeves, *Scientific Enterprise and Christian Faith* (Chicago, 1969).

Charles Hatfield

Mathematics

In the old days, days as old as the twelfth century—the young
lover would on occasion prove the ardency of his love by deeds
of valor. If his true love were within sight when her beauty was
questioned by another man, he might just "break his head—the
other man's head, I mean—then that proved that his—the first
fellow's—girl was a pretty girl. But if the other fellow broke *his*
head—not his own, you know, but the other fellow's—the other
fellow to the second fellow, that is, because of course the other
fellow would only be the other fellow to him, not the first
fellow who—well, if he broke his head, then *his* girl—not the
other fellow's but the fellow who was the—Look here, if A
broke B's head, then A's girl was a pretty girl; but if B broke A's
head, then A's girl was not a pretty girl, but B's girl was."

The moral of this little story by Jerome K. Jerome[1] is that it
pays to know a little algebra! Simply naming the actors enables
the mind to carry the action with ease. If this sounds like a
facetious use of algebra, it nevertheless illustrates a necessary
first step in any mathematical demonstration: giving a different
name to each item to be considered. Mathematicians do this
kind of thing almost automatically. What else do they do?

what is the field?

If we look over the shoulders of mathematicians at work, we discover an almost endless variety of pursuits: analyzing the stresses in the latest supersonic aircraft, predicting the path of the next hurricane, estimating the number of deaths expected in the coming "long weekend," studying the error generated by a computer, developing an inertial guidance system for high-velocity orbits—to name but a few current projects involving the application of mathematics. Projects in pure mathematics are just as numerous, but are difficult to describe without a highly specialized vocabulary. These and many other mathematical activities are undertaken today in behalf of government, of industry, of education, or in some cases, "just for fun." Mathematical discovery—or invention, if you prefer—has accelerated at a dizzy pace during recent years. It is difficult for the layman to believe that there has been more new mathematics published in the last 25 years than in all of time preceding. But it is true.

Today probably more than 25,000 scientists and technicians in this country alone make their daily living by means of mathematics. Some of them see it as a language; others, an art; for still others it furnishes an endless variety of models or patterns; but for all of them it means a method of thinking. Let us look at each of these in turn.

Most persons would agree that mathematics is a *language*—perhaps even a language *barrier* to some. It first names the objects considered (as we saw in the case of the twelfth-century lover) and then begins to study relations within the problem. With its vocabulary partly technical, as is the case for any science, it becomes a hurdle for the beginner who finds that he makes little progress until he masters definitions of basic terms and concepts. But learning these then opens the gate to genuine penetration.

Now there is a bonus for carefully framed definitions of really significant ideas: A carefully chosen symbolism often exhibits a power all its own, whatever the branch of science. The symbol becomes an actual tool for the thinker, an extension of his brain. The symbols and their interrelations become catalysts toward further mental activity, even thinking *for* the user at times. A simple illustration is the use of the Hindu concept of place value[2] in our present number system. Because it does enter symbolically into the thinking process itself, mathematics can often be employed helpfully in other sciences. Laplace called the language of mathematical analysis "the most perfect of all, being in itself a powerful instrument of discoveries; its notations, especially when they are necessary and happily conceived, are so many germs of new calculi."[3] Language so invented for the purposes of analysis proved cleverer than its inventors anticipated. Mathematicians are often criticized for their streamlined model of description. Although its language is minimal, at times austere, mathematics by its very sparseness tries to lay bare the essential nature of the problem or the theory applicable to its solution. Even mathematicians complain about their colleagues' stinginess with paper and ink!

Mathematics is used by so many other branches of science that the name "language of languages" seems to be justified. It is such an important tool in the understanding of nature that more than one mathematician has conceived of God as the first practicer of the art. One writer suggested that through mathematics nature stands revealed before us and "through it the Creator of the world has spoken and the Preserver of the world continues to speak."[4] Without this language, much of the inner harmony of nature would have remained vague or even unknown. This harmony, thought Poincaré,[5] was the sole objective reality, the only truth reachable by mere mortals in their attempt to understand the universe. This concept of truth is appropriate to empirical reality (what we secure by experiment, hypothesis, and theory) but does not embrace all of reality. For the Christian the biblical revelation of God is of an entirely different order, and it is directed to *all* men. It is therefore written in terms all can understand.

why pursue it?

The compelling reason for pursuing mathematics has been for

some the fact that the discipline resembles an art. This probably strikes a new chord with many students, but the criteria of judgment in mathematics will always be in part aesthetic. Mere truth of a theorem is not sufficient to establish it as a part of living mathematics. One also looks for "interest," for "beauty."

But what kind of beauty? And where do we look for it? It is a beauty primarily intellectual, perhaps even cold to most persons, but nevertheless very real to the mathematician. Bertrand Russell, commenting on the truth and beauty of mathematics, observed that "real life is, to most men, a long second-best, a perpetual compromise between the real and the possible; but the world of pure reason knows no compromise, no practical limitations, no barrier to the creative activity embodying in splendid edifices the passionate aspiration after the perfect from which all great work springs."[6]

Mathematics as an art suggests another likeness: the creative process itself. Just as the artist has a strong urge to put brush to canvas, so the mathematician has a zest for putting mind to assumptions. Some of the most significant results in mathematics have been in direct response to such purely intellectual challenges. The discovery of a true theorem and the invention of its proof (often only after hours of hard thinking) are just as surely creative acts as those of novelist, artist, or poet. The result one discovers might not be absolutely new, to be sure, for the first one to discover it may have lived hundreds of years ago. "But," the mathematician thinks, "even though a thousand others discovered and proved the same theorem as I, the thrill *I* experienced in the disclosure remains my own. I did it 'off my own bat.' " The situation resembles that of a thousand artists painting the same scene: Each in his work experiences his own release, his own ecstasy. And, fortunately for all of us, no one profession can monopolize joy.

A third view of mathematics sees it somewhere between art and science—as a model. Or, rather, it *provides* models or patterns. Here, of course, we mean not those of wood, wire, plaster, and string (although these often result) so much as thought-constructs. Hardy wrote that "a mathematician, like a painter or a poet, is a maker of patterns. If his patterns are more permanent than theirs, it is because they are made with ideas."[7] This sounds a little hard on the poet who would surely contend that he uses ideas to make poems. In any case, Hardy's point is the positive one that mathematicians, above all, deal with ideas.

The external world has been the source of many mathematical concepts and theories. But like children reared by wise parents to think independently, these concepts and theories have a way of taking off on their own. Sometimes they soar to heights of development that leave far behind the launching pad of their physical source. Since the material world is hardly simple, the natural scientist often contents himself with the attempt to understand certain selected parts of it. To do this, he streamlines his model of reality, stripping away the inconvenient complications, in the hope that the simplified and idealized model will nevertheless illumine adequately the center of his focus. Newton,[8] for example, treated each planet as influenced only by the gravitational pull of the sun. By thus neglecting the pull of the other heavenly bodies (which was, strictly speaking, quite wrong), he was able to incorporate Kepler's[9] laws of planetary motion into a few elegant equations. Later more refined (because more realistic) models became the basis for some remarkable astronomical predictions in the nineteenth century, one of these being the famous prediction by Adams[10] and Leverrier[11] of the discovery of the planet Neptune.

Now it is not unnatural to expect that measurable quantities of related phenomena might combine into a common formula, which then becomes a kind of shorthand for what is expected of similar occurrences. For example, $s = \frac{1}{2}gt^2$ can be interpreted as expressing a kind of ideal model or pattern for falling bodies. It declares that the distance s in feet fallen by a body in t seconds (ignoring air resistance, dust, moisture, etc.) is given by the right side of the equation, where g is the gravitational constant (whose value is about 32). Thus, if it takes a pebble three seconds to reach the water when dropped from a bridge above, then the latter is approximately 144 feet high. We must say "approximately" because in the real world we do contend with resistance due to air, dust, moisture, etc., and to that extent non-ideal conditions. Thus pure mathematics can pass judgment upon questions of actual fact in the real world often only in terms of approximation to a model.

If the axioms, or initial assumptions, of the mathematical model are only approximately satisfied, we need not get up our hopes that the whole model will fare any better, for the axioms are the *heart* of the theory. Certainty and precision which characterize mathematics generally must be set aside except as ideals, when we try to describe accurately the actual material context of life.

Finally, mathematics provides a method, or better, a collection of methods, for solving problems. Whitehead[12] anticipated that pure mathematics "in its modern developments, may claim to be the most original creation of the human spirit." Its reasoning shapes a conceptual tool for making explicit what is already contained in a set of axioms, just as the nature of a plant is contained in its genetic code. A mathematical system provides a blueprint for a structure yet to be built. Whatever scientists saw mathematics to be in the past, in the twentieth century they regard it primarily as a method sometimes called "postulational thinking," the central nervous system of living mathematics. The conclusions of mathematics do not often make news. When they do, it is because they make us aware of what we had not recognized as implicit in the axioms with which we began. Fontenelle suggested that "mathematicians are like lovers. . . . Grant a mathematician the least principle, and he will draw from it a consequence which you must also grant him, and from this consequence another."[13]

a rational tool

The seventeenth century saw spectacular success in the mathematical conquest of previously unyielding problems encountered in the attempts to understand nature. Model-making and model-testing by means of the new quantitative methods invested science with a new power to rationalize and thus master nature. We can pardon the hope of sweeping reorganization of all areas of knowledge in those days, for today we know not only the power of these methods, but also their limitations. The rationalistic temper (with or without mathematics) provides only one way of viewing the world. Emotional and spiritual modes of looking at the world contribute insights that are just as valid. Numbers are not the key to everything!

All efforts to understand nature seem to begin consciously or unconsciously with assumptions; such is the nature of discursive thought directed upon a particular subject. The scientist and mathematician usually take as their starting point the assumption of *existence* (something "out there" and not merely in my mind); the assumption of *rationality* (one can detect this reality and measure certain of its numerical qualities and then organize it along rational lines); and the assumption of *causality* (the uncovered realities and regularities can lead us to the causes behind them).

In making assumptions or axioms, the mathematician resembles any other scientist. He makes the suppositions and then searches out just where they lead. I believe there is a significant parallel here in the case of the Christian, for he does the same regarding faith. He assumes that God exists (but not without good evidence) as does the Bible ("anyone who comes to God must believe that he exists and that he rewards those who search for him"—Heb. 11:6b, NEB). Then he proceeds to infer consequences of that belief and of others, as found in the Bible. He believes that God has revealed himself, that he has done so preeminently in Jesus Christ, and that the Bible gives us an adequate revelation of God through Christ. These hardly submit to mathematical proof nor to logically tight demonstration, but one sees much confirming evidence in each of these areas if he is not afraid to exert faith. Indeed, "without faith it is impossible to please him" (Heb. 11:6a, NEB). The demonstration is cogent enough. The rub is that not everyone accepts the assumptions, for they imply admission of personal guilt.

parallels

Most people take it for granted that mathematics provides

descriptive techniques for treating our physical world. But when one pauses to ask *why* symbolic systems of mathematics should correspond to some parts of the physical world, more than one scientist of note has refused to take it for granted. For example, E. P. Wigner has observed, "The miracle of the appropriateness of the language of mathematics for the formulation of the laws of physics is a wonderful gift which we neither understand nor deserve. We should be grateful for it and hope that it will remain valid in future research and that it will extend, for better or for worse, to our pleasure even though perhaps also to our bafflement, to wide branches of learning."[14] Such humility, we believe, is part of the Christian's posture in the midst of a world which was created and is sustained by God.

We believe that the correspondence between model and physical reality stems from the manner in which God created the world. And this includes both the passive and the active: his particular handiwork in creating the universe and his shaping the brain and its related structure, the world of thought. To the scientist using models and maps, and who is also a Christian, it makes an incalculable difference that it is God's universe he seeks to model by means of the mind that God gave him and working in the world of intellect which God created along with the mind. Thus the thinker can enter more deeply into an understanding of the creative work of God: understanding more precisely *how* the universe behaves and perceiving in all of it more of God's infinite wisdom. God thus satisfies my intellect and evokes praise from my spirit.

More than one person has observed that the truly incomprehensible thing about this world is that so much of it is comprehensible. Perhaps it is no more surprising than the fact of thought itself. To one who accepts God's sovereignty over and in the world, it seems entirely reasonable that God fitted the mind of man to apprehend his physical environment in more than one mode. For the Christian there are no such things as brute facts in nature, for each structure embodies the creative energy of the Lord God. Each fact, therefore, is some aspect of God's world and as such points in its ultimate significance to the Creator. Placed in this scheme, mathematics is one of the tools, like ear, eye, and hand, that enables us to discern the handiwork of God in a particular manner. And surely this adds intensity to our praise: "O Lord, how manifold are thy works! in wisdom has thou made them all" (Ps. 104:24a, KJV).

Notes

[1] Jerome Klapka Jerome (1859-1927), English playwright and humorist.

[2] Thus, the first 3 in 3,437 stands for 3,000 and the second 3 for 30. This convention enables a third-grader to perform operations far more rapidly than even the most learned mathematicians of ancient Greece and Rome.

[3] Pierre Simon Laplace (1749-1827), French astronomer and mathematician.

[4] Christian Friedrich Dillman (1823-1894), German orientalist and biblical scholar.

[5] Jules Henri Poincaré (1854-1912), French mathematician.

[6] Bertrand Russell, "Study of Mathematics" in *Gateway Books*, Encyclopedia Britannica, IX (New York, 1963), 86.

[7] Godfrey Harold Hardy (1877-1947), English mathematician. The excerpt is from his *Mathematician's Apology* (London, 1940).

[8] Sir Isaac Newton (1643-1727), English natural philosopher and mathematician.

[9] Johannes Kepler (1571-1630), German astronomer.

[10] John Couch Adams (1819-1892), British astronomer.

[11] Urbain Jean Joseph Leverrier (1811-1877), French astronomer.

[12] Alfred North Whitehead (1861-1947), English mathematician and philosopher.

[13] Bernard Le Bovier de Fontenelle (1657-1757), seventeenth-century popularizer of science.

[14] E. P. Wigner, "Unreasonable Effectiveness of Mathematics in the Natural Sciences," *Communication in Pure and Applied Mathematics*, XIII (New York, 1960), 1-14.

Richard H. Bube

Physics

Physics is fun. It combines the fascination of puzzle-solving with the satisfaction of coming to grips with the nature of physical reality. But this isn't possible without real intellectual effort. Students can seldom master concepts in physics by memorization alone. They must be learned by the use of theoretical and experimental techniques that develop a basis for understanding.[1]

Physics emphasizes the development of general principles from the results of particular investigations, as well as the application of general principles to the solution of particular problems. Discoveries in physics are exciting; they often lead to an increase in understanding of an experience that has previously been a mystery. They grapple with the nature of physical reality in a concrete and specific way, challenging the universe to yield its secrets.

purpose in physics

The purpose of physics is to describe the physical universe. A successful description is the first step to partial understanding, as well as to successful control and applications in the domain of engineering and technology. Every science emphasizes a rational and objective approach to its subject. Physics does this to a high degree and incorporates more mathematical rigor in its description of nature than does any other science. Success in physics therefore demands an end to lazy thinking, an end to getting by through parroting little-understood definitions and equations, and the beginning of a real effort to understand the meaning of objective concepts and the proper ways of applying them to real situations. Although mathematics plays a key role in the exposition of physics, something called "physical intuition"—a feeling for the character of the univerce obtained only by relationship and experience—is needed to put living understanding into the mathematical abstractions.

Don't be misled, therefore, into thinking that physics is only a formal discipline that exalts the pure rationality of the mind and avoids any subjective influence of the people taking part in it. This is not the case at all. To pursue physics, a student does not feed input into a vast impersonal scientific machine that inexorably grinds out the truths of the physical universe. Physics, like all science, is a profoundly personal endeavor, requiring the commitment of the participant to the customs and thought patterns of the scientific community.

In many ways this scientific community has characteristics similar to those of the Christian community. The scientific community has a common language—the language of mathematics and of specially defined terms; a common dedication—to the description and understanding of the physical world; a common perspective—to grow in knowledge through the systematic application of theoretical and experimental check and counter-check; a common faith—that the physical world is indeed susceptible to rational analysis; and a common hope—that perseverence and diligence will be rewarded with understanding and progress. No one outside the community can fully comprehend the essential nature of the community; this aspect characterizes the scientific community as truly as it does the Christian community. "Initiation" into the scientific community is not something conferred with the reception of a degree; it is something that takes time and must be earned by demonstrated faithfulness to the perspective of the scientific community.

The pursuit of physics (like every other science) is not rewarded with full success and satisfaction unless coupled with a personal involvement in the mainstream concerns of the scientific community. This involvement is very difficult for a student to achieve. He must therefore be prepared to find that the learning of physics may sometimes require a dull combination of uninteresting details and irrelevant problems—pulleys and weights, falling bodies and electric circuits, light waves and atomic particles. He must learn these things, however, and accept this discipline as a student before he can enter into a full appreciation of what it means to *do* physics. Perhaps he will never get to this point, particularly if his main interests lie in a different area of learning. At least he should be aware that the kind of attraction the physicist sees in physics is something radically different from the routine that sometimes occurs in the early study of physics.

interpretation in physics

Although the equations, laws, and theories of physics are based on experimental data—that is, upon facts—the interpretations of physicists are based upon the ideas of men. Facts never speak for themselves. Each fact that an investigator establishes must be interpreted by him in accordance with his prevalent presuppositions. Although this is certainly true in physics itself, it is doubly true in attempts to draw more general philosophical inferences from the results of physics. It is not stretching the point too much to say that the individual personal faith of the investigator is often a determining factor in interpreting the significance of a particular fact. The more difficult it is to check this interpretation by repeated experiment, the more dominant the personal element in interpretation becomes.

The real world is usually too complicated for the scientist to tackle directly. In order to treat any problem theoretically, therefore, he must (at least at the beginning) simplify the problem greatly. The physicist constructs a conceptual model so that he may apply human concepts, human methods, and mathematical techniques to the solution of the problem. A model represents an actual situation and contains hopefully the most important features of the real situation, but omits many other factors that are believed to be insignificant or those that are unknown to the scientist. The value of such a model is judged by its ability to permit a description of the physical phenomena that will be in agreement with experimental data already at hand, and to predict values for data that may be measured in the future, particularly those kinds of data not used in the formulation of the model in the first place.

The evaluation of such a model is purely pragmatic; if it works, it is good. This is the standard of "scientific truth." To recognize this state of affairs, however, does not minimize or depreciate the significance of "scientific truth." It merely emphasizes the difference between "scientific truth" and "absolute truth." The student should be on guard so that he is not misled into thinking that "scientific truth" translates simply into "absolute truth." Furthermore, a detailed correspondence need not exist between a model acceptable to a physicist and the physical reality that the model represents. Physicists accept as a matter of faith—as a reasonable assumption—that the more accurately a model accounts for or predicts the results of experiment, the more likely the principal features of the model have some correspondence to the principal features of physical reality. But note that this is a matter of faith and of probability, not an assertion of proof or of certainty.

Every investigation of physics intends to discover some kind of physical mechanism for the phenomenon of interest. Whenever physics is successfully applied to a specific problem, a physical mechanism will be found. We should realize, however, that this does not mean that a *full* explanation of the phenomenon has been given. One of the leading problems related to the philosophical inferences derived from physics and the other sciences may be stated as follows: Does the discovery of a physical mechanism rule out other significant ways of describing the phenomenon, ways that correspond to other levels of reality and that are necessary for a consideration of the deep and ultimate significance of the phenomenon? Does physics represent the only valid way of looking at a phenomenon?

All too often we are told that all of existence is ultimately reducible to physics, and that physics therefore can provide ultimate descriptions of all of reality. Since physics can produce only a physical mechanism, the next unfortunate step has been to conclude that physics has shown that God is not only irrelevant but ultimately non-existent. How important it is to remember in this connection that physics deals only with partial descriptions and with partial understandings, with "scientific truth" and not with absolute truth! Partial truths must never be equated with total truth. The assertion that all of reality—even all of material reality—can be described in terms of the laws of physics as they describe the motions of particles or waves of matter, is an assumption that may be accepted on faith, but for which there is neither proof nor really convincing evidence. To assert that all of reality can be described in terms applicable to isolated portions of reality is to assert that the whole is never greater than the sum of its parts. This would seem to be a dangerous assumption and one apparently contradicted on many levels of our present knowledge.

revolution in physics

This century has produced such a revolution in physics and in the philosophical inferences derived from it that no understanding of the significance of physics would be complete without a brief historical perspective.

At the close of the last century, most physicists felt that the major problems in physics had all been solved, and that only painstaking work in increasing the numerical accuracy of physical measurements lay ahead for the physicists of the future. They felt that the description of the entire universe could in principle be reduced to the description of the motions and interactions of the elementary particles of the universe. If the position of each such particle, its velocity, and the forces acting on it, could be determined at any one instant of time, then in principle it was believed possible to predict the whole future course of the universe, as well as to describe the whole past history of the universe.

This faith in the ability of physicists to describe all of physical reality in terms of such precisely known deterministic laws had profound effects on the philosophical inferences deduced from them. On the one hand there were those who felt that the evidence for a completely determined system of natural law afforded the final argument against the existence or at least the necessity of God. On the other hand, there were those who argued that the pattern of deterministic law was exactly what Christians should have expected on the basis of a sovereign God who has predetermined the course of events in his created universe. In either case it appeared that the future of both physics and philosophy were severely constrained, and that continued faith in the moment-by-moment providential activity of God in the world could be maintained only with extreme difficulty.

Defects and inadequacies, at first minor, but rapidly becoming critical, began to appear fairly quickly in this deterministic representation of physics. You may learn about these in a course in atomic physics or in an introduction to a study of quantum mechanics. A variety of physical phenomena can be described adequately only by assuming that observables like electrons, which had formerly been considered as particles, must sometimes be treated as exhibiting wavelike properties. Conversely, physicists discovered that light, formerly considered primarily to be a wave phenomenon, must sometimes be treated as if light energy traveled in particle-like bundles. The whole theoretical framework of quantum mechanics arose from the development of these new ideas with an emphasis quite different from that of the previous determinism. The atomic level of reality was revealed to be characterized by an intrinsic indeterminism, present in principle at every level of physical structure, but a matter of practical concern only when one is concerned with entities of the size of atoms and elementary particles.

This indeterminism can be formulated in several different ways. One way of looking at it is to realize that although an electron sometimes behaves as a particle, and sometimes as a wave, an electron is intrinsically neither particle nor wave, as these words are understood on the basis of common experience. Another way is to refer to the terms of the Heisenberg Uncertainty Principle that states that in any measurement the product of the uncertainty in the position of an electron (for example) and the uncertainty in the velocity of the electron must always have a finite value. To determine both the position *and* the velocity of every particle in the universe at a given time becomes impossible even in principle, and therefore again in principle it is impossible to predict deterministically the future or to describe the past. Defined laws continue to exist, but now these deal with the probability of events and measurements themselves. The net result is that both physics and philosophical considerations derived from physics are much more open-ended today than in the past.

theological implications

To those who had been using the existence of determinism as evidence for the existence of God and of his manner of operation in the world, the shift in emphasis to indeterminism was a blow. In many cases the Christian message had been tied to a certain way of looking at the physical world that was now discredited. But the shift to indeterminism was quickly invoked by Christians to provide an opportunity for God's providential activity on a moment-by-moment basis. Non-Christian philosophers as well have often sought to defend the concept of free will on the basis of the indeterminism in modern physics. As always, the Christian is well advised to make no final commitment to a particular scientific interpretation that makes the validity of his faith and the authority of his witness depend on the final reliability of that interpretation. The ultimate relevance of the contemporary quantum-mechanical view of indeterminism to a problem like free will defies simple correlation and may turn out in the last analysis to be virtually nonexistent.

Sometimes Christian theology is called into question because it involves the postulation and the acceptance of doctrinal or philosophical statements that appear to be in conflict. Such apparent logical conflicts are usually called paradoxes and are not to be confused with logical contradictions. To maintain at the same time that God is both sovereign and not sovereign is a logical contradiction. To maintain that man is wholly responsible for his actions and that God is completely sovereign in bringing his will to happen is a paradox. If the invoking of two apparently conflicting pictures to describe reality more completely occurs frequently in theology, it occurs no less frequently in modern physics, where the use of both the particle and the wave pictures to describe an electron or light leads to some of the same logical problems that characterize theological paradoxes.

the road to belief

Finally, we can appropriately say a general word about the ways that we come to believe things. The principles treated here apply to any science, but particularly to physics, the science most commonly singled out as the prime example of objective rationality. These comments are directed to that often-stated fallacy that physics is devoted to the rational approach to the nature of reality, whereas religion is devoted to an irrational or at least non-rational leap of faith.

First, a clarification of terms seems to be in order. To act rationally in any situation is to act upon a careful and logical assessment of all the available evidence. To act rationally does not mean to take only those actions that are connected by a series of logically provable links; indeed, if this definition should be assumed, it would mean that most of our life would be consigned by definition to irrational behavior. To act irrationally then means to act contrary to or in spite of the results of a careful and logical assessment of all the available evidence. To act meaningfully at all, whether in physics or in Christian experience, always requires a rational act of faith.

If you analyze all the possible ways of coming to believe

something, you will discover two major categories. You believe something either (1) because you accept the word of someone you trust (belief based on authority) or (2) because you have a personal experience sufficient to convince you (belief based on personal perception). These two ways of coming to believe something are equally applicable to physics and to Christianity.

As a student of physics, you will be called on to accept the testimony of other physicists as authoritative. It may be a long time before you can really check out for yourself the validity of even a fraction of the concepts to which you will be introduced. Knowing what you do about the successes of physics and trusting the integrity and reliability of your teachers, you will indeed accept these things on their authority. It would be foolish for you not to respond this way. It is, of course, healthy even in this situation to retain a respectful skepticism, but the only rational course of behavior for you will be to accept in faith, act upon this acceptance, and finally see in your own experience where this acceptance leads you. If your physics teacher is correct in his assessment of physics and if the physical understanding he presents conforms reasonably well to physical reality, you will confirm this in part in your own experience and hence strengthen your faith in the scientific method. If your teacher is misinformed or if physics itself is inadequate, you may be fortunate enough to come to a better understanding of reality in your own experience because at least initially you acted in rational faith on the basis of the knowledge you did possess.

What has been said here about physics can also be said about Christian faith. But this is not an essay on Christian faith, and we cannot pursue this theme further here. Sufficient for our discussion now is the restatement that any act, whether in physics or in Christian living, requires faith and that many times to act in faith after a careful assessment of the evidence constitutes the only rational path to follow.

Notes

[1] The student can find help, at the introductory level, in the following works: Ian G. Barbour, *Issues in Science and Religion* (Englewood Cliffs, 1966); Richard H. Bube, *Encounter between Christianity and Science* (Grand Rapids, 1968); Richard H. Bube, *The Human Quest* (Waco, 1971); David Dye, *Faith and the Physical World* (Grand Rapids, 1966); Malcolm Jeeves, *Scientific Enterprise and Christian Faith* (Chicago, 1969); Donald M. Mackay, ed., *Christianity in a Mechanistic Universe* (London, 1965); William G. Pollard, *Chance and Providence* (New York, 1958); Bernard Ramm, *Christian View of Science and Scripture* (Grand Rapids, 1955); and Aldert van der Ziel, *Natural Sciences and the Christian Message* (Minneapolis, 1960).

Contributors

GEORGE W. ANDREWS (Ph.D., University of Wisconsin) is presently employed as a geologist by a United States governmental agency. He has contributed to the *Bulletin of the American Association of Petroleum Geologists, Journal of Geology, Journal of Paleontology,* and the *U.S. Geological Survey Professional Papers.*

ROBERT D. BAIRD (Ph.D., University of Iowa), School of Religion, University of Iowa, has held two fellowships from the Ford Foundation and one from the American Institute of Indian Studies for the study of Asian religions, in addition to authoring *Category Formation and History of Religions* (The Hague, 1971), co-authoring *Religion and Man: An Introduction* (New York, 1971), and contributing to the *Journal of Bible and Religion, Journal of Religious Thought,* and *History and Theory.*

RICHARD H. BUBE (Ph.D., Princeton University), Department of Materials Science, Stanford University, has written or edited *Encounter between Christianity and Science* (Grand Rapids,

1968), *Photoconductivity of Solids* (New York, 1960), and *Textbook of Christian Doctrine* (Chicago, 1955). He has contributed to numerous scientific and scholarly journals and publications including *Encyclopedia of Electronics, Journal of Chemical Physics, Journal of Applied Physics, Journal of Physical Chemistry, Journal of the Optical Society of America,* and the *Physical Review.* He is currently the editor of the *Journal of the American Scientific Affiliation.*

J. FRANK CASSEL (Ph.D., University of Colorado), Department of Zoology, North Dakota State University, has held a fellowship from the Museum of Comparative Zoology, Harvard University, and has contributed to the *Journal of the American Scientific Affiliation, Audubon Field Notes,* and *Evolution and Christian Thought Today* (Grand Rapids, 1959).

ROBERT G. CLOUSE (Ph.D., University of Iowa), Department of History, Indiana State University, in addition to holding fellowships from a number of foundations, has co-authored or edited *Protest and Politics: Christianity and Contemporary Affairs* (Greenwood, S. C., 1968) and the forthcoming *Puritans and the Millenium, 1600-1660.* He has also contributed to *Teachers College Journal, Harvard Theological Review, Bulletin of the Evangelical Theological Society, Grace Journal,* and the *Westminster Dictionary of Chruch History.*

DOUGLAS D. FEAVER (Ph.D., Johns Hopkins University), Department of Classics, Lehigh University, formerly taught at Yale University and has held fellowships from both the American School of Classical Studies and the Center for Hellenic Studies of Harvard University. His *World to Which Jesus Came* (in Amharic) was published in Addis Ababa (1968). He has also contributed to the *American Journal of Philology, American Journal of Archaeology, Classical World, Yale Classical Studies,* and *Essence of Opera* (Glencoe, 1964). More popular articles have appeared in *His* and *Eternity.*

VIRGINIA LOWELL GRABILL (Ph.D., University of Illinois), Department of English, University of Evansville, in addition to post-doctoral studies at the University of Minnesota, has taught at Western Illinois State University and Bethel College. She is a member of numerous honor societies, a past editor of *His* magazine, and has contributed to *Correct English Magazine, Christianity Today,* and co-authored *Youth Leaders Handbook* (Wheaton, 1951).

CHARLES HATFIELD (Ph.D., Cornell University), Department of Mathematics, University of Missouri—Rolla, has taught at the University of Minnesota and the University of North Dakota and is a past president of the American Scientific Affiliation. He has contributed to the *Bulletin of the American Mathematical Society, Proceedings of the American Mathematical Society, Journal of the American Scientific Affiliation, Christianity Today,* and *His.*

WALTER R. HEARN (Ph.D., University of Illinois), Department of Biochemistry and Biophysics, Iowa State University, served on the faculties of medical schools at Yale and Baylor universities before going to Iowa State in 1955. He is the author or co-author of dozens of research papers in chemical and biological journals on amino acid and peptide chemistry, endocrinology and, most recently, biosynthesis of the bacterial pigment prodigiosin. A member of Phi Beta Kappa and Sigma Xi, he served as a Visiting Biologist to Colleges from 1961 to 1966 under the auspices of the American Institute of Biological Sciences, and in 1965 helped organize an international symposium on a Christian philosophy of science.

CHARLES E. HUMMEL (M.S., Massachusetts Institute of Technology; L.H.D. [Hon.], Geneva College) is president of Barrington College, having formerly served with Esso Standard Oil Company and as executive officer for Inter-Varsity Christian Fellowship. He is the author of *Campus Christian Witness* (Chicago, 1958) and edited *Contemporary Christian Thought* (Chicago, 1964). His studies have also appeared in *Journal of the American Scientific Affiliation, His,* and *Eternity.*

PAULINE B. JOHNSON (M.A., Columbia University; D.F.A.

[Hon.] , Moore College of Art, Philadelphia), Department of Art, University of Washington, has written *Creating with Paper* (Seattle, 1958), *Creative Bookbinding* (Seattle, 1963), and co-authored *Crafts Design* (Belmont, Calif., 1962). Her studies have appeared in numerous journals including *Art Education, Childhood Education, Consumers,* and *School Arts.*

JAMES PAUL KENNEDY (Ph.D., University of Iowa), Director, School of Music, Bowling Green State University, has done post-graduate work at the Matthay Pianoforte School, London, England, and won first prize from the Composers Press, Inc. (1960). A past vice-president of the Music Teachers National Association, he has contributed to *Music Journal, Music Educators Journal,* and *Triad.*

GORDON R. LEWTHWAITE (Ph.D., University of Wisconsin), Department of Geography, San Fernando Valley State College, as a native New Zealander is particularly interested in the historical geography of the Pacific Basin, and has contributed to *New Zealand Geographer, Pacific Viewpoint, Economic Geography,* and *Annals of the Association of American Geographers.*

JACOB A. LOEWEN (Ph.D., University of Washington), a missionary-anthropologist, now serves (while living in his native Canada) as Translations Consultant with the United Bible Societies. He worked for some years as missionary and linguist in Colombia and Peru, and has contributed to *International Journal of American Linguistics, America Indigena, Bible Translator,* and *Practical Anthropology.*

GEORGE I. MAVRODES (Ph.D., University of Michigan), Department of Philosophy, University of Michigan, previously taught at Princeton University. In addition to co-editing *Problems and Perspectives in the Philosophy of Religion* (Boston, 1967), he has written *Belief in God: A Study in the Epistemology of Religion* (New York, 1970), and his essays have appeared in *Analysis, Indian Journal of Philosophy, Journal of Philosophy, International Philosophical Quarterly, Personalist, Philosophical Review,* and *Review of Metaphysics.*

DAVID O. MOBERG (Ph.D., University of Minnesota), Department of Sociology and Anthropology, Marquette University, previously taught at the University of Groningen (Netherlands), Muenster University (West Germany), and Bethel College. He is the author of *Church as a Social Institution* (Englewood Cliffs, 1962), *Inasmuch: Christian Social Responsibility in the Twentieth Century* (Grand Rapids, 1965) and co-author of *Church and the Older Person* (Grand Rapids, 1962). In addition, his work has appeared in *American Quarterly, American Sociological Review, Journal of Gerontology, Journal of Pastoral Care,* and *Journal of the American Scientific Affiliation.*

E. MANSELL PATTISON (M.D., University of Oregon), Department of Psychiatry and Human Behavior, University of California—Irvine, formerly served as senior psychiatrist, National Institute of Mental Health, and more recently, School of Medicine, University of Washington, and is a member of numerous professional boards and organizations. He is the author of *Clinical Psychiatry and Religion* (Boston, 1969) and has contributed to *Christianity and the World of Thought* (Chicago, 1968), as well as to *Christianity Today, Journal of the American Scientific Affiliation, Journal of Religion and Health, Journal of Pastoral Care, American Journal of Psychiatry,* and others. In February, 1969, he was chosen "Man of the Month in Pastoral Psychology."

WALFRED H. PETERSON (Ph.D., University of Minnesota), Department of Political Science, Washington State University, previously taught at Bethel College and the University of Minnesota as well as working as Director of Research Services for the Baptist Joint Committee on Public Affairs in Washington, D. C. He edited *Role of the Christian through Church and State in Human Welfare* (Washington, D. C., 1967) and *Role of the Christian through Church and State in Education* (Washington, D. C., 1966). His scholarly works have also appeared in the *Proceedings of the Minnesota Academy of Science* and *Western Political Quarterly.*

KENNETH L. PIKE (Ph.D., University of Michigan), Department of Linguistics, University of Michigan, is a worldwide consultant in linguistics of preliterate tribes and past president of the Linguistics Society of America. He has written numerous books and essays including *Phonetics* (Ann Arbor, 1942), *Intonation of American English* (Ann Arbor, 1945), *Tone Languages* (Ann Arbor, 1948), *Language in Relation to a Unified Theory of the Structure of Human Behavior,* 3 vols. (New York, 1954 ff.), and *With Heart and Mind: A Personal Synthesis of Scholarship and Devotion* (Grand Rapids, 1962). In addition to teaching responsibilities, he is also president of the Summer Institute of Linguistics, Inc. In 1966 the University of Michigan selected him for the Distinguished Faculty Achievement Award.

DALE D. ROTT (M.F.A., Boston University), Director of Drama, Bethel College, has written and directed numerous plays as well as acted or served in technical capacities in many more. His "So Send I You," commissioned by the North American Baptist General Conference (1964) and "Church Militant" (1966) have set forth a philosophy of the Christian in the contemporary world. His ideas have also appeared in the *Educational Theatre Journal.*

JOHN SCANZONI (Ph.D., University of Oregon), Department of Sociology, Indiana University, has written widely in the area of the Christian and contemporary living. He edited *Readings in Social Problems: Sociology and Social Issues* (Boston, 1967) and has authored *Opportunity and the Family* (New York, 1970) and *Contemporary Black Family* (in press). Monographic studies have appeared also in *American Sociological Review, American Journal of Sociology, Journal of Marriage and the Family,* and the *Pacific Sociological Review.* Recently Wheaton College named him to its Honor Society for "significant contributions" to his field.

ROBERT W. SMITH (Ph.D., University of Wisconsin), chairman of the Department of Speech and Theatre, Alma College, has also taught at the University of Michigan and at the University of Virginia. His monographs, mostly in rhetoric, have appeared in such journals as *American Speech, Anglican Theological Re-*

view, Parliamentary Journal, and *Speech Monographs.*

THOMAS E. VAN DAHM (Ph.D., University of Michigan), Department of Economics, Carthage College, previously taught at Augustana College, Hope College, and Southern Illinois University. *Current Economic Comment, Credit World, Reformed Review,* and *Church Herald* have previously published his essays.

BAIRD W. WHITLOCK (Ph.D., University of Edinburgh), Director of Liberal Studies, Elmira College, has published widely in the scholarly world, including *Aesthetics and Art Criticism, Bucknell Review, Bibliothèque d'Humanisme et Renaissance, Modern Language Notes, Review of English Studies,* and the *Times Literary Supplement.* In 1968, he received the McGraw-Rock Award for Excellence in Teaching.

ROBERT J. WILLOUGHBY (M.A., University of Michigan), Department of Physical Education, Eastern Michigan University, is co-author of *Complete Book of Gymnastics,* 2nd ed. (Englewood Cliffs, 1967), having been a former gymnast. He has contributed to *Mentor, Studies in the History of the School of Education, University of Michigan,* and *Elan.*

WILLIAM YOUNG (Ed.D., Teachers College, Columbia University), Division of Education and Psychology, Barrington College, served for several years on the staff of Inter-Varsity Christian Fellowship and later on the faculty of Haigazian College, Beirut, Lebanon, and has written for the *Scholastic Teacher.*

Those whose names do not appear with the essays but who gave of their professional advice in reading the studies include: John W. Alexander, Inter-Varsity Christian Fellowship (Geography); Ronald D. Anderson, University of Colorado (Education); John C. Bale, Luther College (English); L. Frank Brown, University of Texas (Geology); Wilbur Bullock, University of New Hampshire (Biology); Dewey Carpenter, Louisiana State University (Chemistry); Edward A. Cording, Wheaton College (Music); Donald E. DeGraaf, University of Michigan—Flint (Physics); Ralph T. Eubanks, University of West Florida (Speech); Arnold

W. Flath, Oregon State University (Physical Education); Lee Graber, Florida Presbyterian College (Mathematics); Lars I. Granberg, Northwestern College (Psychology); Arthur F. Holmes, Wheaton College (Philosophy); Frank E. Houser, Whitworth College (Social Sciences); Robert D. Linder, Kansas State University (History); Philip N. Lockhart, Dickinson College (Classics); Wendell Matthews, Carthage College (Art); David O. Moberg, Marquette University (Sociology); Eugene A. Nida, American Bible Society (Anthropology); Dallas M. Roark, Kansas State Teachers College (Religion); William A. Smalley, United Bible Societies, Bangkok, Thailand (Anthropology); Arthur A. Stahnke, Southern Illinois University (Political Science); John Vanden Berg, Calvin College (Economics); Eldad Vanderlip, Westmont College (Language); and Donald J. Veldt, Baptist Bible College (Speech). Robert B. Fischer, California State College—Dominguez Hills, has provided special editorial help.